The Greek Orthodox Waqf in Lebanon During the Ottoman Period

BEIRUTER TEXTE UND STUDIEN

HERAUSGEGEBEN VOM
ORIENT-INSTITUT BEIRUT

BAND 113

The Greek Orthodox Waqf in Lebanon During the Ottoman Period

Souad Abou el-Rousse Slim

BEIRUT 2007

ERGON VERLAG WÜRZBURG
IN KOMMISSION

Umschlaggestaltung: Taline Yozgatian
Umschlagbild: Dr. Ra'if Nassif und Mario Saba
Druckprojektbetreuung: Sara Binay

Bibliografische Information der Deutschen Bibliothek

Die Deutsche Bibliothek verzeichnet diese Publikation
in der Deutschen Nationalbibliografie ;
detaillierte bibliografische Daten sind im Internet
über http://dnb.ddb.de abrufbar.

ISBN 978-3-89913-556-5

 Gedruckt mit Unterstützung des Bundesministeriums für Bildung und Forschung.

Ergon-Verlag, Dr. H.-J. Dietrich
Grombühlstr. 7, D-97080 Würzburg

Druck: Dergham sarl
Gedruckt auf alterungsbeständigem Papier
Printed in Lebanon

ACKNOWLEDGEMENTS

At the beginning of this research I owe thanks to many institutions and people for their support and help in the completion of this study. First of all, I thank the University of Birmingham and the Center for the Study of Islam and Christian-Muslim relations of Selly Oak, in particular my Supervisor Professor Dr. Jorgen S. Nielsen for his help, his encouragement, his advices and specially his patience. I also thank Mrs. Carol Babawi and Mrs. Bernadette Storer.

My thanks go to the institutions Internationales Katholisches Missionswerk missio and the World Council of Churches in Geneva who granted me the scholarship. I thank specially in those two institutions Dr. Tareq Mitri and Dr. Harald Suerman.

I want to thank my friends for their help in reading and editing this research. I think of Dr. Ra'if Nassif, Miss Sameera Bashir, Mr. Sean O'Sullivan and Mr. Michel Moufarrej.

My gratefulness goes to my University Balamand in the persons of Presidents Dr. Elie Salem and Mr. Ghassan Tueini, Vice presidents Dr. Georges Nahas and Georges Sayegh and Directors Dr. Tarek Mitri and Dr. Leila Badr. I hope they will be happy to see and read the results.

To the memory of my friend Yvette Janine Maha and Leyla

TABLE OF CONTENT

LIST OF MAPS

LIST OF GRAPHS

LIST OF DOCUMENTS

PREFACE

Waqfs are one of the main Islamic religious and family establishments. They are deeds bestowed permanently upon families and their descendants and upon religious institutions. They are dedicated to the welfare of society

The waqf institutions of the Christian, as well as the Muslim communities, reached the peak of their expansion during the Ottoman period.

The study of the Lebanese Greek Orthodox waqfs during the Ottoman period is significant because the Greek Orthodox was the most favored Christian community in all the empire. Privileges granted to their church go back to the period of the fall of Constantinople and the nomination of Patriarch Genadios to the patriarchy of Constantinople by Sulṭān Muḥammad al-Fātiḥ.[1] Along with his enthronement, security and continuity were guaranteed to his community. After a difficult period resulting from the consequences of war (looting, displacement of populations, extortion and profanation), the situation progressively returned to normal. A conviviality of sorts and a religious dialogue were established between the enlightened personalities of the two communities. In response to the sulṭān who was seeking information concerning the main dogmas of Christian faith, the patriarch drew up a declaration of faith consisting of around twenty articles. This declaration has reached us by way of a book written in Greek by Theodoros of Monembasia entitled *The String of Pearls of Byzantine Kings*, of which an Arabic translation is available at Balamand Monastery in Lebanon.[2] It relates the history of the Byzantine kings starting with Constantine and ending with the last Constantine. After the story of the fall of Constantinople, the author continues his history of the Byzantine kings and the Ottoman sultans until the time of Sulaymān the Magnificent.

---

1 Antoine Fattal, *Le statut légal des non-musulmans en terre d'Islam,* (Beirut: Imp. Catholique, 1958), 366.

2 "Al-durr al-manẓūm fī tārīkh mulūk al-rūm," Balamand manuscript, no. 187.

This shows that the Greek Orthodox in the empire considered the Ottoman sultans as the heirs of the Byzantine emperors and accepted this situation in the best way they could.

With the occupation of Syria, Palestine, and Egypt, the four ancient patriarchates – Constantinople, Antioch, Jerusalem, and Alexandria – came to be reunited under the authority of the same political power. Of this whole group, it was the oecumenical patriarchate of Constantinople that continued to have a kind of hegemony over the other regions and dioceses. In the patriarchate of Antioch, the inhabitants and the church did not partake much in the Byzantine glory and triumph. Neither did they share the spirit of the crusades, but rather the spirit of the cross. A sermon of Patriarch Ignatius IV describes them as having lived the martyrdom of silence. Through their spiritual, liturgical and doctrinal wealth, the oriental Christians were the launching pad for Christianity as a whole.[3] On the religious level, this wealth was perpetuated in the Ottoman period. On three occasions, the Orthodox Church of Russia called on patriarchs from Antioch to settle problems the church had with the people and the political authorities.[4]

In Mount Lebanon, the Greek Orthodox were not considered an important community. Outnumbered by the Maronites and targeted by Catholic and Protestant proselytism, their presence in Lebanon was limited to commercial cities, harbors, and some rural regions near these cities. Yet they were able to profit from the expansion of the waqfs as much as the other communities. This expansion brought prosperity to the Christian communities and their institutions in Lebanon.

Thus, the waqfs have continued, up to the present, to constitute a heritage of landed, cultural and artistic wealth, a heritage that was progressively built up over four centuries.

---

[3] Ignace IV, *Le martyr du silence*. Sermon of 17th Nov. 1990 at St. Louis des Invalides, (Paris: Service orthodoxe de presse, no. 153), 10-13

[4] Asad Rustum, *Kanīsat madīnat Allāh Anṭākiyyah al-ʿuẓmā*. vol. 3 (Beirut: al-Maktaba al-Būlusiyyah, 1988), 32, 53.

CHAPTER I

INTRODUCTION AND IMPORTANCE OF THE SUBJECT

Studies on the waqf are essential for historical research at all levels. Research on the waqf could constitute an ideal field for multidisciplinary studies in the social sciences. Jurists, economists, geographers, and urban architects can work along with historians and sociologists on the same subjects, using the different sources available for the waqf.

I. 1: Waqfs in the Framework of Historical Research

From the legal point of view, even if the corpus of law governing this institution is well known, the interpretation and the enforcement of these laws have often been astonishingly far-fetched.

It was mainly in the historical field that research on the waqf was the most conclusive regarding the social and economic history of urban and the rural conditions. The variety of sources available on this subject points out the different themes essential to the study of any society: economics, laws, social and moral attitudes, to name only a few. Purchase deeds, sharecropping, establishment deeds, judgments, trials and all sorts of bookkeeping practices have constituted a stepping stone for the study of social classes, prices, and production in the cities as well as in the countryside. This traditional religious institution, often archaic, shows strong persistence in its organization and management. But we sometimes notice that through certain initiatives, the modernization and development of its structures and management has been introduced. The present spread of waqf lands in Lebanon and the Middle East has not been the object of accurate or official statistics. This subject has often remained a taboo as the holders have often been unwilling to disclose openly the effective reality of this heritage. Nevertheless, several limited evaluations have been undertaken; they were mainly aimed at improving waqf productivity. Any project or plan to modernize this institution, in view of benefiting the largest number, must inevitably be based on accurate statistical studies concerning this type of land.

The study of these documents within the framework of a multidisciplinary research could prove to be very useful for the revival of these estates. These documents hold the secret of the prosperity of this institution. In them we can observe, at first, the relation between the waqf and social and economic history.

But, before getting into that subject, we have to distinguish between two different types of waqfs: rural and urban.

Social historical research on waqfs is one way of studying information regarding the different social classes in the Ottoman provinces at that time. In the countryside, peasants, craftsmen, wardens and shepherds are mentioned in these archives, as a class apart from and opposing the notables of different grades: *muqaddams,* emirs and sheikhs. The clergy also is quoted according to its different titles: *shammās, qīs, khūrī, raʾīs, mudabbir, muṭrān, rāhib, mutawaḥḥid.*

In the cities also, the different social strata are listed according to their professions: *al-tājir, al-najjār, al-ḥaddād, al-ṣāʾigh,* or their functions: *al-wakīl, al-qāḍī, al-mutawallī,* etc. These different categories maintained among themselves relations, which were not always stable. As in all traditional societies, this balance of power didn't always refer to different categories. It was mainly between the notables and the clergy that the interests and pacts were either made or broken according to different circumstances. It was during the second half of the 18th century that the peasants' rebellions called *ʿāmmiyyāt* occurred. They were essentially provoked by the increase in taxation and by the rise of bidding on the lease-farming tribute in the provinces of Mount Lebanon. In this context of popular uprisings, the clergy supported the peasant levies. It was the clergy who, with the bourgeoisie, profited from the decline of the local notables and became a new rising social force in the country.

Economically, the waqf had always been considered a stagnant and inactive source of wealth. In fact, the waqf obeys neither the market laws, nor the movement of riches and means of production. The waqfs that were flourishing in the past did not stay that way in all regions. However, they constituted an essential heritage for an eventual policy of communal and economic development.[1] The study of the history of waqfs is essential for understanding the economic history of Lebanon. The waqf documents inform us about the different kinds of agricultural products. The large variety of archives in the monasteries shed light on the history of prices. Price curves can be drawn up over long periods, on the basis of the accounting registers. Prices of production, food products, tools, means of construction, salaries and sharecroppers' shares were registered in the archives and could be listed. Fiscal history and fluctuations of prices can

---

1 Antoine Messarra, ed., *L'église de la réconstruction* (Beirut: CEDROC, 1995), 54.

help the study of relations between political chronology and the different economic crises. Famines, droughts, epidemics, natural catastrophes, and embargoes were among the many factors that had disastrous economic consequences. The population, who often endured the destructive results of these factors, had its own means of resistance that allowed it to survive.[2] Debts, mendicancy, internal emigration, sale of lands and furniture, transfer of properties, and unemployment were often ways of life which the waqfs' bookkeeping practices allow us to look back into. Economic realities noted in the accounts didn't always result in concrete measures. Thus, for example, peasants' indebtedness did not always result in their expulsion. Also, the sudden rise of the taxes collected in the mountain, during the 18th and 19th centuries, didn't always lead to the sale of peasants' properties.

In the urban setting, research on waqf history is also very important for the study of cities' structure and occupancy of space. Urban waqfs form a wide range of immovable properties that were transformed into waqfs for the interest of the communities and the families concerned. Shops, houses, warehouses, *khānāt, sūqs,* kilns, and plots of land are among the many estates belonging to the traditional scenery of the Arab and Muslim city.[3]

The study of waqf deeds, inventories, lease contracts, etc. enables us to understand the evolution of architectural styles of habitat, the transformation of thoroughfares, the expansion of districts, the creation of new suburbs and their development into urban zones. Here too, while studying the waqfs in the city of Beirut, we notice the evolution towards the specialization of districts by the type of habitat. Central districts were dedicated to labor and residence at the same time. In the old cities, the *khānāt* were used as family residences and workshops. With the city's evolution, the downtown *sūqs* came to be dedicated to business and labor.

The various limits mentioned in the transfer of property deeds inform us on the different thoroughfares in the city: street, road, dead end, etc. They are designated by the terms *shāriᶜ, ṭarīq, zārūb, zuqāq, etc.*

Studies of the fiscal system in the archives of the bishopric enable us to know the different strata of the urban society of that period. Notables and important traders controlled the external trade between several Ottoman

---

2 ᶜĪsā Iskandar al-Maᶜlūf, "Zajaliyyāt fī waṣf al-ghalāʾ wa-l-jūᶜ wa-l-ḍīq," *al-Mashriq* (May 1920), 338-348.

3 Randy Deguilhem, "Waqf documents: A Multi-purpose Historical Source; the Case of 19th Century Damascus," in *Les villes ottomanes*, ed. Daniel Panzac (Paris: CNRS editions, 1994), 70.

towns, while bourgeois and small tradesmen formed the middle class ranks that would have an essential role in the political life of Lebanon in the 20th century. Craftsmen and immigrants tried to join the new structures of the rising city.

Concerning the political history of Lebanon, always torn between different ideological and confessional currents, the writing of its political history has always been made on the basis of confessional references, values and priorities.[4] In view of this reality, amplified by the Lebanese civil war, Mount Lebanon's socio-economic history, written on the basis of waqf and family documents, can be regarded as a unifying element in the recording of history. The architectural masterpiece of terraced fields, built throughout the mountain, was the achievement of peasants from all communities. Silk, the essential factor of agricultural and industrial prosperity in Lebanon, was spread over all the Lebanese regions and beyond. With the exception of the Koranic *jizyah,* collected taxes weighed very heavily upon the shoulders of the peasants in all the Lebanese districts of the *wilāyahs* of Sidon and Tripoli.[5]

But here too, some scholars find that socio-economic history was an amplifier of religious and confessional disputes. Confessional conflicts were aggravated by their identification with the social problems of the country. Starting from the 18th century, socio-confessional identification had a decisive impact on the course of events.

In the countryside, almost all of the peasants were Maronite, and the majority of the notables were Druzes; in the cities, the Sunnīs formed mainly the craftsmen and small trader class, while Greek Orthodox worked in trade and the Greek Catholics in finance. In the towns, Jews occupied all the businesses or professions. As for the Shīʿīs, they were peasants also, but chroniclers of that period described them as living a situation of armed conflict with the Sunnī Ottoman *wālīs* of Sidon and ʿAkkā and the Druze emirs of the mountain. Of course this hypothesis assumes many exceptions and demands many reservations. But it also allows us not to "justify" the socio-economic history as being more unifying and objective than it really was. Here too, many polemics have opposed Lebanese historians.

---

4 Ahmad Baiḍūn, *L'identité confessionelle et le temps social chez les historiens libanais contemporains* (Beirut: Librairie Orientale, 1984), 13.

5 Joseph Abou Nohra, *Contribution à l'étude du rôle des monastères dans l'histoire rurale du Liban: recherche sur les archives du couvent St Jean de Khenchara et de 5 autres couvents maronites et melkites (1710-1963)* (Ph.D. thesis, Strasbourg, 1983).

I. 2: Methodology

But the problem of objectivity could be reached by a correct methodology because concerning waqf documents, it is essential to have a history which takes into consideration the different situations and problems.

Because of their nature, their presence in almost all of the Lebanese regions and the fact that they cover a period of at least two centuries, these documents offer an outline of serial and quantitative history. Serial history may be defined as any historical approach that constructs statistical series using homogeneous data extending at regular time intervals over a long period. With serial history the quantitative element truly enters into the field of study. In the traditional method, the numerical figure was used in an isolated and anecdotal manner, but in serial history it becomes the essential instrument for understanding a historical development, both its long-term tendency and its short-term fluctuations.[6]

This claims to be a useful historical method, which is concerned less with the individual fact than with repeated elements capable of being integrated into a homogeneous series. Such series may correspond to or be identified with other series presently utilised by the other human sciences.[7] The archives studied to date do not mention any individual, political, cultural or economic fact. But on the other hand, as an integral part of a homogeneous series, they contain a repetition of elementary facts and numerical data. The series we have cover a period of around thirty to seventy years only (St. John of Dūmā books and Beirut inventories), while other series cover two and even three centuries (our Lady of Balamand and St. Ilyās Shwayyah acquisitions deeds). These series allow us to verify well known historical situations and data included in the documents.[8]

These figures and data, repeated in these archives, may be considered as evidence of a type and a standard of life and of communal relations proper to a society which had its own ways and means of subsistence.

This method allows a more or less great probability of fidelity and precision because it integrates the quantitative information taken from a book into a series of constituted data where the evidence is multiplied.[9] Using a document as a whole gives us a wider margin of accuracy regarding the events we want to describe and the consequences that we can draw. We tend to see in the document what accords with our expectations.

---

[6] Jacques Le Goff, ed., *La nouvelle histoire* (Paris: Retz, 1978), 508.

[7] Pierre Chaunu, *Histoire quantitative, histoire sérielle* (Paris: SEDES, 1978), 121.

[8] Furet, François and Nora Pierre, eds., "Le quantitatif en histoire," in *Faire de l'histoire: nouvelles approches, nouveaux problèmes,* 1 (Paris: Gallimard, 1974), 49.

[9] Chaunu, "Histoire quantitative," 22.

The outcome of a partial use of the documents could result in proving contradictory theses. This method is necessary, especially because the documents of the monasteries and bishoprics are relative to the analysis of the serial and quantitative history.[10]

In fact, we find in these archives the structurally numerical sources, which, once used by the historian, answer the questions that are directly linked to their original field of investigation. For example, the books of accounts, the waqf inventories, and the deeds of acquisition help us to study the expansion of waqfs and their administration.

Colophons of religious manuscripts, deeds of waqf foundation, and trials allowing us to know the evolution of waqfs in their political, religious and human contexts are the structurally non numerical sources that history tries to use in a quantitative and serial way.

This serial history, which allows an accurate study of the past, introduces us to a better reading of the present. And a good reading of the present that fits with the past leads gradually to the future; it is prospective by nature.[11]

This historical method tends to play the collective against the individual, the general against the trivial. This history is less concerned with the history of events such as battles, treaties, kings and their courts, than with the history of anonymous masses, with the ways in which they worked, lived, and loved. It is the history of the day-to-day rather than the exceptional. It seeks to reconstruct the mental atmosphere of past times from the inside, to grasp the mutations of human societies in the transformation of customs, diet etc. It has to a considerable degree used problematical issues taken from other human sciences. It has integrated itself in a wide sociology of the man in society.[12] Since it has moved from the particular to the general, from the aberrant to the significant, history has not ceased to expand its bounds. History is now combined with ethnology, society, economics, psychology, geography etc. in an interdisciplinary movement.[13] If we had to approach the subject of the demography of the Beirut suburbs or the property distribution in the Biqāᶜ in the year 2000, or the difficulties of apple-growing in the Lebanese mountain, we would be dealing with actual socio-economic subjects. Similar problems, of one or two centuries ago, constitute subjects of quantitative and serial history. They give to human sciences a time depth that is the best substitute for an experimentation that is impossible. This new historical method presupposes the overturning of methodological data at the level of space and time.

---

10 Furet and Nora, 51-52.

11 Pierre Chaunu, *De l'histoire à la prospective* (Paris: Robert Laffont, 1975), 283.

12 Chaunu, "Histoire quantitative," 23.

13 Le Goff, 210.

It is a macrohistory, embracing wide fields. It upholds the reality of time and the need for analysis across the arena of world history[14]. In our study on the waqf, which is limited to the Orthodox monasteries of Lebanon, the Ottoman Empire as a whole and the laws of Islam are taken into consideration. The economic situation of the institutions of the Christian minorities is part of a wider geographical and political setting. The waqf as an institution is integrated into the framework of the Turkish and Arab Islamic world, a world whose formal frontiers had less reality than religious affiliation and military hegemony.

This revolution in method has also overturned the concept of time in history. Historical study is shifting its attention from the drama of events in order to identify and formulate problems that can only be grasped in the longer term. Indeed, the history of the slow development of material civilisation has become the history of humanity.

In the framework of the history of monastic institutions, the duration of time appears in a twofold and contradictory manner. Firstly, there is the long term of the traditional rural economy and of popular peasant culture, bound by inertia and ancestral custom. Yet on the other hand, there is the short term, the domain of elite cultures, the source of innovation and challenge. The monasteries in this period were intellectual centres in which the production of cultural and religious writing played a large part in the literary renewal of the Arab world. All this was intimately involved with the slow evolution of the agrarian economy over the long term. The choice of this methodology and this type of history take us away from Lebanon's traditional history, which is often limited to the tales of the deeds and wars of Emir Fakhr al-Dīn and Emir Bashīr. This trend in history lies within the framework of a serial history interdependent with other human sciences and aiming to be an actual part of a wider study on the conditions of development of the waqfs. These conditions raise the problem of an eventual renewal of traditional regional structures, with a view to their greater participation in the economic and cultural development of the country.

The readings of the different data contained in the waqf documents suggest different, indeed contradictory interpretations. Debt adjustments, tax exemptions, and food contributions, all listed in sharecroppers' accounts, suggest that the monasteries of Mount Lebanon played a mainly humanitarian role. On the other hand, the cancellation of sharecropping contracts and the seizing by the waqf of peasant lands in the mountain suggest that the clergy were really part of the landowning class. According to this interpretation, they, along with the *muqāṭaʿjī* notables, monopolised the land as the main

---

14 Chaunu, "Histoire quantitative," 129.

source of production; they, along with the bourgeoisie of the cities, were profiteers who weighed down the indebted peasantry with high interest charges.

In fact, the study of the monasteries' revenues and expenses reveals that the situation was not so clear-cut. The monasteries' land policies, whether conservative or expansionist, depended on the particular situation. Nevertheless, their humanitarian attitude could only make itself felt when their economic condition and the general development of the country permitted it.

The foundation of waqfs was also not a straightforward matter. Present-day inhabitants of the villages surrounding religious institutions often affect a certain moral authority over the lands belonging to the latter, because they claim that their own ancestors had given those lands to the Church by transforming them into waqf. Yet after examining the archives, and particularly the acts of purchase and donation that are preserved in the different monasteries, we notice that the greater parts of the lands were acquired by the accumulated thrift of the monks. For it was they themselves who worked the lands and sold the produce; and with the balance of the income they bought more land.

The serial and quantitative study of the monasteries' accounts, including the series of sharecropping revenues and expenses and the series of acts of acquisition, prompt us to adopt a more relative attitude and a less severe judgement. For the different initiatives and measures taken by the monasteries were often taken under the pressure of particular crises or political situations. The study of the documents in their entirety and in a serial manner should permit us to be more objective in regard to these problems of the waqfs' economic history.

I. 3: The Study of Waqf in the Case of Christian-Muslim Relations

If the problem of objectivity can be solved by the adoption of the methodology of serial history, this is not the case with the problem of the waqfs' socio-economic history as a unifying history. Nevertheless, the waqf documents can contribute to a deeper study of the history of Islamo-Christian relations. The expansion of waqfs among the Christian populations of the empire represents an original aspect of the study of communal equilibrium between the followers of both religions. Paradoxically, it was under the government of an Ottoman Empire considering itself as representing the classical Islamic caliphate that the expansion of the institution of waqfs occurred. The waqfs bookkeeping was recorded in the registers of the Muslim towns' courts of law, where the trials relative to these waqfs were judged. These judgements were often passed in the interest of the waqf. It was not the expansion of the waqfs alone that seemed important, but also the interaction between the two communities that took place along all the steps of the evolution of this institution. The study of the waqf institution in the Ottoman Empire as practiced by the Christian communities gives us an example of the evolution of Islamo-Christian relations over a long period of time. This collaboration between the two communities was also achieved on the levels of waqf management and establishment. Here, it was not the concern for religious dialogue that could order this kind of interaction, but rather it was favored by the needs of the political and fiscal context of that time. The empire's policy towards the waqfs was not the same over four centuries. The restrictive and hostile policy of the Ottoman Porte towards the waqfs during the first period was not limited to the institution in its Christian part. Muslim waqfs also suffered from the Ottoman seizure of their institutions. From the mid-17th century, Christian institutions benefited from the massive transformation of *mīrī* lands belonging to the state and established religious orders to manage these newly acquired properties. Reforms undertaken in the 19th century influenced the Christian and Muslim communities differently. So, on the one hand, the impact the Ottoman measures had on the Christian waqfs was decisive concerning their foundation, expansion and exploitation. On the other hand, measures taken by the Ottoman Empire were not always in accordance with Islamic *sharīʿah* laws concerning waqfs. That is why the study of Christian waqfs in the cities and the countryside is essential for the study of Islamo-Christian relations.

Here too, this subject could be studied through several documents, found in the monasteries and bishoprics, which concern taxation. Some types of documents found in the monasteries are listed in the registers and documents concerning the *mīrī* tax. And we can find documents related to the *jizyah* payment in the *sharīʿah* courts located in the cities. At the end of the 19th century, Muslim-Christian equality, decreed by the different reforms undertaken by the empire, considered the Christians as citizens, who had to serve and participate, together with the Muslims, in the defense of the Empire. But these new reforms did not please everybody. Christians and Muslims had to pay a tax in return for their non-participation in the army. This new *jizyah* paid by the new citizens was called *badal ʿaskariyyah.*

I. 4: Archives and Sources for the Study of Christian Waqf Institutions

Archives and manuscripts that have remained in the monasteries and bishoprics are a very important source for the study of economic, social and regional history. Those Christian religious institutions that were established in the 16th and 17th centuries and evolved under the Ottoman Empire were governed by the *sharīʿah* in an epoch prior to nationalization. Even the interference of the Western powers, facilitated by the Capitulations system, had no meaningful impact on the religious level at that time.

These institutions, i.e. convents, monasteries, and bishoprics, soon became the favoured places for the accumulation of land ownership (land during this period being the major capital and means of production), organization of work, and distribution of revenues. Due to their moral and territorial importance, these institutions also became intermediaries between the population and the state.

In the 18th and 19th centuries, these monasteries and bishoprics were in charge of tax collection in their regions. The fulfillment of these functions demanded an administration, a management and official correspondence, the remains of which have survived in a regrettable condition of decay and neglect. Nevertheless, what we have left is still very useful to us.

I. 4.1: Importance and Limitations of these Documents

The documents we intend to consult for our study of the waqfs of the Greek Orthodox Community in Lebanon are varied and scattered, geographically as well as chronologically. These archives are leftovers of series of judicial administrative and accounting documents that are regarded today as useless. Their presence in the monasteries and bishoprics is merely accidental.

We rarely have in our possession a consecutive series of related documents or records that could make us discover the evolution or that would indicate changes in a specific situation and at a given period. The documents, which form a chronological set, are not the same everywhere.[15]

In Beirut, archives date back only to 1870. They cover the urban zone of the city, and also the rural zones of Mt. Lebanon that since 1902 have become an independent diocese known as the Diocese of Jubayl and Batrūn.[16]

We have purchasing agreements and waqf sale bills, but it is obvious that they do not cover all the territories of the waqf, even at the beginning of the 20th century. On the other hand, we have found inventories, made at the end of the last century, which recorded the land and commercial estates of every church or charitable organization.[17] Here also, all the lands or waqfs of the city were not listed in the inventory.

---

[15] Daniel Crecelius, "The organization of waqf documents in Cairo," *International Journal of Middle Eastern Studies*, no. 2 (1971), 268.

[16] Georges Birberī, *Nashʾaṭ abrashiyyat Jubayl wa-l-Batrūn wa mā yalīhā* (D.E.A. thesis, Institute of St. John of Damascus, Balamand, 1993).

[17] *Maḥfūẓāt Dayr Sayyidat al-Balamand al-baṭriyarkī wa Dayr al-Nabī Ilyās al-baṭriyarkī, Shwayyah wa Dayr al-Qiddīs Yūḥannā al-Maʿmadān Dūmā* (Beirut: University of Balamand, 1995), Bey 1380-Bey 1359-Bey 1418.

At the Balamand Orthodox monastery, founded in 1603 in the old buildings of a Cistercian abbey, scattered purchasing agreem ents and accounting records are extant. The purchasing agreements are in a rather bad condition, torn and damaged by humidity, and their contents are barely decipherable. However, a 19th century monk rewrote these agreements in the monastic register.[18] It is not possible to tell whether the register includes all the agreements concluded by the monastery, since it has not been compared with the scattered agreements.[19]

We have also found accounting records related to the upkeep of the lands of this monastery. But these records cover a period extending from the end of the 19th century to the beginning of the 20th century (with many omissions). On the other hand, these daily accounting records are a kind of accounting journal in which all the purchases and expenditures were registered in a haphazard way. Other, better organized, records were called "the general ledger." Other registers use the two pages to record – face to face – the weekly or monthly expenditures and revenues of the monastery.[20]

The monastery of St. John of Dūmā, located 700 metres above sea-level in the region of Batrūn, and belonging to the diocese of Jubayl and Batrūn, was deserted for a long time. Its documents were obviously damaged due to the fact that it became a barracks during the Lebanese war of 1975-1990. Not a single purchasing agreement or waqf deed was found in this monastery. But fortunately we have found in a religious manuscript (Triodi) an "annotation" related to the foundation of the monastery and to the establishment of its waqf. This agreement, written in small characters on a large page, describes in detail all the measures that were taken and the acquisitions that were made in order to settle a community of monks. Clothes, ritual objects and religious manuscripts are mentioned there in the same way as the carefully delimited agricultural lands.[21] In addition, the monastery of St. John Dūmā has a set of accounting records that enabled us to outline the annual balance sheet, which included all the expenditures (salaries, constructions, food, upkeep, etc.) and revenues (essentially agricultural rents and revenues from the fulfillment of vows). In these accounts, every land of the waqf has its own inventory, which includes

---

[18] Ibid., document Bal 48.

[19] Ibid., documents Bal 49 to Bal 372.

[20] Ibid., documents Bal 1 to Bal 47.

[21] *al-Makhṭūṭāt al-ʿarabiyyah fī-l-adyira al-urthūduksiyyah al-anṭākiyyah fī Lubnān* (Beirut: Center for Antiochian Orthodox Studies, N.d.), vol. 1, 74-75.

its production and revenues as well as the expenditures and salaries resulting from agricultural exploitation.[22]

The archives of the patriarchal monastery of St. Ilyās of Shwayyah in the Matn also include purchasing agreements and many other documents like land agreements, trial sentences, and land limitation agreements. These agreements form a set of relatively concentrated documents that may be considered as irrefutable proof of property at a time when the land registry did not exist. They cover three major regions where the lands of the monastery were located: the region full of pine-trees and orchards directly surrounding the monastery; the region of Abū Mīzān; and the region of Qinnābah. The agreements relating to cultivation provide an example of what kind of relationship existed between the tenant farmers and the ecclesiastical authorities.[23]

In the same way, accounting records of different kinds and different periods have provided us with information about the land and the fiscal and economic organization relating to different kinds of agricultural exploitation. Based on these registers, other economic analyses of the prices and evolution of salaries could be made.[24]

I. 4.2: Documents Related to the Waqf of Beirut City

These documents are very diverse. The ones that we plan to use are the purchasing and waqf agreements, the inventories, various agreements, and the text of the law. These different sources give us an idea regarding the different ways of administering the waqfs, and the role of the waqfs in the urbanization of the city and in the organization of the summer resort industry in the mountain. They also shed some light on the evolution of the land policy of the waqf and its role in urban life through the educational, medical, and social services provided by the concerned associations and institutions.

We are going to describe briefly each kind of these documents.

I. 4.2a: The Purchasing and Waqf Agreements

These agreements are concerned with the acquisition of real estate through purchase or endowment.

The majority of the estates were acquired by the waqf through purchase. The bishopric and the associations, which controlled the waqfs,

---

22 Ibid., documents Dou 278 to Dou 339.

23 "Maḥfūẓāt Dayr Sayyidat al-Balamand", documents Eli 1 to Eli 154.

24 Ibid., documents Eli 137 to Eli 174.

dedicated part of their budget to the acquisition of new real estates and made them profitable either by direct exploitation or by renting them to a third party. Other acquisitions were dedicated to the construction of new schools or to the clinic, which later became a hospital. There are two categories of purchasing acts, those concluded locally or by mutual consent between the two parties, and those that had more official aspects and were made under the auspices of the court of Islamic law (*sharīʿah*) in the city.[25]

Such a distinction is due to the content and style of the agreement itself. These agreements are also distinguished by their writing, the paper used and the witnesses who signed them. The two categories of acts included all the details necessary to the identity of each: the buyer and the seller or to that of their official. The nature of the acquired land is also mentioned, and some included a description of the acquired buildings and their contents. Information concerning the locality and the boundaries on the four sides of the acquired place are also recorded in detail.

As to the price of the acquired real estate, it is recorded in terms spelling out the exact sums paid and received by the two parties. The acts are dated according to both the Hegira and to the Oriental Christian calendars.

In the case of the agreements on the spot, only the Christian year is mentioned.

The endowment agreements are not so numerous but their content is much more elaborate. Many conditions are included in the text of the deed of endowment to make it available. Special words must be used to define those specific conditions. The endowment is made in favor of the poor of this or that waqf of the community. The text states that if the community had no poor, the endowment should then used for the common good of any community.

The juridical citation of the physical and mental well-being of all the faculties of the donor as well as expressions concerning the validity and the irrevocability of the act take up a great deal of the text.[26] The reason for the great emphasis regarding this matter was to avoid or prevent any possible contesting of the donation that could arise in the future on behalf of the heirs of the donor or other injured parties.[27]

---

25 *Maḥfūẓāt abrashiyyat Bayrūt li-l-rūm al-urthūdhuks*, 2 vols. (Beirut: University of Balamand, 1998-99), 1. Deeds have been registered in *al-Wikālah*, register Bey 65 to Bey 69.

26 Salīm Harīz, *al-Waqf: dirasāt wa abḥāth* (Beirut: Lebanese University Publications, 1994), 30.

27 Ibid., 22.

The land agreements are of different kinds, but the ones that we are most interested in are related to the organization of the city and to its urbanization. The bishopric had launched the planning of a whole part of the city centre, with the help of other communities of the city – the Catholics, the Maronites and the Armenians – and of some interested families, mainly the Sursuqs. Many roads were opened and the old houses were destroyed and replaced by shops and buildings (*ḥārāt*) with many businesses. We can identify four kinds of agreements.[28]

Doc 1 - Deed of Acquisition of the Waqf of Beirut from the Archives of the Sharīʿah Justice Court – Year 1290-1291 H N 290*

[28] "Maḥfūẓāt abrashiyyat Bayrūt," vol. 2 (1999), documents Bey 951 to Bey 1534.

Other agreements were concluded between the bishopric and some private individuals. They were mainly agreements that set down the boundaries and limits of the lands (boundary agreements), and they were usually concluded in the aftermath of conflicts arising between two owners of contiguous lands. These conflicts were usually settled out of court, ending in the conclusion of agreements that drew the boundaries of the land of each party. Other land agreements were also concluded by the bishopric in Sūq al-Gharb. This village had depended initially on agriculture for survival, but by the beginning of the 20th century it became more dependent on the summer resort industry.

The waqf lands that the bishopric owned in the region were divided into plots and sold to the inhabitants. The bishopric put some investments into the construction of a family hotel (Locanda) in the region. We have 23 purchasing agreements made by the inhabitants of the village, dating between 1905 and 1910, of lands that belonged to the waqf. On the other hand, other agreements were concluded at the same period in order to build a hotel and to exploit it before the bishopric decided once again to sell it.[29]

I. 4.2b: The Inventories

There are seven inventories. Each one of them included the list of goods and properties of the waqf inside the city. This waqf could be a church, or a charitable organization. These associations, which had their own communi ty services, established institutions – schools or hospitals – that have lasted till the present. Unfortunately, these inventories were not provided with dates. But they were issued because it became necessary to inscribe them in the official register of the land registry of the *wilāyah* of Beirut. It was also important to make a list of the waqfs during the nomination of a new bishop after the death of Bishop Ghifrāʾīl Shātīlā and the election of Bishop Jirāsīmūs Masarrah. This fact has enabled us to date them back to around the end of the 19th and the beginning of the 20th century, like all the rest of the documents belonging to the bishopric and related to the waqfs. As these waqfs were established, they were used for the benefit of the poor of an institution or a church, or generally for the common good. These inventories include information on the nature of the waqf (buildings, *khānāt*, *ḥārāt*) and its premises or fields. In the case of buildings, the number of doors is mentioned; as for lands, the surface area is inscribed. The location or the district of the waqf is also indicated. These inventories give special importance to the delimitation of the waqfs by defining the four boundaries.[30]

---

[29] Ibid., vol. 1, documents Bey 65 to Bey 69.

[30] Ibid., vol. 2, documents Bey 1387-Bey 1389.

I. 4.2c: Law Texts

A special register, which goes back to 1865, was kept in the bishopric. It contained all the laws and statutes controlling the activity of religious institutions and charitable organizations. The end of the 19th century was in fact a period of cultural and religious development, marked by the creation of associations that were responsible for institutions like schools, hospitals or orphanages. Other associations turned to religious teaching and, for this purpose, they established public libraries, organized conferences, and went further to publish weekly religious and cultural magazines. All these associations were run mainly by the laity, despite the fact that they were directly related to the bishopric. The laity did not only play a major role in the management of the waqf and the relations with the official authorities, but also in the growth of associations and institutions of the community. Lay members of the notable families of Beirut were invested with more powers because of the community councils set up by the Ottoman during the reforms of Khaṭṭ-i-Humayun (1856). The community council of Beirut had its status mentioned in the register.[31]

I. 4.3: St. John of Dūmā. Balance-Sheets

As to the balance sheets of St. John Monastery of Dūmā, we have for each year 2 written pages; one dealing with the annual expenditures, the other one with the income of the same year. These accounts are made through daily statements under each heading. The reference to each heading is noted in the balance sheet, which refers to the page of the book where all the details related to each element of this balance sheet are written. We have a series of these accounts extending from 1890 to 1927. Even the years of the First World War are covered. The accounts are noted in *pāras* or in Ottoman piastres even for the years after 1918, the year which witnessed the fall of the Ottoman Empire and the beginning of the French Mandate.

The person responsible for this accounting was the superior of the monastery who signed the accounts and made the balance sheet. The Bishop of Beirut, Ghifrāʾīl Shātīlā, to whom the monastery was answerable, used to review these accounts often. He appended his signatures and his seals after showing that he had revised these accounts and noting in letters the amount of the balance sheet. After 1902, this monastery became subject to the bishopric of Jubayl and Batrūn, which had become independent from

31 *Register of Associations*, Bey 1722 (17/24).

Beirut, and beginning with 1904, we notice the signature of Bishop Būlus Abū ʿAḍal.

In the expenditures' page, the superior had obviously divided the accounts into three themes, well defined by the partial operations, which affect the sum of one part of these expenditures. The first theme concerns salaries. The second includes various expenditures related to the cattle plus the expenditures called "of table" (kitchen and food). The third theme is dedicated to the expenses of the upkeep of agricultural lands, which are part of the monastery's waqf. Every property is designated by the name of the place where it is situated.

The first theme of the salaries enumerates 2 kinds of persons to whom the monastery paid salaries. The terms used are different. Monks, seminarians, priests, deacons and even the superior received the price of a garment. The granted sum of money was considered as being equal to the price of a garment. Its value varied according to the person concerned. Other names that received salaries from the monastery were registered with the number of months of work and with their kind of work. Servants, workers, cooks and game wardens receive a salary proportional to the number of months of work and kind of services.

In the second theme, headings do not constitute a uniform unit. Added to the food expenses, there were the cattle expenditures and sometimes the sums dedicated to the construction of the St. Nicolas Church. Later on, the expenses of the restoration of the monasteries and those previewed for the trial of the Maronite waqf of Mār Yaʿqūb, were also added to the same operation.

As to the third theme, concerned with the expenses of the maintenance of agricultural lands, we have six estates plus the mills, which required an annual upkeep. These lands are listed as being vineyards or orchards located in some very precise places in the village; the estates surrounding directly the monastery are the most extensive ones and are listed as being "within the monastery."

The page dedicated to the revenues of the monastery is very concise. Its headings are the same as those described in the third theme. The main revenues of the monastery consisted of the yield of the various agricultural estates. But here, the superior did not only point out the location. He has also indicated the kind of production that gave that particular yield: fruits, vegetables, and grapes. These accounts included also three sources of revenues. They were incomes resulting from the sale of the cattle, which varied from year to year.

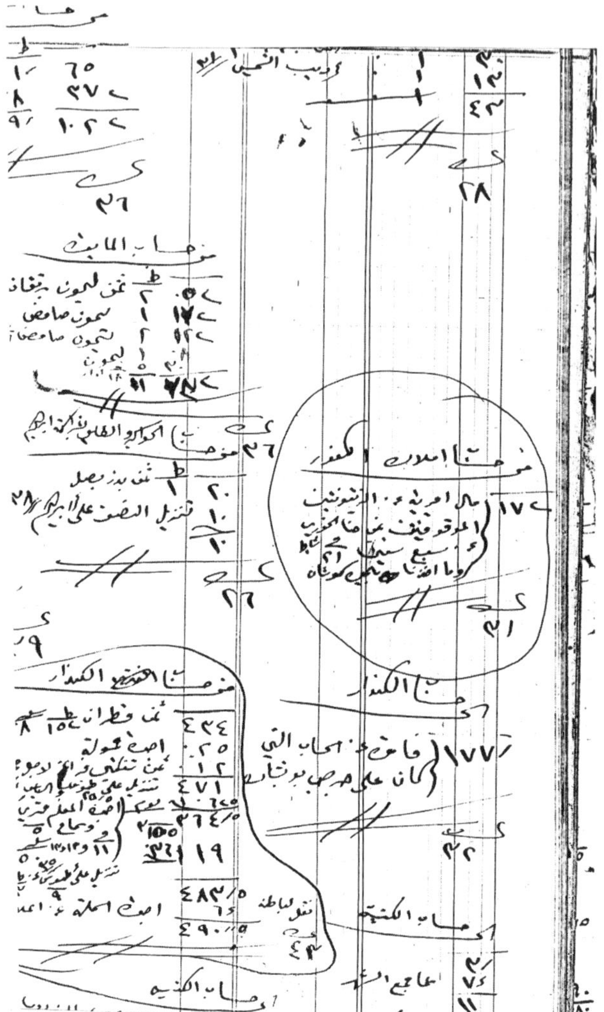

Doc 2 - A Page of the Account Book of the Monastery of St. John the Baptist, Dūmā

The mills are also included as giving the monastery a variable income. The less important income was that of the church which was also marked under the heading of the expenditures.

These accounts will help us make a detailed report on the various forms of agricultural exploitation that the monastery enjoyed. They are essential to understanding how the budget of the monastery functioned during a period, considered very important as to the political changes that occurred in the region as well as to the economic crisis endured by the population.

I. 4.4: Land Record of the Monastery of Balamand

The land records of the monastery of Balamand are a main source for studying the economic role of the monastery and tracing the evolution of land transactions between the monks and the inhabitants of the region.

An important aspect of rural history is revealed through these records. The importance of the role of the official authorities of Tripoli in the establishment and evolution of that waqf may be inferred from the agreements, trials and formalities enclosed with the land transactions in these records. Every detail pertaining to these waqfs, established through the centuries, is reported in this hand written record preserved by the superior of the monastery. This record was written by Father ᶜĪsā Ḍūmiṭ al-Ṣarrāf, known as the monk Iṣaʾyā, of the city of Hanah. It was commanded, as mentioned by the author, in 1869 by Patriarch Irotheos during his visit to the monastery. This measure was taken to prevent the disappearance of essential proofs validating the ownership of the lands of the monastery. The second half of the 19th century was marked by crucial changes in the ownership of the lands of the Ottoman Empire and Mount Lebanon. In Mount Lebanon, we witness throughout the century many disputes over land and farmers' revolts. Shortly before the composition of the record, the landed problems of the monastery prompted the issue of special act emanating from the Ottoman authorities of Tripoli in order to delimit the lands belonging to the monastery from those surrounding it. But the register of the monk Iṣaʾyā revealed the existence of many properties belonging to Balamand spread out all over the region of Kūrah and even in Tripoli. These pages were not all written by the monk Iṣaʾyā; in fact, at the beginning of the register, he mentioned that he had completed his work on the 20th of November 1870. Other monks came to complete and fill the empty pages left by the monk Iṣaʾyā.

Land purchasing and sale agreements, limitation agreements as well as trials, were mentioned in this record by various superiors of the monastery until 1945 and right after the deeds of the 19th century.

This register starts with very old purchasing agreements of the 17th century, which mention only the names of the seller and buyer with the location of the purchased estate, its price and the date of the deal. These thirty acts are written on the width of the page; each three acts on one page. The remaining 345 pages of the register are dedicated to sale, purchasing or exchange agreements, trials, and landed deals dating back to the 18th, 19th and 20th century.

وثيقة رقم BAL 48

Doc 3 - Deed of the Greek Orthodox Monastery of Balamand

All these formalities are written in the register according to the villages and cities where they were concluded: Tripoli, al-Mīnāʾ, Bṭurrām, Amyūn, Bishmizzīn, Kfar Ḥazīr, Kfar ʿAkkā, Bṣarmā, Kfar Qāhil, al-Zuhayriyyah, Wādī al-Mashāniq, ʿĀbā, Fīʿ, Barghūm, al-Ḥurayshah, and the mills.

But not all of these acquired properties are included in the official delimitation agreement passed to the monastery in 1814 by the governor of the city of Tripoli, Muṣṭafā Āghā Barbar. Among the documents of this register, we have the agreements concluded under the aegis of the official authorities (landed transactions, trials, limitation and exchange) and the agreements made locally between the monastery and the inhabitants of the region under the supervision of the superior and the sheikh or *mukhtār* of the village.

The farming agreements and the cancellations of contracts are included in this second category. The problem of tax collection led also to serious problems related to exactions imposed by the authorities on the monastery.

The choice of archives has been practically imposed by the availability of documents. Most of the archives of monasteries and episcopal sees have been destroyed by disasters, by time, or by spring-cleaning initiatives. For example, during the civil war in Lebanon, the episcopal sees of Tripoli and Mount Lebanon were sacked and burned in the course of the fighting, and their archives perished in the fires. During the battles in Kūrah in 1976, the manuscripts, archives and icons of the monastery of Balamand were stolen; fortunately, they were restored, but not until 1987.

In examining the institutions we have selected, their sites, and the hierarchy to which they are attached, we are struck by their diversity. Indeed, the sites, altitudes, products, and working methods of the different institutions reveal varied forms which may be reflected in the functioning of other Greek Orthodox religious institutions during the Ottoman period.

For example, with regard to altitude, Beirut is on the coast, whereas Our Lady of Balamand is at 200 metres in the region of Kūrah. St. John Dūmā and St. Elie Shwayyah are both in the mountain: the former is at 900 metres in the caza of Batrūn and the second is at 1100 metres in the caza of Matn.

As for agricultural products, all regions grew the Mediterranean trio of wheat, vines, and olives. However, the most important culture was that of the mulberry-tree, which rose to become a monoculture in the 19th century. Each region and each monastery exploited the culture that was best favoured by the local soil. For example, pine trees were grown at the monastery of St. Elie Shwayyah, where they were suited to the local sandstone. The villages surrounding Balamand profited from their chalky soil by giving priority to olive-growing and the production of olive oil. Whereas at Dūmā, the monastery of St. John was able to profit from plots located in rocky districts in order to grow wheat and vegetables.

These different monastic foundations depended administratively on different ecclesiastical authorities. Thus the two monasteries of St. Elie Shwayyah and Our Lady of Balamand depended on the direct authority of the patriarch. These were two important seats for the residence of the patriarchs of Antioch during their pastoral visits in the dioceses. As for the monastery of St. John the Baptist of Dūmā, until 1901 it depended on the bishopric of Beirut, but from 1902 it was included among the waqfs of the bishopric of Jubayl and Batrūn (Mount Lebanon).

Until 1901, the waqf of the city of Beirut was both urban and rural. From the beginning of the 20th century, the diocese of Beirut lost its control over the great monasteries of the mountain, but kept some property in the new suburbs of the city. This twin urban-rural aspect of the waqf of this diocese reveals a conflict between city and countryside, during a period when Beirut was in a state of transition, changing from a small local town into a capital city. The waqf is an indicator of this change, a witness to the social and economic upheavals of this watershed-period.

I. 5: Problematical Issues

Research undertaken on the waqf, either generally as an element of urban and rural social history, or more particularly as an element of Islamic Middle Eastern society, has emphasised different aspects of its development. For some the main characteristic of the waqf was its immobility. Thanks to the waqf, properties and domains that one desired to keep intact could be preserved from partition and confiscation.[32] Because of this immobilisation of property, large sections of the population were withdrawn from productive activity and supported at the expense of society. Therefore, the massive accumulation of property in mortmain was a cause of economic stagnation. The effect of the waqf was frequently the inefficient exploitation of vast lands, whose very extent deterred the introduction of more modern methods of agricultural exploitation.[33]

Other researchers have been more positive in their evaluation of the waqf; they consider that it has rendered a great service to the Near East both in the struggle against misery and poverty and by encouraging scientific studies. In a region where social policy was limited to religious

---

[32] Claude Cahen, *L'Islam: des origines au début de l'Empire Ottoman* (Paris: Hachette Littératures, 1997), 176.

[33] Antoine Abdel Nour, *Etude sur deux actes de waqf du XVI et du XVII siècles des wilayaets de Damas et de Sayda* (Thèse de doctorat 3ème cycle, Paris, 1977), 74.

obligations, the waqf and its attached foundations played a great role in the stability of social life.[34]

The waqf has always been a living institution in the Arab world; it was far from being simply a factor of immobility and backwardness in a conservative setting. The foundation of a waqf did not by any means result in a permanent withdrawal of real estate from circulation. The continuing demands of the market obliged waqfs to be administered with a great deal of flexibility. At first this flexibility was manifested in an informal customary way. Later it was codified in the *sharīʿah* and the laws of different states and communities. Legal judgements giving particular interpretations in the form of *fatwās* were imposed in favour of one social group or another depending on the changing balance of power between them.[35]

Other researchers have pointed to the expansion of waqf that came with the access of Mount Lebanon to the international market during the period when Lebanon became an important producer of silk. As has been noted, the expansion of waqf came with the need to commercialise silk production. One of the central issues of the impact of European economic expansion on agricultural structures in the Ottoman Empire concerns the formation of large agricultural estates. The growing demand for raw materials on the world market fostered efforts towards the integration of small landholdings into larger units of production and an increasing commercialisation of agricultural production. This commercialisation coincided with a tendency towards crop specialisation and a differentiation among the rural districts.[36]

The expansion of waqf is also connected with the conflict between town and country. The waqf played the linking role and the essential agent in the formation of relations between these two groups, which in social and economic terms were so distinct from each other. The waqf opened the way towards the exploitation of the countryside by numerous beneficiaries from different social classes, who would otherwise have been unable to exploit the peasantry. An element of stagnation prevented the crisis from being overcome.[37]

---

34 Louis Gardet, *La cité musulmane : vie sociale et politique*, 2nd ed. (Paris: J. Vrin, 1961), 236.

35 Randy Deguilhem, ed., *Le waqf dans l'espace islamique: outil de pouvoir socio-politique* (Damascus: IFEAD, 1995), 15-26.

36 Van Leeuwen, Richard, "Monastic Estates and Agricultural Transformation in Mount Lebanon in the 18th Century," *International Journal of Middle Eastern Studies* 23 (1991), 601-617.

37 Rudolf Vesely, "Procès de la production et rôle du waqf dans les relations ville-campagne," in *Le waqf dans l'espace islamique*, ed. Randy Deguilhem, 229-241.

In this thesis we shall attempt to study the waqf property belonging to certain foundations of the Greek Orthodox community in Lebanon by following the different stages of their development:

The foundation or restoration of waqfs in Mount Lebanon followed the example of several monastic institutions, which in the 16th and 17th centuries remained places of contemplation and prayer. By means of private donations (*mulk*) or public grants (*mīrī*), these foundations responded to a challenge that was occurring in all the provinces of the empire.

The expansion of waqf foundations in the countryside corresponded to a direct initiative on the part of notables and clergymen. In many cases, waqfs were the direct fruit of popular piety expressed by individual donations. However, they were also the fruit of the accumulation of landed estates, which had been preserved from partition among heirs. Waqfs also resulted from the demand for raw materials (in this case silk) and the requirements of the international market, which suited the establishment of large estates as efficient units of production.

The expansion of waqfs in the cities took place thanks to Ottoman reform initiatives that sought to introduce laymen into the administration of church affairs. Urban waqf expansion was limited to the Christian communities and was a clear sign of their prosperity (by contrast, urban waqfs belonging to the Muslim communities were in decay).

This prosperity was also a sign of the imbalance of relations between the town and the countryside. Soon the rural population began to migrate to Beirut, causing a separation between the city and its hinterland in Mount Lebanon. This separation in turn caused a change in the policy of waqf expansion; indeed, a movement now began to sell waqf property.

The administration of waqfs and the transfer of authority from clerics to laymen will be studied through the accounts of the monastery of St. John Dūmā, written at a time when monasteries were attempting to establish schools on their properties. In addition, the study of the accounts of the Aleppo waqfs and the rents of properties belonging to the waqf of the Beirut diocese will permit a better understanding of how the waqf functioned in the context of a rapidly expanding city.

Therefore, separate studies on the foundation, expansion and administration of the waqfs of several institutions should reveal whether and to what extent the waqf was growing or declining. We may also study the waqf's evolution in the context of relations between town and countryside; finally, we may consider how far the waqf responded to the needs of the market economy, which was represented in Mount Lebanon mainly by the predominance of mulberry-growing

The essential role of the monasteries and waqfs has its source in history. For centuries, pious foundations among both Christians and Muslims have served as a kind of social safety net and as a guarantee of economic recovery during periods following violent conflicts and natural catastrophes such as earthquakes and plagues. Two specific examples will illustrate the point. In the 17th century, the waqfs of Tripoli were the main base for the rebuilding of the city and its socio-demographic fabric in the wake of its destruction by the wars between the Maʿn emirs and the *muqāṭaʿjīs,* the local governors. The latter came from the Sīfā family[38] until the first half of the 19th century. Likewise, for more than four centuries the monastery of Our Lady of Balamand was a place of refuge for the inhabitants of Kūrah and Tripoli. Greek Orthodox families fleeing wars, epidemics (plague in 1770, 1785, 1809, 1813 and 1853; cholera in 1865) and earthquake would often stay for several months in this monastery. During these periods of forced leisure, the guests would read the monastery's manuscripts, inscribing marginal notes that described the events of the time and dated the length of their stay.[39]

These foundations, based on vast waqf estates, played a very important role on several levels. On the religious level, they did much to conserve and perpetuate the faith of the Church. Indeed, during the period of Ottoman occupation, any public manifestation of the Christian faith was regarded by the authorities as a form of proselytism. Since town and village churches became run-down and difficult to repair, Orthodox believers began to frequent remote clifftop chapels and monasteries. Every important feast of the Church became an excuse and an opportunity to take flight into depopulated country areas and mountainous places. The celebration of the Office could take place there more freely and in a far more secure atmosphere. The vigils and feasts which preceded and followed the liturgies were also occasions for the faithful to meet, discuss current affairs and comment on the great problems of the hour.[40]

One consequence of this frequentation of the monasteries was that the monks took in hand the whole religious life of the *rāyas*, a notable phenomenon both in Asia Minor and the Syrian provinces during the Ottoman era. Everyone knew the importance of Balamand in relation to Tripoli, and

---

38 Khālid Ziyādah, *Tārīkh al-muqāṭaʿāt al-lubnāniyyah fī al-qarn al-thāmin ʿashar* (Beirut: N.p., 1995), 305-320.

39 Rashīd Ḥaddād and Fāyiz Furayjāt, *Fihris makhṭūṭāt dayr al-Balamand* (Beirut: Dār al-Kalimah, 1970), 59.

40 Asterios Argyriou, *Les exégeses grecques de l'Apocalypse: L'époque turque (1459-1821)* (Tessaloniky: Etaireia Makedonikon Spoudon, 1982), 56-57.

that of Ṣaydnāyā to Damascus. Believers who frequented these monasteries were generous in giving to them, especially if they would be buried nearby. The three monasteries of Kūrah, Sayyidat al-Nāṭūr, St. James Diddih, and Our Lady of Balamand shelter the graves of families from the city of Tripoli to this day.[41]

On the economic level, from the 18th century the monasteries became centres for gathering harvests and allocating labour. Lands acquired by purchase or donation were intensively exploited. The monks, who had previously worked on the land, tended to give up their work to sharecropping peasants and to turn to increasingly diverse activities.

The peasants received land, tools, plants and seed from the monasteries and gave in exchange half of their yield in the case of silkworms, or one-third of yield for vineyards. The sharecroppers, who were often indebted to the monasteries, awaited the sale of their crops to free themselves from their financial obligations. They could, on the other hand, stock up with food supplies throughout the year, giving payment at the end of the season. The accounts of sharecroppers preserved in the monasteries' registers attest to the importance of these purchases, which were mostly imported. The entire Lebanese cereal production met only a quarter of the population's needs.[42]

The lands acquired by religious institutions were redistributed to the peasants, who worked them and delivered their crops to the monasteries. After being gathered, the produce of the surrounding areas would be sold throughout the country by the ordinary channels of commerce. Certain monasteries functioned as commercial companies, some of which are still thriving. They had agents in all the towns and villages of the region, whose business was to dispose of the monasteries' produce. The latter was not limited to silk and agricultural staples, but included other food products such as wine, oil and raisins, and also religious books, which were printed in some of the convents.[43]

On the fiscal and financial level, the economic growth of the monasteries and their relative prosperity, in addition to their spiritual and religious functions, conferred on them a financial and political dominance in the country. Because of their wealth and importance, the monasteries acted as bankers for both deposits and credits. The trust which they inspired among the people in general and their relatively neutral position, at a distance from

---

41 *Archives of Balamand, the Cemetery Registers*, Bal 38 to Bal 39.

42 Dominique Chevallier, *La société du Mont-Liban à l'époque de la révolution industrielle en Europe* (Paris: Geuthner, 1973), 42-43.

43 Joseph Abou Nohra, "Rôle des monastères."

the country's political conflicts, made them safe havens where Christian emirs, financiers, townsmen and merchants could deposit their fortunes during difficult periods. The chroniclers of the period tell us that the Greek Catholic inhabitants of Zaḥlah deposited their savings at the monastery of St. John Khinshāra, while the Greek Orthodox deposited theirs at St. Elie Shwayyah. In 1794, however, the soldiers of Emir Bashir II, during their war against the Abīllamaᶜ and the people of Zaḥlah, pillaged both these monasteries, seizing their deposits.[44]

The monasteries also advanced loans to their sharecroppers and other inhabitants of the neighbouring villages. These credits might be given to tide them over until the harvest season, but more importantly they were made for the payment of taxes levied by the local and central authorities. In becoming the principal landowners, the monasteries became, in their own areas, the chief tax collectors too.[45] This function was at first under the control of the *muqāṭaᶜjīs*. But with the coming of the *mutaṣarrifiyyah* and the drawing up of new land registers in the Mountain, the monasteries came into direct contact with the state and collected taxes from all the people living on their lands. Land registers and receipts of payment by persons and by areas have been preserved in the monasteries, providing ample proof of the fiscal role played by the religious authorities in both rural and urban areas. These authorities acted as intermediaries between the state and the peasants in the collection of taxes; the latter were thereby spared visits by the soldiery of the emirs, who would often organise paramilitary campaigns to replenish their treasuries. These were being increasingly squeezed by the rival bidding for the tribute of Mount Lebanon, provoked by conflicts among the ruling families.

On the cultural level, the first school in Mount Lebanon was established in the monastery of Ghūsṭā ᶜAyn Waraqah. At the Synod of the Maronite Church in 1736, those participating were urged to educate and enlighten the people.[46] From that period, ecclesiastical officials encouraged the foundation of schools in the convents and monasteries of Mount Lebanon. Among the Greek Orthodox, the first clerical school, providing a university-level education, was founded in 1833. It was

---

44 ᶜĪsā Iskandar al-Maᶜlūf, *Tārīkh madīnat Zaḥlah* (Beirut, 1911), 135.

45 Souad Slim, *Le métayage et l'impot au Mont-Liban aux XVIII et XIX siècles* (Beirut: Dār al-Mashriq, 1993), 112-113.

46 Nasser al-Gemayel, *Les échanges culturels entre les Maronites et l'Europe: du Collège maronite de Rome (1584) au Collège de ᶜAyn-Warqa (1789)*, vol. 2. (Beirut, 1984), 786.

followed by the School of the Three Doctors, founded by the archbishop of Beirut in 1835.[47]

But long before schools began to be officially established, the monasteries had possessed libraries in which manuscripts of great value had been copied and stored. These writings, which included patristic, theological, historical, monastic and especially liturgical works, constituted a cultural treasure by means of which visitors, whether lay pilgrims or religious, might deepen their faith and understanding. This patrimony still preserves the record of a long tradition of popular piety in which believers of all categories and backgrounds made donations to the monasteries. Moving witness to this may be found in innumerable inscriptions borne by icons or written on the pages of manuscripts. Pages left blank at the beginning or end of manuscript books carry the marks of the calligraphic and handwriting exercises of young novice copyists. Whole margins are filled with detailed descriptions of the circumstances which led the readers, whether guests or residents, to profit from reading the Holy Scriptures and the works of the Church Fathers.[48]

Travellers at the end of the 18th century had already remarked on the role of the monks in acquiring manuscripts, noting that they would frequently send out one of their number to search for important literary and scientific works of the time. These same travellers also noted the progress that had been made in reading and writing during this period. The knowledge and practice of reading spread rapidly among the people of the areas where convents and monasteries had been established.[49]

The monasteries played an essential role in the development of culture and the spread of teaching. In this sense, the establishment of schools in convents and monasteries during the 19th century was a natural continuation of the role that they had fulfilled for centuries in an informal manner. The new educational institutions took their place in the continuous religious and cultural tradition of the monasteries and episcopal sees.

In the second half of the 19th century, efforts on behalf of teaching came to assume a wider scope. Catholic and Protestant missions from the West gave a spur to the educational activities of the different religious communities in Lebanon. The institutions created by the Western missions were tied to those foreign powers, such as France and Britain, which enjoyed special privileges under the Ottoman system of capitulations. Teaching became

---

47 Jamīlah Kustī, *Madrasat Zahrat al-Iḥsān: khaṣāʾiṣ al-nashʾah wa-l-taṭawwur min khilāl "ʿIqd al-jumān" (1881-1928)* (D.E.A. thesis, Lebanese University, Beirut, 1993), 63.

48 Ḥaddād and Furayjāt, 60.

49 M. Delaroière, *Voyage en orient* (Paris: Debécourt, 1836), 155.

an ideological instrument linked to different political interests and movements. Thus, the teaching provided by Maronite institutions and French Catholic missions was able to win friendships for France throughout Syria, while the British and American Protestant missions trained supporters of the Western democratic political model. Official Islamic teaching, for its part, was directed towards preserving a Muslim culture and the unity of the Ottoman Empire.[50]

In the setting of the Greek Orthodox Church, schools founded by charitable associations and by the Imperial Palestine Society were established in parishes beside churches and presbyteries. These schools insisted on the teaching of the Arabic language and very often carried, besides their religious name, the qualification of "National."[51]

These different institutions permitted the cultural and technical training essential to the birth of an economic elite that would form the new middle class, and an intellectual elite that would take responsibility for the administration of the country.

---

50 Sāmī ʿAun, *Abʿād al-waʿy al-ʿilmī: dirāsa fī al-fikr al-ʿarabī al-ḥadīth* (Beirut: al-Maktabah al-Būlisiyyah, 1986), 10.

51 Yūsuf Asʿad Dāghir, *al-Madrasah al-Muskūbiyyah al-Manshūrāt al-Urthūdhuksiyyah* (Tripoli: Dār al-Kalimahh, 1982).

CHAPTER II

LEGAL AND HISTORICAL BACKGROUND

II. 1: Christian and Islamic Origins of Waqf

Throughout the Ottoman period, the waqf, as an institution, was an essential element in the structure of landholding in the provinces, in the distribution of the means of production and of income among the different social classes, and in the general organisation of society. Conversely, the relationship between the different kinds of landed property, together with the measures taken by both central and local authorities over a period of four centuries, greatly affected the evolution of the waqf. The word "waqf" may be applied to two distinct concepts. It may refer to the juridical act by which property is made over to a religious or charitable foundation. The owner renounces his right of disposal and stipulates that any income be used for worthy and authorised ends.[1] This juridical act includes the stopping of all transactions with regard to the property, which has become, as it were, "arrested" or "imprisoned." It may no longer be subject to sale, legacy, mortgage, donation or division leading to subsequent appropriation; yet it may still be leased for the short- or long-term and it may be exchanged.[2] Such property, duly established by juridical act, carries the name and status of waqf. The usufruct may be dedicated to a religious foundation, whether mosque or church, a charitable institution devoted to the poor, or to the children and posterity of the founder. In the first two cases, it is known as a charitable waqf or *waqf khayrī*. In the third case, it is known as a family waqf, *waqf dhurrī* or *waqf ahlī*.

The concept of "arrested" religious property, known as "waqf" in Islamic *sharīʿah* law and in the writings of various Muslim jurists, corresponds to the definition of Church property which appears in the records of Church councils from the start of the fourth century.[3] This institution, which, during the rule of successive Muslim dynasties, was managed by Muslim town councils, also existed among the various Christian commu-

---

1 Encyclopédie de l'islam, Nov. ed., s.v. "Waqf."

2 Harīz, 8.

3 Nadīm Ḥaydar, "al-Awqāf," *al-Nūr*, no. 7 (1984), 7.

nities living under Muslim rule. Under the *sharīʿah* law upheld by different Islamic governments, Christian religious and charitable institutions saw remarkable growth and prosperity. The Koran contains several instances of praise for the piety and modesty of Christian monks secluded in their monasteries.[4] Muslim historians often describe the festivities celebrated on the occasions of the feast-days of the monasteries' patron saints, at which Christians and Muslims would meet after long pilgrimages. Some of these popular celebrations have survived to the present. The caliphs would often come to participate in these festivals, despite the prohibitions of religious authorities.[5] The tradition of monastic life was ascetic; it aimed at the freeing of the soul from its servitude to the cares of the earthly body. Over the centuries, the piety of the faithful brought an enormous accumulation of landed wealth into the possession of monasteries whose members were sworn to voluntary poverty. Even today, one may see the extent of this wealth in the great monastic houses that were built throughout the region, usually in remote places, and always on sites well placed from which to contemplate the natural world and its Creator.

This landed wealth, classified in Byzantine Orthodox canon law as church property, and in Islamic *sharīʿah* law as waqf, saw important developments in the Ottoman period. The administration of these lands was subject throughout to a double jurisdiction. The Christian minorities of the empire, who had retained a degree of autonomy under the aegis of their religious leaders, remained subject to their own laws in matters of religion and personal statute.[6] Property matters and economic questions related to the land register were dealt with by the town tribunals of the *wilāyah* and so came under the purview of Islamic *sharīʿah* law. This law contained several chapters and articles concerning goods and lands dedicated to religious foundations. Such property, immobilised as waqf, was marked in the Ottoman state registers alongside other landed property coming under the different legal status of *mulk, mīrī, matrūkī* and *mawāt.*

These registers were made and consulted with the main purpose of fiscal distribution and tax collection in all the provinces of the empire. The *defterdar*, the official of the registers, whose position was equivalent to that of a finance minister, was responsible for them.[7] On the local scale, the registers were marked, kept and maintained in the courts of justice at the adminstra-

4 Koran, *Sūrat al-Māʾidah* 5:82.

5 Faraḥ Furzlī, *Ṣūrat ghayr al-muslimīn fī kitāb Ṣubḥ al-Aʿshā fī ṣināʿat al-inshāʾ*. (Ph.D. thesis, Kaslik University, 1983), 196-197.

6 Furzlī, 25.

7 Alphonse Belin, "Sur la propriété foncière en Turquie," *Journal Asiatique* (1861), 408.

tive centres of each *wilāyah*. The *ʿulamāʾ*, either the *qāḍī* or the *muftī*, were responsible for dispensing justice according to Islamic *sharīʿah* law. It was their duty to record all details concerning land, such as location, boundaries and produce. These registers also recorded changes in legal status.[8] The foundation deeds of waqf property, together with rental and exchange contracts, were kept, either in original form or as copies, in the patriarchates, bishoprics, monasteries and convents of all the Eastern churches. Like the Islamic courts of justice, the bishoprics had an important judicial role, although it was limited to resolving internal church matters and questions of personal statute. The monasteries and convents kept these deeds and registers as legal proofs in case of conflict or judicial process. These institutions traditionally played a role, albeit customary and informal, in the administration of justice. Deeds and land registers concerning waqf were, then, kept and used both by the official Islamic authorities and by the local churches. It would be of interest to explain both the Christian origin of church property and the Islamic origin of the concept and legal status of waqf.

II. 1.1: Church Property

The existence of landed property connected with religion in general, and particularly with temples and cultic places, goes back to the dawn of antiquity. In Egypt and Mesopotamia, the wealth accumulated by donations and sacrifices bestowed to the pagan gods, together with the domain lands of the royal-theocratic state, constituted the economic base of society and the chief source of investment in agriculture, crafts and commerce.[9] With the coming of monotheism, the Hebrews established temples dedicated to the cult of Yahweh and obligations to donate the first-harvests, first-fruits and first-born of all cattle to the One God. The first-born among the Jews were also dedicated to the temple but were replaced by animal offerings.[10] Several prophets made harsh remonstrances to Israelites who neglected to make their offerings. Both threats and rewards made by Yahweh on this matter were also related by these same prophets and taken up in the writings and sermons of the Church Fathers.[11]

It is quite plausible, therefore, that the property of the Church should have had a continuous connection with the property and donations dedicated to pagan and Jewish temples.

---

[8] Charles Issawi, "British Trade and the Rise of Beirut, 1830-1860," *International Journal of Middle East Studies* 8, no. 1 (1977), 25.

[9] Jean-Louis Huot, Jean-Paul Thalmann and Dominique Valbelle, *Naissance des cités* (Paris: Nathan, 1990), 47-48.

[10] *Exodus* 22:29.

[11] St John Chrysostom, in *Mattheum,* 66:3, PG 58, col. 630.

In an article on waqfs, Bishop Georges Khuḍr, taking an anthropological perspective, traces the idea of the waqf to the institution of public property in the primitive cultures of Africa and India. In such cultures, lands belonging to no one in particular were held by the community as the heritage of its ancestors. The essential aim of this custom was to perpetuate the group, by reinforcing both ties between its living members and fidelity towards its forefathers through a supposed identification between the community and the land. Land that was identified in this way with the group's cultural and ethnic identity could not be transferred to individual ownership. It could not be disposed of except for the sake of survival in times of disaster.[12]

Nevertheless, it seems that the early Church was unaware of such forms of landholding. The Acts of the Apostles describe donations and sharing of goods in kind and money among the early Christians. These gifts were intended to support the oldest poorest members of the new and growing community.[13] The legalisation of Christianity by the Emperor Constantine in 312 allowed Christians to recover churches and other property belonging to them. From 324 Constantine began to decree legislation regulating the relations between Church and State and granting privileges to encourage missionary activity. An organised and coherent corpus of laws was passed to facilitate the expansion and unity of the new religion. Special laws gave to the *corpus christianorum*, later called *ecclesia*, the right to receive donations and legacies. Goods were assigned to the Church. From 313 the emperor decreed for the Church the same regulations governing donations which applied to pagan temples. An edict of 321 greatly simplified testamentary procedure; the testator's bequests to the Church would henceforth be valid even if they had not been drawn up in legal form. Fiscal immunities granted to ecclesiastical property displayed the emperor's concern to encourage liberality towards the Church, which was now endowed with a privileged status that the pagan cults had never attained.[14]

This favourable attitude was the start of close and mutually supportive relations between the Church and the Byzantine State. Emperors and notables continued to make donations to the Church and to pass laws favouring the growth of ecclesiastical property.

In 534, the Emperor Justinian, who considered himself the protector of the Christian faith, legally defined three main sources of Church

---

[12] Georges Khuḍr, "al-Awqāf," *al-Nahār*, 14 June 1994.

[13] Nadīm Ḥaydar, 7.

[14] Charles Pietri, "Constantin et l'inflexion chrétienne de l'Empire," in *Histoire du Christianisme : spécialement en Orient*, ed. H. Musset, vol. 2 (Harissa: Imp. Saint Paul, 1949), 212.

property: donations, comprising lands and buildings with their revenues; taxes imposed by the State on the property of pagans and heretics; and legacies, especially ecclesiastical, which had not been bequeathed, or for which heirs were lacking.[15]

More detailed laws on Church property were decreed by the councils of the Church. Article 15 of the Council of Ancyra, held in 314, forbade the sale of Church property by clerics. The Council of Carthage in 419 likewise formally prohibited the sale of Church property. One exception however was allowed: if land were unproductive, yielding no revenue, and if the needs of the community were urgent, the bishop might sell the land after consulting the other bishops of the archdiocese, thereby avoiding sole responsiblity before God and the community. The number of bishops who were to be consulted is given as twelve.[16]

Article 32 of the same council forbade priests and bishops from acquiring landed property for themselves; any who did so or who received property as a personal gift must bequeath it to the Church in his will. Any who sought to recover land he had bequeathed would be degraded and deemed unfit to fulfil their clerical duties.

Article 33 stipulated that if a legacy were made to a village, it might not be recuperated by the central institution.[17]

Article 24 of the council held at Antioch in 341 recommended that all members of the clergy should be able to identify Church property in detail.

The Councils of Ancyra and Carthage decreed stiff penalties against parish priests guilty of selling Church property. Any sale would be cancelled and the Church must return the purchase price to the buyer, without receiving any compensation for the value of crops the buyer may have sold during the period of appropriation. If, however, the value of crops should exceed the purchase price of the land, the buyer would no longer have the right to recover the sum he had paid.[18]

Article 24 of the Council of Chalcedon in 451 decreed that convents, monasteries and attached farmlands should be protected. Monasteries might not be converted into temporal residences for the use of princes or nobles.

The councils also took up the question of relations between the Church and nobles. In a council held at Constantinople at the time of Patriarch

---

[15] Nadīm Ḥaydar, 10.

[16] Ḥanāniyyā Ilyās Kassāb. *Majmūʿat al-sharʿ al-kanasī aw qawānīn al-kanīsa al-masīḥiyya al-jāmiʿa* (Beirut: Manshūrāt al-Nūr, 1985), 676.

[17] Ibid., 680-681.

[18] Ibid., 133.

Photius, complaints were lodged against nobles who dedicated their own residences as monasteries, yet continued to live in them in the same manner as before. In the time of Pope Gregory the Great, born in 540 at Rome, nobles whose ancestors had founded convents were exercising their authority over these convents and the attached lands. The Pope decreed that consecrated monasteries must not be exploited for the profit of nobles.[19] Gregory the Great undertook an administrative reform of Church property that benefited their rural inhabitants. He reformed the patrimony of all parish churches in the West; all administrators were henceforth to become *defensores*, i.e. clerics sworn to evangelical poverty who must defend and protect the Church's rural tenants against all forms of public or private injustice.[20]

Ecclesiastical property was by then already becoming the object of lay covetousness. The Seventh Ecumenical Council of 819 took up the problem of monasteries, convents and episcopal sees occupied and converted into hostelries and inns during the Iconoclastic Controversy. Article 13 ordered the despoilers to return the property of their own free will; if not, they would suffer expropriation and excommunication.[21]

Prompted by forcible occupations of this kind, the Seventh Council required bishops (and abbots) to appoint administrators to Church property. In Constantinople, this function was undertaken by a *codinos* or *economé* charged with the receipt of revenues and the surveillance of patriarchal expenses.[22] This requirement certainly expressed the desire to leave the bishop free to devote all his time to the spiritual and parochial care of his flock, but it also reflected the wish to protect Church property from acquisitive bishops and their relatives. The very real problem of connivance between the clergy and lay notables was treated by this council. Article 12 recognised the bishop's right to administer Church property under God. Yet the same article warned abbots and bishops against transferring lands to temporal princes and notables, to themselves or to any of their relatives. If they did so, their action would be null and void and they would be deprived of their functions for having squandered wealth that he had not gathered. If any of his relatives were living in straits, they must help them just as they would all the poor. This clause was aimed at some members of the clergy who were seeking by means of such transfers to gain the support of governors and officials for their own promotion in the ecclesiastical hierarchy.[23]

---

19 Ibid., 427.

20 *Dictionnaire encyclopédique du christianisme ancien*, s.v. "defensores," 1106.

21 Kassāb, 820.

22 Ibid., 133.

23 Ibid., 819-20.

Imperial legislation and Church councils were not the only encouragement to liberality on the part of the faithful. The Church Fathers praised almsgiving and criticised property in their teaching. The Christians of the first centuries had created numerous institutions for relief and mutual aid: hospitals, asylums, hostelries and funerary services were dedicated to the relief of the poor. Christianity accomplished a revolution in social values by giving dignity to the wretched. This assistance, practised on a wide scale, affected the life of Christian communities, the spread of Christianity and the socio-political makeup of the cities.[24] Christian preachers of the fourth and fifth centuries called for the practice of almsgiving. This often led them to violent diatribes against greed and even against the right to own property. They saw property as unjust from its origins and by its very nature. St. John Chrysostom asserted that in the beginning God made nobody either rich or poor. The origin of possessions was certainly the result of injustice.[25]

Gregory of Nyssa referred to the lost paradise, praising the state of primitive equality that existed before the fall:

"There was no death; sickness did not exist; "yours" and "mine," those hateful words, were absolutely banished from life. Just as the sun was for all, the air for all, praise for all, and above all the grace of God for all, so in equality too was offered the free sharing of all goods. [...]"[26]

Deprived of any basis, property was seen as a mere usufruct, permitted by God so long as its beneficiary acted as a manager in the interest of all. The excess wealth of the rich should therefore revert to the poor. Bāsīl of Caesarea affirmed:

"You have seized the goods that were placed under your management. [...] To the starving belongs the bread which you keep, to the wretched the money you hoard. [...] Thus you oppress so many people whom it is in your power to help."[27]

During the fourth century, in an environment permeated with language of this kind and slanted towards social assistance, the bishop became one of the most powerful figures in the urban scene. As the protector of the weak and of certain trades, organiser of great public works, and arbitrator

---

24 "Christianisation et nouvelles règles de la vie sociale," in *Histoire du christianisme*, 693.

25 St. John Chrysostom. "In Epistulam I ad Timotheum 12:4, PG 62, cols. 562-4," in *Les pères de l'église*, ed. J. Liébaert (Paris: Desclée de Brouwer, 1986), 104.

26 Gregory of Nyssa, "In Ecclesiastem 6, PG 44, col. 708," in *Les pères de l'église*, 64.

27 Basil of Caesarea, "Homilia in Illud 7, PG 31, cols. 276-7," in *Riches et pauvres dans l'église ancienne*, ed. F. Quéré-Jaulmes and A. Hamman (Paris: Bernard Grasset, 1962), 76.

of disputes between private citizens, his power equalled, if not exceeded, that of the most influential lay notables. In a Christian society the bishops upheld the Romano-Hellenistic tradition of noble largesse. This custom had encouraged aristocrats, as a means of maintaining their status and popularity, to offer their fellow citizens public monuments and amusements. Bāsīl of Caesarea, founder of the Basiliads, called on all nobles to vie with him in humanity and magnanimity towards the poor.

The evangelical call to charity thus expressed itself in the ancient form of competition between urban benefactors. Noble pride was deeply involved. The munificence of Christian clerics and laymen recalled the desire for prestige and fame (or notoriety) of the classical tradition.

II. 1.2: Waqf According to Islamic Sharīʿah

Many researchers and historians of the Muslim world have taken an interest in the institution of waqf within the framework of Islam. In view of the spread of waqf and the importance of waqf foundations, several attempts have been made to define and explain the waqf in all its aspects. According to tradition, the Islamic waqf stems from the Prophet and the first caliphs, although the rulings of Islamic juridical schools diverged on certain details of waqf. Certain *ʿulamāʾ* derived the concept of waqf from charitable institutions already existing in conquered lands, such as the Byzantine Empire and in Medina. Much later there was another case of adoption by Islam of local legislation. The original concept of waqf property saw a remarkable expansion as the faculty to dispose of such property developed. Waqf was applied to real estate, but it was extended to money wealth also.[28]

During the Ottoman period, cash waqfs, or *waqf al-nuqūd*, were widespread and popular throughout the lands that had previously been Byzantine provinces. *Waqf al-nuqūd* meant the establishment of a trust with money, the income from which would pay the salary of a teacher or preacher. Most military and religious officials and provincial governors ruled in favour of their validity, and no one spoke out against them. The practice was considered to be quite as sound (*ṣaḥīḥ*) as any other waqf. Therefore it should be treated as irrevocable (*lāzim*).

The use of *waqf al-nuqūd* marked a revolution in *sharīʿah* endowment law; its legitimation, rationalised on the basis of customary practice, was a prime example of positive law in action within the *sharīʿah* Islamic system of law. However, there are few examples of this practice in the Syrian provinces until the eighteenth century. The Syrian scholar Ibn ʿĀbidīn

[28] *Encyclopaedia Universalis*, s.v. “Habous.”

wrote in his *Radd al-mukhtār* in 1660: "waqf of dirhams is practised in Turkish lands and not in our lands."[29]

In a society where health, education and welfare were entirely dependent upon gift and endowment income, this practice was fully legitimated, and we can find references to cash waqf in many Syrian *maḥkamah* deeds.

Although the waqf institution was essentially religious, waqfs were often founded for straightforward material reasons, in particular to avoid confiscations and to circumvent *sharīʿah* laws on the partition of legacies. Laws and customs developed over the ages, establishing certain general conditions: a waqf must be eternal and irrevocable (*muʾabbad, lāzim*) and must respect the principle of *qurbā*, by being instituted for a charitable end (that which brings one closer to God).

Like any other traditional institution several centuries old, the waqf had to adapt to the usages and practices of different periods and regions within the bounds of Islam. Legislators of the Ottoman period adopted *waqf al-nuqūd*, which required the payment of rent with interest. Donations of money in coin had to be profitably invested – such donations were a common practice in the Byzantine Empire before the Ottoman occupation.

II. 1.2a: Definitions of Waqf

The various definitions of waqf all insist on two fundamental elements:

1. the non-transactional nature of the property transformed into waqf.
2. its destination for pious ends.

According to Claude Cahen: "The permanent waqf is a foundation made by the owner of a property as a pious deed, guaranteed by the law, an irrevocable benefice made for designated beneficiaries."[30]

Mohammed Qadri Pacha gives another definition: "To constitute a waqf means to withdraw a piece of private property and prevent it from returning to its original condition. The usufruct must go to the poor or to a particular work of charity or of public interest, either at once or after the decease of the named beneficiaries."[31]

Gibb and Bowen in their book *Islamic Society and the West* define waqf as follows:

> It is a practice made by caliphs and sultans from a relatively early time consisting in devoting some part of the revenues of the privy purse to religious objects. But the bulk of the revenues of the religious institutions were

[29] Jon E. Mandaville, "Usurious Piety: the Cash Waqf Controversy in the Ottoman Empire," *International Journal of Middle Eastern Studies* (1979), 289-308.

[30] Cahen, 175.

[31] Gérard Busson de Janssens, "Les waqfs dans l'Islam contemporain," *Revue d'Etudes Islamiques* (1951), 5-72.

derived from private charity principally in the form of permanent endowments of land and other immovable property by a deed of restraint (waqf). The property so restrained was thereby withdrawn from all further transfer of ownership and its usufruct devoted to a specific object designated by the donor."[32]

The *Dictionnaire de l'Islam: religion et civilisation* gives the following definition:

The juridical institution known as "waqf" mainly in the legislation of the Middle East, and as "*habous* property" in the states of the Maghrib, originates in the precepts of the Koran. The designated waqf property must be devoted to a pious work or to a foundation of general interest for an unlimited time. But it is accepted that the donator may keep the right to grant the use (or usufruct only) of this property to persons of his choice and eventually to himself."[33]

These different definitions introduce us to the two different kinds of waqfs: those founded by sultans and governors from State lands and those founded by individuals from their own property. The first is known as *waqf ghayr ṣaḥīḥ* and the second as *waqf ṣaḥīḥ*. They also give us an idea of the beneficiaries of waqfs, who are divided into two categories:

1. Individuals, such as the descendants of the donator. This kind of family waqf was termed *waqf dhurrī* in the legislation.

2. Public institutions: mosques, hospitals, schools, caravanserais etc. In this case the waqf corresponds generally to the donations made by Christians to their churches.[34]

Besides these usual donations, the objects for which waqfs were founded were almost innumerable. Many waqfs were founded for the supply of money to the needy, dowries for orphan girls, the payment of debts for imprisoned debtors, the provision of excursions for children in spring-time, the burial of the indigent, while others were founded in aid of the armed forces.[35]

II. 1.2b: The Islamic Origins of Waqf and its Relation to Other Types of Property

The Islamic origins of the waqf must be sought in the beneficent impulse so characteristic of Islam. A tradition of the *sunnah* links the origin of

---

32 H.A.R. Gibb and Harold Bowen, *Islamic Society and the West: a Study of the Impact of Western Civilization on Moslem Culture in the Near East*, vol. 2 (London: Oxford University Press, 1951), 165.

33 Christine Barthet, "Habous," in *Dictionnaire de l'Islam: religion et civilisation* (Paris: Albin Michel, 1997), 338.

34 Cahen, 175-176.

35 Gibb and Bowen, 167.

the waqf to a verse of the Koran, naming it *ṣadaqah muḥarramah*.[36] The practice of waqf was a development of the Islamic obligation of almsgiving known as *al-zakāt*.[37] According to general Muslim opinion, no waqfs in either buildings or land existed in Arabia before Islam. The *fuqahāʾ* dated this institution to the Prophet, although they found nothing in the Koran to authorise it. Compared with other practices, the traditional justification of the waqf was very tenuous, although jurists affirmed that the companions of the Prophet and the first caliphs practised it. In a tradition of Anas ibn Mālik, it is reported that the Prophet wished to buy some gardens from the Banū al-Najjār on which to build a mosque, but the latter refused the price offered and gave the land for the love of God.[38]

According to a tradition of Ibn ʿUmar, who served as a principal source of reference for the jurists, the caliph ʿUmar acquired lands (*arḍ*) of great value at the partition of Khaybar. He asked the Prophet if he could give them as *ṣadaqah*, to which the Prophet replied, "Keep the land itself and dedicate its produce to pious ends" (*ḥabbis aṣlahā wa-sabbil thamarātahā*).[39]

The waqf appeared also as a form of common property dependent on the community. Land conquered by force (*ʿanwatan*) was never considered as privately owned, either in theory or in practice. The right of ownership was accorded neither to individual Muslims nor to non-Muslims. By the very fact of conquest, this land became the common property of all Muslims and was subject to *kharāj*. The assignment of such land as *al-tamlīk* naturally conferred only limited rights of ownership.

The same was true of assignment of revenues, whether *kharāj* or *ʿushr*, in lieu of pay in the form of *iqtāʿ al-istighlāl*, since *kharāj* lands were held in alienable trust for all Muslims. The only right accorded to the imam was that of leasing the usufruct in the name of the *bayt al-māl*, while retaining full ownership of the land itself.[40]

II. 1.2c: Different Legislation and Byzantine Origins

In the absence of any legal text relating to waqf throughout the first century of Islam, the *sunnah* assimilated the customs and laws in force in pre-Islamic Arabia and the recently conquered provinces. The *sunnah* of

36 According to the Shāfiʿī tradition (Encyclopédie de l'Islam).

37 John Robert Barnes, *An Introduction to Religious Foundations in the Ottoman Empire* (Leiden: E.J. Brill, 1986), 154.

38 al-Maqdisī, ʿAbd al-Raḥmān Ibn-Ibrāhīm, *Al-ʿudda, sharḥ al-ʿumdah fī fiqh imām al-sunnah Aḥmad Ibn-Ḥanbal al-Shaybānī* (Cairo: al-Maktabah al-Salafiyyah), 280.

39 *Encylopédie de l'Islam*, Nov. Ed., s.v. "Waqf."

40 Barnes, 28.

local tradition, and of Medina in particular, was codified by the consensus of the region's Muslim community, and this consensus came to serve as legal principle.[41] It is surprising that the earliest jurists do not agree on the essential elements of the waqf. Disputes revolved around matters of acceptability, inalienability, irrevocability and other problems.[42] At the local level, Mālik recognised the Medinese practice of giving charitable legacies to anonymous collectivities, known as *ḥabs fī sabīl allāh*, or contributions to Muslims engaged in holy war, and charitable gifts bequeathed to the poor in general. Mālik also recognised the practice of *ṣadaqah mawqūfah*, the provisional waqf that reverted to the donor's heirs upon the extinction of the original beneficiary's line.

The Shāfiʿī tradition for its part contested the opinion that the waqf remained the property of the founder and his heirs. Shāfiʿī seems to have been the first to promote the rise of later theories of waqf.[43]

Abū Yūsuf's use of reasoning by analogy and his acceptance of the *sunnah* of local tradition facilitated the establishment of family waqf, a practice born of communal custom and the desire to continue pre-Islamic convention regarding the division of inheritances.[44] Aḥmad ibn Ḥanbal's reliance on tradition was not just a conservative trend in the development of Islamic law, but the finalising of legal precedent and the culmination of Muslim jurisprudence as an unfolding dialectic. After his time there were no additions to the corpus of Islamic law regarding waqf. Any innovations were quite contrary to Koranic inheritance law regarded as *bidʾah* and equated with heresy.[45] Any waqf could be considered as favouring one member or another of the family.

Legislation therefore received a fixed juridical form in the 11th century. It should be added that in the conquered lands the Arabs found the basis of a system of public support in churches, convents, hospitals, orphanages and hospices. The early jurists may have had this kind of property in mind as the realisation of the charity prescriptions contained in Islam.[46]

Legal precedent was readily found in Justinian's legislation governing *piae causae*, which accorded point for point with the conditions respecting the creation of family waqfs. This Byzantine legislation was incorporated

---

41 Barnes, 19.

42 *Encylopédie de l'Islam*, Nov. Ed., s.v. "Waqf."

43 Ibid.

44 Barnes, 19.

45 Ibid.

46 *Encylopédie de l'Islam*, Nov. Ed., s.v. "Waqf."

into the corpus of Islamic law by the celebrated Ḥanafī jurist and first chief *qāḍī* of the Abbasid dynasty, Abū Yūsuf Yaᶜqūb.[47]

We see here the adoption by Islam of local, especially Byzantine, legislation in the provinces and of the primitive customs of the tribes of Medina in Arabia. The foundations reserved for mosques, charitable institutions and family waqfs had much in common with Church property. Like the latter, they were managed by the authorities who administered religious affairs.

Placed under the bishop's authority, the property of the Church was inalienable. Draconian legislation made its sale difficult, if not impossible. The waqfs, reserved for similar religious and charitable ends, were managed by the *muftīs* or *qāḍīs* who presided over the law courts in the main towns. Islamic *sharīᶜah* legislation intended to reinforce the irrevocability of waqfs was introduced by Abū Yūsuf after his journey to Medina, where he had been able to observe many Muslim waqfs.[48]

II. 1.2d: The Principal Aims of Waqfs.

Waqfs were founded to please God and to come closer to Him. The terms regarding the religious aims of waqf are clearly formulated in the acts of donation. But apart from its sacred purpose, the waqf was frequently utilised as a way of sheltering property from the State's appetite for confiscation; such property was often important, and its tenant would then become an administrator (*wālī*). Large families often had recourse to waqf in order to avoid the disintegration of their territorial patrimony. The purpose of waqf in this case is to assure the integrity of the property against division among heirs, including daughters (who would carry their inheritance into their new family when they married). Muslim inheritance law not only prescribed the division of an estate among children, but also took into consideration the claims of distant relatives. A large property could not be preserved under this system. Even if estates could be joined and enlarged by fortunate succession and marriage, there remained all the same a great mobility of landed property. The aim of the waqf therefore was to immobilise such property.[49] However, the founder of the waqf could not establish more than one-third of his fortune in waqf, whether in the form of a *waqfiyyah* or of a testament.[50]

It is certain that the waqf was utilised as a means of evading Koranic law concerning the distribution of legacies. Shurayḥ, one of the earliest

---

47 Barnes, 154.

48 *Encylopédie de l'Islam*, Nov. Ed., s.v. "Waqf."

49 Cahen, 175-176.

50 Abdel Nour, "Etude," 23.

Muslim jurists, contested the unlimited acceptability of waqf. He attributed to the Prophet a formula which forbade all actions of waqf on shares reserved for heirs: *lā maḥbas ʿan farāʾiḍ Allāh*, or "no withholding of inheritance shares prescribed by God."[51] When property was established as waqf, the donator excluded it from the share to be bequeathed to his heirs, dedicating it to a designated third party and the line of that party if it were a family waqf. Abū Yūsuf's initiative in introducing the *al-dhurrī* waqf contravened the legal provisions of his master Abū Ḥanīfah and the teachings of several other traditional jurists of that period. Abū Yūsuf's innovations were quite contrary to Koranic inheritance law. In this respect, Abū Yūsuf bowed to popular will, the influence of custom and tribal tradition and, most probably, to elite interests. But at that time these practices were still quite rare and the evolution of the waqf as an institution was very slow. The consequences of the immobility of property were not yet so clear and widespread as they would become at the dawn of the modern era.[52]

II. 1.2e: The Conditions of Waqf and its Extinction.

It seems that the principal rules for establishing acts of waqf, and the various clauses relating to waqf legislation were established from the 10th century onwards and regarded as obligatory. They are found in acts of waqf made today.[53] The underlined formula at the end of the act of waqf insists on the fact that the waqf is inalienable, eternal, and immutable. Very strict conditions are required for the waqf to be regarded as valid. These conditions had to be clearly formulated in the act of waqf itself; their application was overseen by the *ʿulamāʾ* and religious officials who executed the testaments (*waṣiyyah*) or acts of donation (*waqfiyyah*). Precise terms had to be used; the elaboration of the legal stipulations and formulae was mainly undertaken by the Ḥanafī school.

The first condition for the validity of waqf concerned the person of the founder. The constituent of a waqf must have the absolute right to dispose of his fortune. He must be capable of disposing of property – that is, he must be free, adult, and healthy in mind and body. These conditions had to be expressly included in the act of donation or foundation of waqf: *ḥurr*, *bāligh*, *ʿāqil*, free, adult, healthy.

The second condition concerns the aim of the waqf. It is only valid if it established for purposes of charity, religion or public interest. A pious

---

51 *Encylopédie de l'Islam*, Nov. Ed., s.v. "Waqf."

52 Cahen, 177.

53 Khadr, Mohamed, "Deux actes de waqf d'un Qarahanide d'Asie centrale," *Journal Asiatique* CLV (1967), 313-314.

or humanitarian end (*qurbā*) is the absolute condition of waqf.[54] This principle is unanimously admitted by ḥanafī *ʿulamāʾ* .The waqf must be made "in the way of God," in order to be pleasing to Him and to come closer to Him. Without this pious intention it has no validity.[55]

It follows that foundations made by non-Muslims are only valid if their aim is not contrary to Islam – for example, if they are not destined for churches or monasteries.[56] Therefore during the Ottoman era, Christian waqfs were all founded and named in favour of the poor of the church or of the monastery.

The third condition concerns the relation between the constituent of the waqf and the property thus established. The constituent must have unlimited property rights. Very often, the constituent stipulates in the act that the property should remain for himself. This immobilised property then becomes the full property of the donator.

Waqf should last forever (*muʾabbad*). In acts of waqf, this condition is realised by the stipulation that the income should go to the poor after the death of the founder and the extinction of his line; henceforth the waqf is inalienable.

Waqf should take effect immediately; a waqf must not be tied to any condition that postpones its taking effect until the death of the founder.

The act of donation is an irrevocable juridical act (*lāzim*). However, according to Abū Ḥanīfah, the foundation of waqf is revocable except in the case where it only takes effect upon the death of the founder. For this reason, the ḥanafī founder always brings a fictitious suit against the waqf administrator in order to reintegrate the waqf into his property. The judge then has the choice of applying the doctrine of Abū Ḥanīfah or that of Abū Yūsuf; however, favouring the latter because it upholds the principle of irrevocability, he invariably confirms the waqf and rejects the demand for reintegration.[57]

If the object of the foundations ceases to exist – if, for example, a hospital or *madrasa* were destroyed – the revenues should be applied to another charitable purpose, which is frequently specified in the *waqfiyyah* itself.[58]

---

54 ʿAbd al-Karīm Zaydān, *Aḥkām al-dhimmiyyīn wa-l-mustaʾminīn fī Dār al-Islām* (Baghdad: University of Baghdad, 1976), 484.

55 Muḥammad Fārūq al-Nabhān, *Al-ittijāh al-jamāʿī fī-l- tashrīʿ al-iqtiṣādī al-islāmī* (Beirut: al-Risālah, 1988), 346.

56 Zaydān, 486.

57 Muḥammad ibn Aḥmad ibn Juzayy, *Qawānīn al-aḥkām al-sharʿiyyah wa masāʾil al-furūʿ al-fiqhiyyah*, ed. ʿAbd al-Raḥmān Ḥasan Maḥmūd (Kairo: ʿĀlam al-Fikr, 1985), 400.

58 Gibb and Bowen, 175.

A vast number of waqfs have been founded since the beginning of Islam; if the rules of irrevocability and perpetuity had been followed, no doubt all landed property would have become waqf long ago. Of course this was never the case, because in every period waqfs have excited the appetites of the powers-that-be, and more or less outright confiscations have always been numerous. It seems that changes of government and invasions were a good opportunity to make a clean state and start anew. But it is also remarkable that waqfs dating from the start of the Ottoman Empire in the 16th century remain in vigour today.[59]

II. 2: Ottoman and Lebanese Backgrounds

II. 2.1: Waqfs during the Ottoman Period

Having dealt with the Byzantine and Islamic origins of the waqf, it is necessary to return to the local and regional situation. The State *de facto* was not always identical with the State *de jure*, just as actions taken on the ground did not always conform to the decisions, whether political or religious, taken by the central authorities. Islamic religious rulings on waqf jurisdiction and the stopping of *ijtihād* were not in practice fully applied by the Ottoman government, whose changing laws and decrees repeatedly upset the situation.

Almost from its earliest beginnings, the Ottoman Empire tried to take control of waqf administration and to extract from them the maximum profit. The changes in the land register effected by the Ottoman administration were essentially aimed at organising the running of the provinces, and assuring both territorial defence and fiscal levies. These three functions were combined in the *tīmār* system, which granted military fiefs to provincial governors and the army cavalry.

Indeed, recent research has proved that the basic aim of the new laws was to protect the economic interests of the landowning class, although the old Ḥanafī law safeguarded the property rights of independent peasants.[60]

The policy of the Ottoman Empire towards waqfs developed in three distinct stages:

---

59 Abdel Nour, "Etude," 35.

60 Baber Johansen, *The Islamic Law on Land Tax and Rent: The Peasants' Loss of Property Rights as Interpreted in the Hanafite Legal Literature of the Mamluk and Ottoman Periods* (New York, N.Y.: Croom Helm, 1988), 4.

II. 2.1a: The First Period

When the central Islamic lands were conquered by the Ottomans in the early sixteenth century, two different policies were adopted towards conquered land. In provinces that had been under Christian rule, Ottoman laws greatly affected the landowning structure. At the beginning of the reign of Salīm II, for example, the revision of the Salonika land register ordered by Abū Suᶜūd led to the confiscation of the property belonging to the monks of Mount Athos. Lands that they had traditionally owned as *mulk* were now registered as belonging to the *bayt al-māl*. The land that the monks had originally purchased from the peasantry was now rented from the Ottoman treasury on payment of an investiture fee called *ṭābū*. The land would remain in the possession of the monks as before; they would continue to cultivate it and enjoy usufruct, but they no longer possessed the right of ownership, which would have allowed them to alienate land in any manner without having to ask permission from the central government. The lands were now part of the state domain, a radical change in the conditions of land tenure for the monks of Mount Athos.[61]

Abū Suᶜūd's legislation was contrary to customary practice, which granted privileges and tax exemptions to monastic establishments and other religious foundations. Ottoman subjects were hardly in a position to object. They could not appeal to Islamic law because they had never previously been subject to it; unlike in Syria and Iraq, the Ottomans were free to deal with Rumelia and Anatolia in the manner they desired without being restrained by ancient traditions sanctioned by the *sharīᶜah*. Far from being restricted by the holy law, the State used its religious authority to expropriate private arable land. During this first period, many waqf lands were converted into *tīmārs*, particularly those whose income had been allotted to the poor, but which had fallen into disuse.[62]

The second policy was applied to provinces that had been regulated by Islamic land law before the Ottoman conquest. Here, the incorporation into the state domain of lands that were *mulk* and legally *kharāj* was out of the question. The provinces of Sidon (including Beirut), Syria, Aleppo, Baghdad, Basra, Mosul and Tripoli became *mustesna eyaletler* provinces, exempt from the normal fiscal practices of Ottoman administration. Yet even in those provinces, waqf donations were subject to review by the central government, which recorded all waqf landholdings in its central land

---

61 Paul Lemerle and Paul Witteck, "Recherches sur l'histoire et le statut des monastères athonites sous la domination turque," *Archives d'histoire du droit oriental* (1947), 411-472.

62 Barnes, 40.

register. They were either confirmed or, if they had ceased to fulfill their function, abolished.[63]

The aims behind the foundation of religious endowments were twofold: to preserve the family patrimony intact for future generations (*dhurrī* waqf), and to expand the landholdings of religious institutions. Placing *mulk* property in waqf had the effect of circumventing Koranic rules regarding inheritance and avoided the likelihood of confiscation by the state.

The Ottoman government, however, now asserted its right to supervision and control of waqfs established from *mulk* land.

Such a degree of control over *mulk* and waqf property worked well enough in the sixteenth century when the Ottoman Empire reached its zenith and the state's power became virtually absolute. It has been estimated that the size of waqf and *mulk* holdings in the first part of the century was relatively modest: in 934/1528, they amounted to some sixteen percent of the total state revenue. The majority of the endowments were created for religious or charitable ends and not for the benefit of individuals and their posterity.[64]

Even in Egypt, where lands had long lain under the jurisdiction of Islamic law, the new land reforms were also applied and, reluctantly, accepted. The *qanuname* decreed by the Ottoman governor Ali Pasha in 1553 introduced many changes in the traditional land code dating from the Mamluk period. By closely verifying existing land deeds and other documents, the Ottoman rulers transformed waqf and *mulk* into state property on an extensive scale. The end result of the land law of 1553 was to restore to the treasury some 300 taxable *muqāṭaʿahs* which had been alienated for various reasons in late Mamluk and early Ottoman times. The recuperation increased treasury revenues by over 80% during the last years of the century, allowing the Egyptian government to send over twenty million *pāras* annually to the Porte.[65]

A landowning class, composed mainly of Cairene rentiers and high-ranking military and civilian officials, had already come into being, having bought lands from the treasury during the Mamluk period. Although they had paid a high price in order to acquire lands that were virtually exempt from taxation, they had enhanced their prestige and social status.

Waqf land constituted from such properties was not subject to *kharāj* but to the much lower rate of *ʿushr*. The *muftī* Ibn Nujaym, a member of the

---

63 Barnes, 41.

64 Barnes, 42.

65 Stanford Shaw, "The Land Law of Ottoman Egypt, a Contribution to the Study of Landholding in the Early Years of Ottoman Rule in Egypt," *Der Islam* 38 (1962), 116.

Egyptian *ʿulamāʾ* and a well-known scholar considered that the new measures were aimed at abolishing waqf and charitable institutions and would impose *kharāj* taxation on waqf lands. In 1553, shortly before the promulgation of the new Ottoman *qanuname*, he wrote an important treatise, *al-tuḥfah al-marḍiyyah fī al-arāḍī al-miṣriyyah.* This defended *mulk* and waqf land property, and thereby the landowning class of officers, religious scholars and rentiers that had benefited in previous times and against whom the impending *qanuname* was being prepared.

On the evidence both of the *qanuname* and of Ibn Nujaym's treatise, it is clear that property could legally be turned into waqf. Obviously, the government had taken over much land from peasants and other landowners, whose longstanding property rights had thereby been rendered precarious.[66]

II. 2.1b: The Second Period

The state of conflict between the government and waqfs was not to last. During two centuries, from 1600 to 1800, while the empire underwent a protracted decline and political power slipped from the hands of the sulṭān and central government, the condition of waqfs changed greatly. The number of land endowments grew considerably, so that at the end of the nineteenth century, foreign observers estimated that anywhere from two thirds to three fourths of the empire's land had been transformed into waqf. The annual income of those lands in the area of modern Turkey has recently been evaluated at 50 million Turkish pounds.

The same situation prevailed throughout the Arab provinces of the empire. In the mid-nineteenth century, waqf land constituted half of the cultivated land in Algeria and one third in Tunisia. As late as 1927, it made up one eighth of the cultivated land in Egypt.[67] During this period, most waqf land was classified as *waqf ghayr ṣaḥīḥ* in contrast to *waqf ṣaḥīḥ*, which had been formed out of *mulk* land.

During this period, the majority of waqf foundations became semi-familial. Such kinds of waqf (*ahlī* or *dhurrī*) were religious foundations whose principal beneficiaries were the founder and his descendants to the extinction of his line, after which the endowment reverted to the poor. Semi-familial waqf was prebendary, in that the founder appointed himself and his posterity to various official and administrative posts, such as sheikh or *mutawallī*, which went with religious or charitable institutions. The proliferation of family waqfs in Egypt during the nineteenth century obliged

---

[66] Johansen, 93.

[67] *Encylopédie de l'Islam*, Nov. Ed., s.v. "Waqf."

the muftī of Alexandria, Muḥammad al-Jazāyirlī, to issue a ruling in 1262/1845 that governors could forbid the institution of properties in waqf in order to prevent "the fulfillment of depraved aims and practices."[68]

During the course of the eighteenth century, ninety per cent of new waqfs were created by the *askeri sinif* ruling class, which comprised the civil as well as the military aristocracy, the religious class of the *ʿulamāʾ* and members of rank belonging to the various *tarikats* or dervish brotherhoods. The *rāya* class, consisting of the Muslim and non-Muslim peasantry in the countryside and the merchant and artisan classes in the cities, founded only ten per cent of the waqfs created during the eighteenth century.

This situation is clearly apparent in Lebanon, particularly in the case of Balamand in the seventeenth century.[69]

In the cities, all kinds of real estate were used in creating waqfs. Documents show that any kind of property from which revenues could be derived was established in waqf. Commercial buildings such as stores, boutiques (*dukkān*), warehouses (*makhzan*), inns (*funduq*), khans and coffee houses (*qahāwī*), were often mentioned in waqf documents. Other kinds of structures such as dwellings (*dār* and *bayt*) were likewise put into waqf, with single rooms or the entire dwelling rented out to generate an income for the waqf's designated beneficiaries. In rural areas, agricultural properties of various kinds (*bustān, junāynah, ḥaql, ʿawdah, karm, ʿalqah, ḥākūrah*) likewise formed the basis of waqf capital.[70]

The Christian and Jewish minorities living in the cities made up the greater part of the merchant and artisan class. The interest derived from the liquid assets they had turned into waqf frequently went to the support of church or synagogue. Very limited, by contrast, was the number of religious endowments created by Muslim *rāya* engaged in trade or industry. Such waqfs made up ten per cent of the total number created by the *rāya* class, and only two per cent of those that designated *wakīls* to their endowments.[71]

A widely held opinion considers that waqf land was exempt from taxation during the Ottoman period and that this exemption was the principal reason why so much land and other property was given in waqf.

This opinion is still generally accepted, even though it has been proved that the Ottoman treasury did indeed demand taxes from waqf properties of

68 Harīz, 23.

69 Barnes, 43.

70 Deguilhem, 70.

71 Barnes, 43.

all kinds. The treasury upheld its right to tax all lands that had become inalienable and perpetual in waqf. No individual had the right to appropriate state revenue on his own initiative and direct it to a religious foundation. The state alone reserved the right to alienate revenue for a pious endowment or any other purpose.[72]

Nevertheless, the expansion of waqf property constituted a real threat to the treasury. Well aware of the problem, the Ottoman government developed a kind of waqf that would favour the treasury by allowing it the ultimate right of ownership.

II. 2.1c: The Third Period

The situation changed drastically with the onset of the so-called Tanzimat period of 1839-1876, during which the Ottoman Empire instituted a wide ranging policy of reform, the result of both political pressure from the European powers and of a real desire for modernisation on the part of enlightened Ottoman rulers. The Tanzimat Khayriyeh or Beneficent Reforms, introduced on 2 November 1839 in Istanbul's Gulkhaneh Park, was a watershed in Ottoman history, marking the beginning of a series of legislative reforms. Some of these reforms were truly revolutionary for an Islamic state. According to the Khaṭṭ-i-Sherif of Gulkhaneh, Christians, who had been considered as *dhimmī*-subjects since the beginning of Islam, would have the same status and rights as Muslims. This decree abrogated the chief politico-legal characteristic of the Muslim community – its dominant status in law.[73]

The reforms also introduced a series of measures which would have a great impact on religious foundations, and which were also considered at the time as revolutionary. The Tanzimat greatly affected the foundation, taxation and management of waqf institutions.

The Tanzimat legislation introduced different legal possibilities for founding waqfs. After the Land Code of 1858, it was legally accepted that waqfs could be officially established with *mīrī* properties held under a *sawād ṭābū* contract.[74] In the nineteenth century, waqf real estate was treated in practically the same manner as private *mulk* property. It even became possible to include waqf property in a legacy if that property was held with a *sawād ṭābū* contract. Despite the fact that *mīrī* land held with a *sawād ṭābū* contract was reclassified as *mulk* by the 17 Muḥarram 1284/

---

[72] Barnes, 47.

[73] Edward Engelhardt, *La Turquie et les tanzimat*, 2 vols. (Paris: A. Cotillon et Cie, 1882-1884), 1.

[74] Deguilhem, 95.

1867 decree, full rights of disposal and inheritance were granted over it. The 1867 legislation permitted the inheritance of this type of *mīrī* property even when it had been put into waqf.[75]

In this situation, the state remained the ultimate owner of these properties.

Before the Land Code of 1858, it had been common practice to found waqfs from *mīrī* properties. Normally constituted by governors and officials, they were considered as *waqf ghayr ṣaḥīḥ*. Waqfs prior to 1858 were far from being exclusively founded from *mulk* private property, the only acceptable type of property permitted by the *sharīʿah* to be converted into waqf. So the 1858 Land Code, whose principal aim was to increase the interest of sharecroppers, individuals working lands they did not own, created new circumstances by which various former legal constraints were lifted.[76]

From the point of view of taxation and state revenues, the situation was extremely prejudicial to the imperial treasury, since the vast majority of landed waqf property was *mīrī*, state lands whose revenues had been alienated by former sultans and governors and made waqf. It was imperative for the Ottoman State to rectify this state of affairs by creating a central administration for all waqfs throughout the empire in order to obtain the revenues of *mīrī* lands which had been diverted to other ends. This was without doubt the principal motivation of Sulṭān Maḥmūd's creation of the Awqaf Humayun Nezarati, the Ministry of Waqfs, in 1858, the peak year of reform. The ostensible reason for instituting this ministry was to create a central administration for waqf properties, which were under the control of a multitude of administrators and subject to a plethora of abuses.[77] The importance of the 1858 Land Code for the Ottoman government and its taxation policy lies in the fact that it legitimated and rendered taxable certain customary practices such as waqf established with *mīrī* property. It thereby gave the government more control over a larger percentage of land and other property in the empire.[78]

The most important change brought about by the Tanzimat towards waqfs was made in the field of administration. Since Umayyad times, the administration and supervision of waqfs had been the special province of the *qāḍīs* and other religious officials appointed as *wakīls* by the donors. But because of their flagrant abuse of the responsibilities laid upon them,

---

[75] Deguilhem, 72.

[76] Ibid., 71.

[77] Barnes, 95.

[78] Deguilhem, 95.

and the growing loss of revenue to the Ottoman treasury, waqf affairs were removed from their jurisdiction and placed under a secular administration responsible to the Ministry of Waqfs.[79]

According to the wording of the decree, the transition was to be gradual, and indeed the Ottoman government proceeded very cautiously in the transformation of waqf administration.[80] Respected notables, whose high rank would make them acceptable to the populace and who were found to be capable and competent for the office, were to be appointed as *muʾajjalāt nāẓirī* in charge of waqf affairs.

Ottoman rulers turned to local notables for the handling of waqf affairs essentially because of their wealth and position. It was hopefully assumed that persons of means would not be tempted to divert waqf revenues to their own purposes, and further that since they were experienced in the affairs of their province, they would be qualified to oversee local religious endowments. These assumptions were mistaken on several accounts. The local notables were too distant from Istanbul to be reliable, and their appointment to new duties appeared to many of them as merely an opportunity for self-aggrandizement. Even when they were honest, they were, more often than not, incompetent; the end result was almost always a loss of revenue to the treasury.[81]

Consequently, this reform in the administration of waqfs was not only prejudicial to the Ottoman treasury, but was also the principal cause of the waqfs' decline. Many waqf institutions fell into ruin because they had passed into the hands of corrupt and incompetent administrators. It was obvious that the control of waqf revenue exercised by the Ministry of Waqfs led to a decline in the number of religious foundations who held valid *berat* patents were given salaries and rations for life on the understanding that they would not interfere with waqf affairs or the collection of revenues.

This was another source of loss in waqf revenue. A number of European observers commented unfavourably on the situation. As MacFarlane puts it:

The reformers who are uprooting religion, and respect of it, in every direction have utterly destroyed the security which mosque, and mosque alone, could give to any land property. They have destroyed the independence of the Turkish "Church," if I may so call it. They have laid their greedy hands on nearly all waqfs of the empire and are undertaking to provide out of the common state treasury for the subsistence of the ule-

---

[79] Barnes, 102.

[80] Ibid., 106.

[81] Ibid., 132.

mas, mollahs, college or medresseh students, to repair bridges, khans, medressehs and mosques, and to do governmentally that which the administration of the waqf had done or ought to have done. Hence with very few exceptions we see the heads of the mosques and medressehs in abject poverty and the rabble of religious students in rags. The most beautiful minarets are shamefully neglected and hurrying into decay. Bridges, khans and fountains which were in a tolerably good state of repair no farther back than the year 1820, are now destroyed and useless. It is notorious that since the waqf have been administered by the government, nothing has been done to maintain the works of public utility.[82]

As can be seen therefore, the government's policy and legislation regulating waqfs was undeniably being redefined with a view towards making waqf properties turn in a better profit. This was part of the general Tanzimat reform drive towards progress and an acceptance of foreign influence.

A relationship may be seen between Ottoman attempts to exploit the empire's lands, including waqf lands, more efficiently, and the gradual but growing economic interlinking of the empire with the West. Contacts with the expanding European industrial economies, which were in search of raw materials and new markets abroad, affected life in the Ottoman Empire during this period in ways both overt and unseen. Efforts to expand profits and promote private property by means of new legislation raise the question of the extent to which the Ottoman Empire was now functioning as a peripheral part of the developing capitalist world economy.[83]

It need only be said here, however, that Istanbul's attempt to control waqf administration failed; the waqfs were in effect cut off from their religious roots by the introduction of greedy and incompetent secular administrators. Customary practices, however, such as long term rent contracts, do not seem to have been greatly affected by the new legislation. Both *sharīʿah* rulings and secular government statutes largely corresponded to actual business practices. In general, it seems likely that the law adhered to customary and *ʿurf* waqf usages rather than the other way around.[84]

II. 2.2: Situation of Waqf in Mount-Lebanon

The situation of the waqf in Lebanon in more recent times was not as it had been during the four centuries of Ottoman rule. While its development corresponds in certain respects to that of the Ottoman waqf, it differs in others. The current arguments in the field of Lebanese historical studies

---

[82] Charles MacFarlane, *Turkey and its Destiny: The Result of Journeys Made in 1847 and 1848 to Examine into the State of that Country* (Philadelphia, 1850), 396.

[83] Deguilhem, 95.

[84] Ibid., 94.

as to whether the status of waqf land was primarily *mīrī* or *mulk* has been overshadowed by the fact of the sheer extent and importance of those lands. The situation differed in each region, district and village, and varied with time, but there is no doubt that waqf lands covered a large part of Lebanon, extending over half of the cultivated land surface of the mountain.[85]

Even from the beginning of the 17th century, we can observe a definite correspondence between the development of Christian waqfs and the successive demographic increases and upheavals which took place in Mount Lebanon.[86] The *mīrī* and *mulk* origins of the waqf may also be traced to this particular period in the Ottoman Empire. Relatively few documentary acts of waqf have been uncovered, and these are all concerned with the foundation of waqfs; the expansion of the different institutions took place progressively according to a very astute purchasing policy which was also encouraged by political and economic developments in the country.

The institutions and lands in Lebanon that profited from the status of waqf were mainly the monastic establishments which, from their beginnings as little hermitages in the mountain were to grow into vast agricultural domains. The stages in the evolution of waqf that we have already noted in the Ottoman Empire as a whole occurred in Mount Lebanon also, if not at exactly the same times.

In the seventeenth century several factors helped in the foundation and expansion of waqfs. The massive emigration of Christian families from the north of the country and their settlement in the central and southern regions of Mount Lebanon[87] was at first encouraged by the presence of small local churches, and later directly organised by the monastic institutions, which welcomed the newcomers to their lands, offering them shelter and work, and granting them sharecropper status.

In the course of the seventeenth century too, there took place throughout the Ottoman Empire a major transformation in administrative organisation and taxation. The ending of an expansionist imperial foreign policy based on *jihād*, combined with successive economic crises and a decline in population, all affected the entire system of provincial organisation. The *timar*, which was at the same time a military, administrative and fiscal institution, gave way to a tax-farming system capable, it was hoped, of replenishing the Ottoman treasury, now chronically exhausted by the empire's continuing and mostly unsuccessful wars.[88]

---

85 Ibrahim Aouad, *Le droit privé des Maronites aux temps des émirs Chéhab 1697-1841 d'après des documents inédits* (Paris: Geuthner, 1933), 18.

86 Chevallier, "*Société du Mont-Liban*," 10.

87 Ibid., 12.

88 Robert Mantran, *Histoire de l'Empire Ottoman* (Paris: Fayar, 1994), 225.

The ending of the *timar* system in the provinces of the Ottoman Empire did not take place smoothly, least of all in Mount Lebanon. The passing of power from the Sunnī Sīfā *muqāṭaʿjī* of ʿAkkār to the Druze Maʿn governors of Mount Lebanon brought with it the widespread destruction of villages and crops in the north of the country.[89] The seventeenth century saw the conversion of military fiefs (*timars*) entrusted to the old governors belonging to the military cavalry into *mīrī* lands entrusted to the new tax-farming district governors or *muqāṭaʿjīs*.

Mīrī lands lying in war-ravaged districts were unproductive. They would be gradually handed over to the inhabitants of villages that were becoming repopulated by waves of migrants coming from the north and to the monastic institutions which were established during this period beside the villages.

Ottoman land law specified that lands inside and up to one league around villages were *mulk* belonging to their owners with full property rights. Pasturages, forests and wasteland lying outside and between villages were classified as *mīrī* land.[90] On becoming waqf, these lands were terraced and planted with trees, fruits and cereals, either directly by the monk-labourers or by the peasants who had become sharecroppers.

Such a change in the status of these lands could not have come about without the approval of the official Ottoman authorities that governed the countryside from the towns. Transfers had to be recorded in the Ottoman state registers (*defter*) held by the judges of the courts located in the provincial capitals. These were Islamic *sharīʿah* courts charged by the Ottoman state with administering the cities, providing justice and in general dealing with day to day problems. The *ʿulamāʾ* of these courts were closely related to notables of this region and living in the cities.[91]

One of the principal characteristics of the waqf in Lebanon during the Ottoman period may be seen in the link created by the granting of *mīrī* lands to religious institutions. One may see in this a traditional alliance between the clergy and governing officials, who showed themselves particularly generous during the seventeenth century in granting extensive lands to religious institutions in Lebanon. Although they were not themselves Christian, but belonged to the Druze or Sunnī communities, these tax-farming governors greatly helped Christian communities and monastic orders to spread throughout the mountain.[92] This was so even though the general

---

89 Kamal Salibi, *Modern History of Lebanon* (Delmar, N.Y.: Caravan Books, 1965), 4.

90 Wilhelm Padel and L(ouis) Steeg, *La legislation foncière ottomane* (Paris: A. Pedone, 1904), 11, 17.

91 Charles Issawi, ed., *The Economic History of the Middle East 1800-1914: A Book of Readings* (Chicago, Ill.: University of Chicago Press, 1966), 27-28.

atmosphere in the country was unfavourable to the foundation and expansion of religious institutions. Indeed, some oral traditions and even written accounts, such as diaries or annals, state that convents in Kisrawān were built in secret at night by lamplight.[93]

Conflicts and friction with the Sunnī authorities over these foundations were common in the first half of the 17th century. But with the growth in political authority of the *muqāṭaʿjī* sheikhs of the Mountain, greater facilities were accorded to the churches and monasteries.

An example of this collaboration between government officials and clergy in Mount Lebanon is illustrated by the case of the Kisrawān district, where the Khāzin *muqāṭaʿjīs* contributed to founding and developing several waqfs. Such privileges were not always recorded in writing and were often determined by local tradition. In general, the founders or their descendants remained in control of the monasteries they erected, while *muqāṭaʿjīs* were able to interfere with the administration of monasteries founded in their districts. This authority on the part of officials over monasteries in Kisrawān was strengthened by their influence in the election of patriarchs and the nomination of other ecclesiastical dignitaries, particularly *muṭrāns* (metropolitan archbishops). According to custom, no patriarch could assume his functions without the formal consent of the Khāzin sheikhs, while in some dioceses the latter had their protégés chosen as *muṭrāns*.[94]

The founding of waqfs and especially monasteries offered the governing class several advantages:

1. Waqfs contributed to the consolidation of the *muqāṭaʿjī's* authority in his domain, as they were legally protected against confiscation by the state.
2. Monastic estates were often instrumental in the reclamation and cultivation of land and therefore attracted peasant families from other regions, contributing to the expansion of the cultivated area. This new land was subject to taxes, which meant a gain both to the Ottoman treasury and to the *muqāṭaʿjī* personally.
3. The inhabitants of monasteries were accustomed to providing officials with annual gifts (*ʿīdiyyat*); they also provided financial aid and gifts to the bishops and the patriarch by the levy of a special tax, the *nūriyyat*.
4. Monasteries were also founded as an insurance against the impoverishment of the founder, his family or other relatives.[95]

---

92 Mārūn Karam, *Qiṣṣat al-milkiyyah fī al-rahbāniyyah al-lubnāniyyah al-mārūniyyah* (Beirut, Dār al-Ṭibāʿah al-Lubnāniyyah, 1972), 73.

93 Ibrāhīm Ḥarfūsh, "Tārikh dayr Mār Shallīṭā," *al-Mashriq* (April 1902), 299.

94 Van Leeuwen, 601, 605, 617.

95 Ibid., 607.

Both clergy and *muqāṭaʿjīs* therefore had an interest in the preservation of waqfs. But in Mount Lebanon, throughout the seventeenth century up to the reforms of the Lebanese Maronite Council in 1736, even peasants found it socially and economically beneficial to install monasteries in or near their villages. Some such convents were mixed. Special aisles for women were constructed not too far from those for men. Old couples would go there to live out their last years with their companions; they would often donate money or lands to the convents.[96] The latter were also important to new immigrants from the north, who were looking for a place to live and some work before settling down permanently.

In the eighteenth century, demographic changes and political developments, both internal and external, had a very important impact on the expansion of waqf lands. The problem of the security of lands and properties continued to be a principal factor in the growth of waqf lands. The French traveller Volney, who visited Mount Lebanon at the end of the 18th century in the course of his travels in Syria and Egypt, remarked on the respect for private property in the Maronite country of Mount Lebanon, which had been largely spared from Ottoman fiscal oppression. Speaking of the waqfs a little later on, Volney states that donations to religious institutions were simply a way of preserving the security of property and assuring its usufruct for life. The peasant donor could lease the land so placed in mortmain or continue to cultivate it as a sharecropper.[97]

This statement may be taken as clear proof of the insecurity of both lands and their owners. Peasants converted their lands to waqf to religious institutions, in particular monasteries, hoping thereby to rid themselves of the crushing tax burden, not to mention arbitrary confiscations, which characterised this period.

The same donors would attempt to reclaim ownership of their lands once the state of affairs became more favourable, but the courts always ruled in favour of the religious institutions, maintaining the lands in waqf.[98] The situation reveals the simplicity of the peasants, ignorant as they were of the laws that governed the status of their own lands.

On the level of waqf administration and of relations between clergy and officials, the situation was to change completely from the early eighteenth century. The reforms of the Council of Catholic Churches, held at Lwayzah

---

96 Sabine Mohasseb, *Histoire de l'expansion foncière du couvent Mar Challita au Kesrouan* (M.A. thesis, St Joseph University, Beirut, 1987), 45.

97 C.F. Volney, *Voyage en Syrie et en Egypte pendant les années 1783-1785* (Paris, 1804), vol. 1, 421; vol. 2, 269.

98 Ilias al-Qattar, *Les conditions sociales au Liban au début du XIXème siècle* (M.A. thesis, St. Joseph University, Beirut, 1974), 123.

in 1736, were primarily intended to avoid lay interference in church affairs. This council placed churches, monasteries and waqfs under the jurisdiction of the bishops.[99] Nevertheless the patriarch retained the ultimate right to have a monastery taken back under his own jurisdiction.

In practice, these decisions could not be applied at once. They were intended above all to prevent the interference of lay officials in the nominations of prelates by reorganising the ecclesiastical hierarchy and by redefining the responsibilities of bishops and patriarchs.

Lay officials retained the right to present candidates to clerical posts although the nomination of prelates now lay exclusively within the competence of the ecclesiastical authorities.[100] Lay founders of waqfs could not lay any claim to the revenues of their foundations and the privilege of founders of monasteries was restricted to the right to appoint the first superior and the right of presentation. Further regulations were aimed at preventing monks or their relatives from acquiring personal interest in monastic property.

The regulations introduced by the council reflected the principles of Canon Law formulated by the Council of Trent; they did not, however, provide an all-embracing legislation for the whole range of legal and administrative practices connected with waqfs.

The council, while it limited the rights and prerogatives of lay officials with regard to waqf estates, did not attempt to block the cession of *mīrī* and *mulk* lands in the mountain to religious institutions. Indeed, important internal developments were bringing about an upheaval in the relative confessional transformations of the population, favouring the expansion of waqfs. Likewise, the situation abroad, both in the East and in the West, necessitated a new organisation of agricultural properties in which the waqf was to play a much greater part.

On the internal political level, the bitter and longstanding conflict between the rival Druze parties of the Qaysīs and the Yemenīs was brought to a climax at the battle of ʿAyn Dārā in 1711, won by the Emir Ḥaydar Shihāb, which marked the victory of the Qaysite party. The chiefs of the defeated Yemenite party were forced into exile. The defeat, however, affected not only the leaders of the party but also the whole of their following, including their families, military retainers and clients. A large number of Drūzes in the mountain, known for their sympathy or collaboration with the Yemenite party, were forced to emigrate. Entire estates and villages were abandoned by the Drūzes in their departure for the Hawrān.[101] The demographic gap was rapidly filled by Maronites from the north and by

99 Van Leeuwen, 606.

100 Ibid.

101 Salibi, 8.

Greek Catholics from Damascus and Aleppo, who progressively moved into the southern districts of Mount Lebanon – the Matn, the Shūf, the district of Jazzīn, and the area to the east of Sidon.

In the second half of the eighteenth century, another event, connected to the internal politics of Mount Lebanon, completed the revolution in the demographic transformation of the country. The 1760s were marked by struggles between the Shihāb emirs and the Shīᶜa Ḥamādah sheikhs who were governors of the districts of Jubayl and Batrūn. The Emir Yusuf Shihāb, who had recently converted to Christianity, finally drove his rivals into the northern part of the Biqāᶜ Valley.[102] Following this victory, the Shihāb emirs granted several estates to the Lebanese Maronite Order on advantageous conditions that were aimed at stimulating the recultivation of abandoned agricultural lands and the reclamation of wastelands.

In 1766-67, an important transaction was concluded between Yūsuf Shihāb and the Maronite Order, comprising a donation of four deserted monasteries and their estates, together with several churches. The Daḥdāḥ sheikhs, who had also profited from the redistribution of the Ḥamādah estates, gave the Order another monastery in Jubayl.[103] The Order provided a new centralised framework for the exploitation of agricultural lands and a similarly centralised system of finance. The possessions of the Order were relatively independent from the patronage of leading families, and so remained immune from political rivalries. These factors together explain how the Maronite Order succeeded in building an efficient organisation that brought new elements into the agrarian structure of Mount Lebanon.

The expansion of waqf lands in Lebanon owed much also to the fiscal policy of the Ottoman Empire, which was administered locally by the Emir governors of the mountain. Efforts for integration were made in response to external pressure in the form of increased demands for taxes from the governors; such efforts were usually limited to attempts to introduce new general taxes or to regulate the export of silk. These tendencies became visible from the first half of the eighteenth century, after Ḥaydar and Milḥim Shihāb had established their authority over Beirut in 1729 and 1749 respectively.[104]

Mount Lebanon suffered an economic decline from the 1750s onwards. Economic activity was affected by the overall economic recession of the

---

[102] al-Khūrī Manṣūr al-Ḥattūnī, *Min tārīkh Lubnān: nubdhah tārīkhiyyah fī al-muqāṭaᶜah al-kisrawāniyyah* (Beirut: Awrāq lubnāniyyah fī khidmat al-tārīkh, 1956), 183.

[103] Ibid.

[104] Van Leeuwen, 603.

Ottoman Empire, a result of the depreciation of the Ottoman currency and the increasing rapacity of state officials. Aḥmad al-Jazzār, governor of both Acre and Damascus for intermittent periods between 1780 and 1804, succeeded in stirring up political strife in Mount Lebanon and extorted large sums from his rivals, the Shihāb emirs. Continuous warfare hampered economic activity and laid a heavy financial burden on the population. The emirs Yūsuf Shihāb (1763-1790) and Bashīr Shihāb (1790-1840) were forced to find ways to increase tax revenues, secure their position and meet the demands made by the provincial governors. Both resorted to new taxes, imposing extraordinary levies and doubling or tripling the *mīrī* tax, which forced the peasants into the vicious circle of borrowing money and selling their crops in advance.[105] At the end of the Egyptian occupation of Syria and Lebanon, the *mīrī* taxes were levied up to 16 times per year in addition to the personal taxes paid by Christians and Muslims called *fardah*.[106]

On the level of external influence, the general situation in the East encouraged the expansion of waqfs in Mount Lebanon. After the disruption of long distance Asian trade during the Turco-Persian wars of the 1720s, new opportunities for Syrian silk production arose. Increased French trade with Syria and Egypt and the creation by Syrian Melkite Christian merchants of an efficient Syro-Egyptian trade network widened the commercial radius of producers in Mount Lebanon. Although little data exists on the Syrian silk trade during this period, presumably contacts with the international and regional markets through Damascus and Damietta ensured the marketing of increasing silk production in the mountain.

Christian waqfs played an important role, economically as well as socially. The clergy freed itself to a large extent from lay interference, thanks to its closer relations with the Shihāb emirs.

This development was mainly due to the latter's economic requirements, which in the eighteenth century forced them to find ways to reintegrate and restructure the exploitation of their estates. One way was to revive existing waqfs, making use of the efficient mechanisms provided by Christian religious foundations as an alternative to the tax-farming system, which could no longer meet the growing fiscal demands of the central and provincial governments. The exceptional status of monastic lands enabled the emir governors to devise a flexible policy with respect to taxes and the legal status of land, thereby strengthening the role of waqf institutions as an innovative force.[107]

---

105 Henri Guys, *Beyrouth et le Liban: Relation d'un séjour de plusieurs années dans ce pays*, 2 vols. (Paris: Challamel Ainé, 1850), vol. 2, 146.

106 Ibid., 248.

107 Van Leeuwen, 613.

CHAPTER III

ESTABLISHMENT AND EXPANSION OF WAQF ESTATE

III. 1: Foundations of Waqf Estates in Rural Monasteries

The exact date when waqfs were established in the Ottoman Empire, particularly in Lebanon, is difficult to ascertain. It would be more appropriate to talk of renewal of the Christian waqfs in the region. The monasteries and convents of the mountain seem to have been established around the end of the 17th and beginning of the 18th centuries. But the economic take-off of the Greek Orthodox monasteries seems to have occurred later, in the second half of the 18th century, when the purchase of land increased, resulting in an important expansion. We have already seen that the substitution of the *iltizām* system for the *tīmār* system favored the expansion of the waqfs in the Ottoman Empire, especially in Mount Lebanon. Although the monasteries had existed in the mountains as far back as the first centuries following the Ottoman occupation, their hold on agriculture, through the control of the waqf estates, was limited. In spite of the existence of documents (*firmans* or deeds of establishment) relating to the establishment of monasteries during the 17th and 18th centuries, several proofs confirm their existence earlier. Monks have always lived at the sites of these monasteries, which were often only caves dug into the rock or remains of earlier buildings. Data on architecture or heritage have ascertained the existence of monastic life in these places. Archival sources related to fiscal matters have often completed the data. Manuscript colophons also report stories and details about these monasteries. The concluding colophons of these manuscripts or their bindings give us supplementary proofs as to the existence of a monastic life prior to the official establishment of the monastery.

Locally, the most favored version is the one asserting the existence and continuity of these monasteries since Justinian's time. The actual heads of these monasteries like to state that their institution was established in the Byzantine period, considered to be the golden age of the Christian orthodox religion. But the historical context does not allow us to accept such an assertion. The country and nearby regions, passing under the domination of different dynasties and peoples, could not have provided the monastic institutions with the calm and security they needed.

We have thus seen that in the Ottoman Empire, the waqf estates benefited from the change of the fiscal and administrative system. Sultans and local governors granted waqfs to their lineage.[1] To increase the daughters' and wives' inheritance, waqfs were often registered in their names. This practice was generalized in the Turkish Ottoman and Arab worlds. The waqf formula was used in wills, to by-pass the rules of the Koran on inheritance of wives, daughters and other children or in order to favor specified members of the family.[2]

What, then, was the situation in Mount Lebanon? The lands turned into waqfs were essentially *mīrī* lands, formerly dedicated to the *tīmār*. The change of the *tīmār* administrative system into *iltizām* was decisive for the expansion of waqf estates. Here too, during the 16th century and the first part of the 17th century, mountain monasteries and convents were established on *mīrī* lands depending on the emirs and *muqāṭaʿjī* sheikhs. Already in the 16th century, the largest part of the lands was dedicated to *tīmārs*.

North Lebanon, which benefited from a certain degree of autonomy under Ottoman administration, illustrates the evolution of waqfs and the Ottoman policy towards them. The census of waqfs in north Lebanon was carried out by Ottoman authorities in 1519 as part of the census of the *wilāyah* of Tripoli.[3] The names of several waqf-holding families show them as belonging to the Mamlūk period. In this census no mention is made of Christian waqfs, although they existed at that time. However a convent of the medieval period, that of Our Lady of Kaftūn, is mentioned as part of the waqf of the Tripoli mosque.

Eight kinds of waqfs are mentioned, belonging to families, individuals, fortresses, mosques, *madrasahs*, *zāwiyahs*, the cities of Cairo and Jerusalem, and lastly miscellaneous waqfs. Family waqfs came first in terms of revenues; they were the providers of the fortresses whose annual revenues came to 78,378 aspers. The most common were the religious and family waqfs. Waqfs dedicated to military fortifications were not very common. Waqf lands dedicated to eight fortresses were scattered in 35 different villages or farms. In a mountainous land only recently occupied and possibly harboring unforeseen dangers, the surveillance of the countryside formed part of the administration of this province by the *tīmār* system. Religious waqfs, those dedicated to mosques, *zāwiyahs* and *madrasahs*, provided

---

1 Barnes, 43.

2 Crecelius, 270.

3 Issam Khalifeh, *Des étapes décisives dans l'histoire du Liban* (Beirut: Librairie Avicenne, 1997), 35-52.

a total annual revenue of 26,665 aspers, hardly a third of the revenue of fortress waqfs. It is clear therefore that in this period, military priorities were foremost even in the organization of waqfs.[4]

The 1519 census also records the revenues derived from *tīmārs* of north Lebanon, which totaled 2,702,760 aspers. The importance of the *tīmār* for the regions is obvious. Waqf revenues amount to only one eighth or 12.5% of the taxes contributed by the region's *tīmār*, which is comparable to the sixteenth per cent of the total revenues that waqfs contributed in the whole empire at that time.[5] In practice then, the autonomy of Mount Lebanon did not distinguish it from the rest of the empire. For the Ottomans, autonomy was only a practical means of governing different provinces and raising a maximum of revenue for the treasury, while avoiding as far as possible friction with the local population.

We can go through the case of several Greek Orthodox and other monasteries and see how these monasteries, originally *tīmārs* and then *mīrī* lands, were turned into waqfs. These *mīrī* lands were given out or sold to tax farmers through the bias of emirs or sheikhs aiming to expand their exploited and productive agricultural lands so that they could be more taxable.

III. 1.1: Balamand Monastery

The installation of Greek Orthodox monks in Balamand was officially confirmed in a document going back to the year 1603. This installation and rehabilitation is reported in the first page of the records kept by the monastery superior. The document specifies that after three centuries of desertion, the Cistercian abbey was rehabilitated by the Greek Orthodox who brought in some innovations and transformed the premises and buildings according to their liturgical requirements and their activities. This initiative was the result of an agreement between the Orthodox hierarchy, the notables of the region of Kūrah, the monks, and the inhabitants of this region. According to this document, the rehabilitation of the monastery was decided by the metropolitan bishop of Tripoli, Kīr Yuwākīm, and the metropolitan bishop of Beirut. The Kūrah notables gave their approval. Sheikhs Abū Ṣāliḥ, Sulaymān al-Yāzijī, Yūsuf Pāshā and the notables of the village of Fīᶜ – Ḥājj Farḥāt and Ḥājj Buṭrus – are the notables mentioned in this document.[6] The presence of Sulaymān al-Yāzijī seemed to have been decisive in the reopening of the monastery. In fact, this notable was known to

---

4 Khalifeh, 50.

5 Barnes, 42.

6 Land Register of Balamand, 1.

have occupied the position of secretary of the Ottoman *wālī*, Yūsuf Pāshā Sīfā. There is no way for us to know whether the Yūsuf Pāshā mentioned in the document was himself the governor of Tripoli.

"Balamand Monastry"

Moreover, the document is full of praise for Sulaymān al-Yāzijī in recognition of the help and donations he granted to the monastery, then deprived of all commodities and furniture. Along with his charitable gifts, the essential contribution of this notable lay in the finalization of official formalities allowing the establishment of this monastic community. The raising of a church or monastery required a special permit from the *wilāyah* of Tripoli. The transfer of estates and establishment of monastery waqfs required the same formalities, which were facilitated by the presence of an influential secretary.[7]

However, the Ottoman archives of 16th century mention Balamand monastery long before the year 1603, the presumed date of its establishment. From the beginning of the Ottoman period, according to the first census of 1519 (register Tapu Defteri, no. 68), Mazraᶜat Dayr al Balamand is already quoted. The word *mazraᶜah* designates either a farm or a hamlet. In this case it referred to the lands surrounding the monastery, but we do not know if

[7] ᶜĪsā Zurayq, "Maṭbaᶜat al-Balamand," *al-Manār* (1901).

the monastery itself was a part of it. According to the census, these lands were part of Muḥammad Kānāfānī's *tīmār*. They were mainly planted with wheat, oats and a few olive trees. The tax due was set at 300 aspers.[8]

The monastery is mentioned once again in the Istanbul archives, during the second Ottoman census of 1571. At that time, Balamand was administered by the inhabitants of Batrūmīn village, who were dependent on the *tīmār* of the Fortress of Tripoli. Taxes were set at 400 aspers for that year. This increase of 100 aspers during a little over 50 years was due either to a production increase or higher taxes in the region.[9]

Thus, the lands surrounding the ruins of Balamand monastery during the 17th century were *tīmāriyāt*. Some people consider this term to come from the Greek language: *tīmāriyāt* meaning lands where thyme grew. In the Ottoman organization, the term *tīmāriyāt* designated lands granted as military fiefs to governors entrusted with the administration and tax collection of a region. Therefore, 1603 would be the year in which the monastery lands changed their status from *tīmār* to waqf.[10]

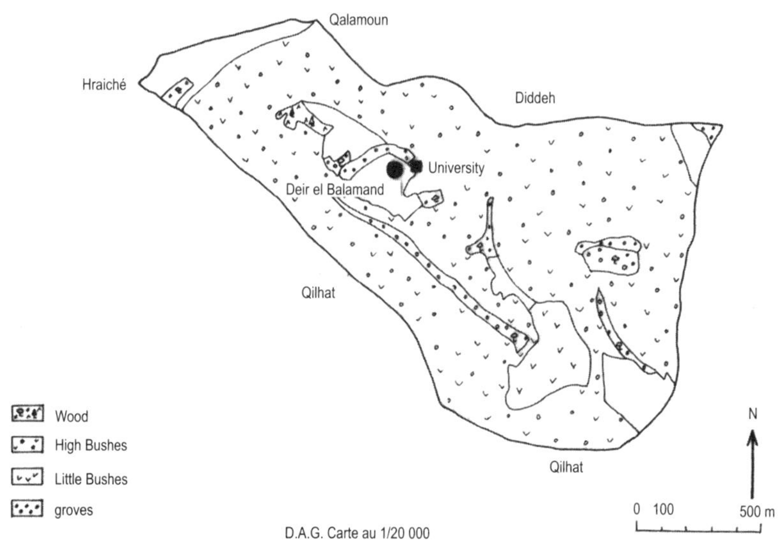

Map 1 - The Domain of the Monastery of Balamand

---

8 Nāfiẓ al-Aḥmar, "Dayr al-Balamand: Taʾsīsuhū wa dawruhū ʾabr al-tārīkh," in *Jawānib min tārīkh al-kūrah fī-l-ahd al-ʿuthmānī,* ed. R. Sābā (Beirut: N.p., 1999).

9 al-Aḥmar, 319.

10 Souad Slim, *Balamand: histoire et patrimoine* (Beirut: Dār an-Nahar, 1995), 25.

Several other data concerning the religious heritage of this monastery prove the existence of Greek Orthodox monks in Balamand before 1603.

These proofs are essentially Arabic and Syriac manuscripts that have caused much polemic among historians. Orthodox chroniclers and historians assert that the monastery was completely deserted during the three centuries between the departure of the Crusaders and Cistercians and the arrival of Orthodox monks.[11] But western historians assert that Syrian non-Chalcedonian monks lived in Balamand. There was quite a large number of them in the region of Tripoli where their bishop lived. It has been often reported that Chalcedonians, later called Greeks, lived in towns, while Syriac-speakers and Maronites lived in rural areas, possibly with the exception of Tripoli.[12] The wrong interpretation of a Syrian manuscript sent to Balamand, and preserved now in the Bodleian library at Oxford, strengthened the assumption of the presence in the monastery of Monophysite Syriac-speakers. In fact, this document was a Melkite manuscript transcribed in Syriac. The Arab Syriac manuscript of the Oxford Bodleian is recorded under number 87. According to the Greek Orthodox ritual by monk Yaᶜqūb from the village of Ḥardīn, it is a triode written in year 7000 of Adam's era (1492). It was sent by the bishop Gregorios of Damascus to the hermit monks residing in Balamand, near Tripoli. But the same bishop specifies that should it be difficult to dispatch the manuscript to the monastery, its price should then be paid.[13]

Other manuscripts prove also that the presence of Greek Orthodox monks was previous to the beginning of the 17th century (1603). These manuscripts were transcribed in Balamand by the monk Makāriyus al-Ḥalabī: "al-Istishārī" (no. 82, dated 1598), and, "al-Qindaq" (no. 8, dated 1599). Father Joseph Naṣrallah also mentions that a Syriac manuscript *octowikhos* (*pentecostarion*) kept in the Syrian Catholic convent of Dayr al-Shurfah, was transcribed in Balamand in 1597.[14]

The expansion of the monastery's lands started immediately with the beginning of this period. The monks already installed there had started acquiring lands before 1603. Another text following the colophon relating to the foundation of the monastery, written by the *proestos* Simeon,

---

[11] Ilyās al-Ḥalabī, "Nubdhah tārīkhiyyah ᶜan dayr al-Balamand," *al-Kalimah* (1907), 360-361.

[12] Henri Lammens, *Tasrīḥ al-abṣār fī mā yaḥtawī Lubnān min āthār*. vol. 1, 2nd ed. (Beirut: al-Maṭbaᶜah al-Kāthūlīkiyyah, 1913), 155.

[13] R. Payne Smith, *Catalogus codicum manuscriptorum bibliothecae bodleianae pars sexta, codices Syriacos, Carshunicos Mendaeos* (Oxford: Clarendon Press, 1864), Triodi, no. 87.

[14] Joseph Nasrallah, *Histoire du mouvement littéraire dans l'église melkite du Vème au XXème siècle: contribution à l'étude de la littérature arabe chrétienne (1250-1516)*, vol. 4/1 (Paris, 1992), 51.

informs us of the replacement of superior Makāriyūs al-Dīrānī by monk Yūḥannā, second *hygoumené* of the monastery. The first purchases of lands for the benefit of the monastery started with this monk. In this period, 25 monks lived in Balamand. They were mainly from Amyūn village monastery, which was abandoned and progressively went to ruins. Balamand monastery started to enjoy a period of development and prosperity, as attested by the expansion of its lands and the quality of its acquired cattle. According to Simeon, the monastery, in ruins and deprived of everything, could, thanks to the exemplary way of life of the Christians in the Tripoli area, notables and especially monks, acquired a flock of a hundred goats and three to six cows. Vineyards, mulberry trees and olive trees were also planted and the monastery received as waqf an olive orchard of 200 trees, in the village of Fīᶜ.[15] All this occurred only 8 years after the community foundation in 1603, corresponding to the year 1610 (7118 of Adam's era) as quoted at the end of monk Simeon report.[16]

III. 1.2: St. John Monastery of Dūmā

Regarding the monastery of St. John of Dūmā, there is a colophon relating the steps of its foundation in 1785. This colophon, written on the last page of the "Triodi" manuscript, relates the arrival of the Orthodox monks to this monastery. It was the priest Aftīmūs, superior of the monastery, designated by Beirut bishop Yuwwānikūs the Cypriot, who arrived at the monastery together with a group of monks coming from St. Ilyās of Shwayyah monastery.[17] These were monk Andrāwus Abū Fayṣal from Amyūn village, monk Ṣarāfīm al-Maᶜlūf of Zabbūghā, deacon Buṭrus Maᶜlūf of Kfar ᶜAqāb, priest Sābā of the city of Tripoli al-Mīnāᵓ and several others. As a first step the endeavors of these monks centered on the acquisition of lands because the monastery had none and was going to ruins. The only buildings were the church and the large kitchen basement used for the conservation of food and supplies. The acquired lands seemed to be those surrounding the monastery and representing its main estate, commonly called, al-Kindār. This estate is limited on the west and north sides by cliffs and rivers. It is also surrounded by *mīrī* lands belonging to al-Baklik estate.[18] Were the lands listed in this colophon originally *mīrī* lands? Two notables mentioned in the colophon seem to have been involved in the setting up of this estate. One of them was Abū Nabhān who used to sell land and orchards in the

---

[15] Zurayq, 360.

[16] *Land Register of Balamand*, 1.

[17] *Makhtūtāt al-ᶜArabiyyāt*, Triodi no. 6.

[18] Ibid.

region of Bahassīs. The two historians, father Qusṭanṭīn al-Bāshā and ᶜĪsā Iskandar al-Maᶜlūf state that he (Abū Nabhān) was of the Ḥamādah family.[19] This Shīᶜī family was in charge of the *iltizām* in the northern region of Mount Lebanon, until their expulsion from it by Emir Yūsuf Shihāb. It seems here that the foundation of St. John of Dūmā monastery coincided with the upheavals the mountain witnessed during the 18th century.[20] The lands abandoned by the Ḥamādah, who withdrew towards the plain of the Biqāᶜ, had to be redistributed to the monasteries of the Maronite Lebanese monks orders all over the districts of Jubayl and Batrūn. The Greek Orthodox, who were the majority in the higher regions of Batrūn, especially in the villages of Dūmā, Kfar Ḥildā and Kfūr, must have had their share too. The words used in the colophon do not suggest any donation on behalf of the Shihābs.[21] In fact, this new establishment of St. John's waqf was done under the aegis of Emir Yūsuf Shihāb's secretary, sheikh Abū Fāris Simᶜān al-Bīṭār, from the village of Ghazīr in Kisrawān. He (sheikh Abū Fāris) had supervised, on his own, the establishment of the boundaries of the property of monasteries and given the deeds thereof. The colophon first enumerates the different plots acquired, starting the sentences by emphasizing the word "we have bought" (*ishtarayna*); this word was used four times. "We have established estates for the monastery" is also used once in the text; and "we have planted" (*ansabna*) is used four times. The borders of the acquired lands are then set.[22] A specific term, *jaddadna*, was also used to designate new acquisitions. It means "we have renewed" and is used 6 times, twice concerning lands and four times concerning objects.

The repetition of these expressions show the monks' insistence on explaining their estate had not been given out as waqf but had been won thanks to their efforts and labor at a time when al-Baklik *mīrī* lands were bestowed on religious orders only in return for the *mīrī* tax payment.

These lands comprise not only the central estate surrounding the monastery but also parcels located in the nearby villages. These parcels were enlarged by acquisitions finalized later on. The essential object of these acquisitions was the purchase of mulberry orchards. In this document, acquired or newly planted mulberry plots are enumerated ten times. There are also four orchards and vineyards and two *ṣalīkh* (uncultivated) lands. The

---

19 Qustantīn al-Bāshā, *Tārīkh Dūmā*, 2nd ed. (Beirut: al-Maktabah al-Būlisiyyah, 1991), 297-298; al-Maᶜlūf, "Zaḥlah," 507.

20 Ibid., 219.

21 Tūmā al-Bīṭār, *Tārīkh dayr al-qiddīs Yūḥannā al-Maᶜmadān Dūmā wa urthūdhuks al-minṭaqah* (Dūmā: Dayr al-Qiddīs Yūḥannā al-Maᶜmadān, 1991), 34.

22 Triodi no. 6, colophon. Dūmā Monastery.

colophon also mentions buildings already existing or being raised on these lands: three mills, three houses and one stable.[23]

How can we justify the fast installation and dazzling development of a waqf that was not supported by any order, that had a relatively limited number of monks and whose (waqf) lands had to be purchased? The colophon specifies that this was done thanks to the charities of the Christians, the labor of the monks, the help of God, and the care of St. John the Baptist. In this period, the necessity to take over the monasteries and to grant them waqfs could join the overall efforts because the problem of populating the mountain depended on them.[24]

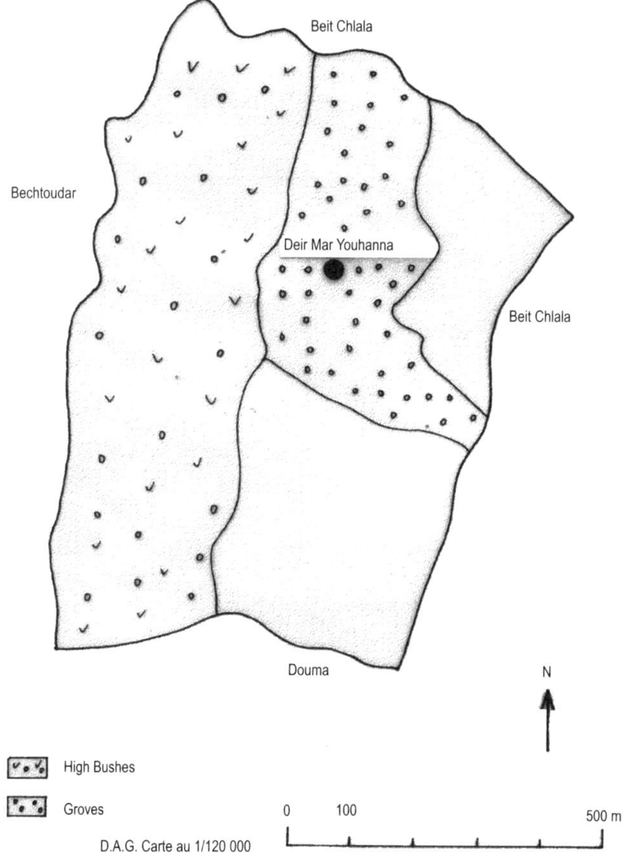

Map 2 – The Map of the Domain of the Monastery of St. John Dūmā

23 Ibid.

24 al-Bīṭār, 29-30.

Peasants and inhabitants coming from Syria and the north of the country settled down in places where their communities could receive them and give them work. Conversions occurred according to these settlements. Often, the inhabitants embraced the community or even the religion of the monastery or the institution controlling the location. Shīʿīs, Drūzes, Maronites and Orthodox moved with their chiefs depending on the conditions of the period, either fleeing wars or trying to get a job on new lands with the aim of owning them later on. During this 18th century, Dūmā monastery and the Orthodox villages seemed to have been a kind of border zone between Shīʿīs and Maronites.[25]

Lands were not the only acquisitions made by the monasteries. Several other items are listed in this colophon. Here also, the term "we have renewed" is used the most. The objects necessary for cult celebration and agricultural chores were essential for the restarting of monastic or everyday life. There were also kitchen utensils, three cauldrons, four pots and ten copper plates, earthenware jars as well as three liturgical costumes, manuscripts, a large chalice and a large ornamented silver crucifix. Kitchen utensils were listed among manuscripts and worship items. Writings in the colophon confirm that these manuscripts, just like the lands, were regarded as waqfs. Sometimes the items were stamped with the name of the waqfs and the date of acquisition or donation. So the listing of liturgical items among manuscripts, kitchen utensils and agricultural exploitation is justified by the fact that all these articles were regarded as waqf.[26]

In Dūmā as well as in Balamand, several proofs confirm the existence of a monastic life in St. John monastery before 1785. First are the archeological data we find inside the monastery. The north-west wall stones of the church are of a very large size, their length sometimes reaching one to two meters with a width of half a meter. This type of construction probably went back to the Roman period and was financed by the state in order to serve as a temple. Later on, the Christians might have reused these stones to build their church. At the entrance of the church, above the door, a Byzantine cross is engraved in the rock.[27]

In Dūmā too, manuscripts give us proof concerning the monastery's old age. In 1765, priest Yūsuf al-Jubaylī acquired an *euchologion* for the monks "established here." The colophon does not specify the location. In 1770, a note mentions that this manuscript was given as waqf to St. John

---

25 al-Bīṭār, 29-30.

26 Triodi no. 6, colophon. Dūmā Monastery.

27 al-Bīṭār, 31.

of Dūmā. So, even if the monks who had left the monastery of St. Ilyās of Shwayyah were already established in Dūmā in 1765, they had to wait around twenty years before they started to expand their estate.[28] Was this due to a more favorable situation? It was during 1770, in fact, that St. Ilyās monastery started its land expansion. Was it the problems between Catholics and Orthodox that had hindered the return of the monks to their restored monastery?

Another manuscript belonging to the monastery of St. Ilyās mentions in its colophon that it was transcribed in St. John of Dūmā monastery in 1595 almost two centuries before the new establishment in 1785.[29]

Thus, we can consider there were several stages in the establishment of Orthodox monasteries. This applies for Balamand, St. Ilyās of Shwayyah and St. John of Dūmā.

We lack any example of family waqf among the Orthodox community, although it was very common practice in the Sunnī and Maronite communities. Yet, according to the historian ʿĪsā Iskandar al-Maʿlūf, it appears that the Maʿlūf family of Dūmā had strong links with the monastery of St. John of Dūmā until the second half of the 19th century. Several superiors and monks of this monastery came from this family.[30] Also, this family came from the Matn village of Muhaydsah, in central Mount Lebanon, close to St. Ilyās of Shwayyah monastery from where the monks came. Among the new founders listed in the colophon, two monks came from this family. It was mainly members of this family who felt concerned by the foundation of the monastery and donated waqf lands. And it was mainly they who undertook the protection of the land against the attacks of the Shīʿīs living in the nearby village of Kfar Ḥildā.[31] We could not trace any monk coming from any other Dūmā family.[32] Did the Maʿlūf find a certain interest in the faithfulness they had for their monastery? Were they a part of the sharecroppers? Was it simply an aspect of family belonging? Or was it a simple coincidence of the historical context of the period, the monks and the Maʿlūfs arriving from the same region and at the same time?

---

28 al-Bīṭār, 30.

29 *al-Makhṭūṭāt al-ʿArabiyyāt*, Colophon of the Typicon, no. 34, 8.

30 al-Bīṭār, 35.

31 ʿĪsā Iskandar al-Maʿlūf, *Dawānī al-quṭūf fī tārīkh banī al-Maʿlūf* (Baʿabdā: ʿUthmāniyyah, 1907-1908), 220.

32 al-Bīṭār, 35.

III. 1.3: St. Ilyās Monastery of Shwayyah

Concerning the establishment of the monastery of St. Ilyās of Shwayyah, we know that the first parcel was acquired in 1595.[33] But the subsequent acquisitions started only one century later. On the other hand, the chroniclers of that time inform us that the expansion of the monastery was slowed down, first by the Greek Catholic schism in 1724 and then by the earthquake in 1759. The development of this monastery did not start effectively until 1770, relatively late, in comparison to the Maronite and Greek Catholic monasteries.

"St. Ilyās Monastery of Shawayyah"

But all these stages of the monastery seem to have been preceded by older ones. The actual building is, in fact, built on older foundations, consisting of seven cells and two rooms that may have been used as entrance and church. The doors of these cells get progressively smaller. The entry door can be seen from the one at the far end. All the cells have rocky walls and a very small window, just enough to let in air and light. The stones used to build up some of these cell

---

33 *al-Maḥfūẓāt al-ʿarabiyyah fī al-adyira al-urthūdhuksiyyah al-anṭākiyyah fī Lubnān*, 2 vol. (Beirut: Balamand University, 1991-1994), the first deed in the archives of St. Elias Monastery, 183.

walls are rough and unpolished and used exactly as they have been extracted from the quarry set in the same cliff where these cells are dug. So here too, architectural elements prove that the monastery existed before the extant written documents and the archives. In this monastery, there are also manuscripts that were transcribed during the 13th and 14th centuries, but their colophons do not specify if they had effectively been written in the monastery.

This monastery is one of the few having a common wall with another Maronite monastery that depended on the order of Mariamite monks (previously monks from Aleppo separated from the order of the Lebanese monks).

This ecumenical coexistence has been reported to us by the chroniclers of the region as being the result of a donation made in 1612, by a notable from the Maṭar al-Jumayyil family of Bikfayyā to a monk of his family, named Ilyās. This same family might have also donated bordering lands to an Orthodox priest akin to it named Buṭrus al-Klink. This priest added these lands to the ones he inherited from his family and built a monastery.[34] This version omits the presence in the monastery archives of the first purchase deed dated 1596. It also ignores the great age of the cells that were constructed before the year 1612.

This closeness of Greek Orthodox and Maronite monasteries is common, especially in the Matn region, where for example we have the monastery of Dayr al-Ḥarf, dedicated to St. Georges, built side by side with the Maronite church.

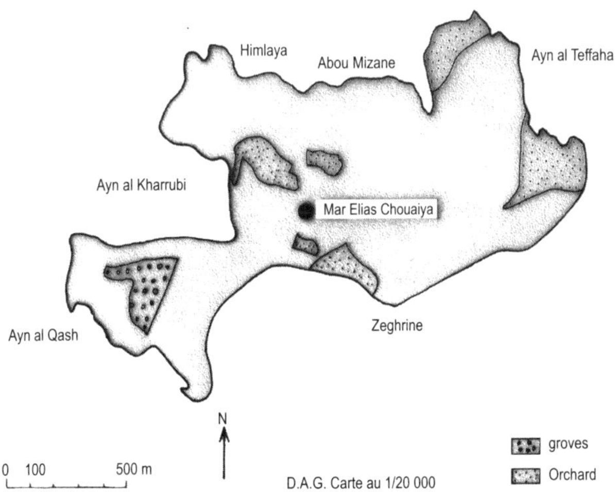

Map 3 - The Domain of the Monastery of Mār Ilyās Shwayyah

34 al-Maʿlūf, "Dawānī al-Quṭūf."

III. 1.4: St. Georges Monastery of Dayr al-Ḥarf

Here, the presence of a Druze prince was important for the monastery's expansion. But well ahead of its development, this monastery seems to go back to the Mamlūk period, shortly after their military invasions and punitive campaigns against the Shīᶜīs and the Maronites of the mountains. Wihbi ibn Muḥsin al-Lakhmī, a Christian believer, left his village in the Hawrān, during the first years of the 14th century and arrived in the village of Rās al-Matn where St. Georges appeared to him several times. He decided then to become a monk in this location. In 1326 his brother joined him.[35]

Another verbal tradition attributed the construction of the church to a Druze emir. The latter, from the Tanūkh family, came by the monastery in 1409, while he was on his way to a battle. He saw a light and inquired about it. He was told it was St. Georges's light. He then vowed to build a sanctuary if he won the battle. On his way back, triumphant, he met monk Wahbah, who lived there at that time and told him about his intentions. He built a church and gave lands to the monks so that they could live from the benefits of their estates. It is important to notice here the popularity of both St. Ilyās and St. Georges in the Christian and Muslim mentalities of the region. Both were identified by the population as al-Khuḍr, quoted in *sūrah* 18 of the Koran.[36] They are represented in the icons with their weapons, which gave them their popularity among Drūzes and Ottomans. During the whole Ottoman period, especially during its first part, most of the churches, if not all of them, were raised in the name of this saint.[37]

For these four cases of establishment and expansion, notables, *timariots*, *multazimūn*, *muqāṭaʿjīs* or sheikhs of the Druze or Sunnī communities, sold leased, or gave state-owned lands whose administration was entrusted to them. The Sīfā, Shihāb, Tanūkh and Abīllamaᶜ families in turn entrusted these lands to the monasteries, aiming thereby at increasing their share of the taxes collected in the different regions of the Lebanese mountain. In fact, the tax farmers kept for their own benefit, a part of the tax collected which was 2% or 5% of the total amount. Starting from the 19th century, they stopped paying their taxes and instead, made the peasants pay them in their place.[38]

In spite of proof that the monastery did pay taxes some historians still believe that fiscal exemption generated numerous donations in favor of

---

35 Houda Kassatly, *La communauté monastique de Deir el Ḥarf* (Balamand: Université de Balamand, 1996), 19-20.

36 Ibid., 21.

37 Victor Sauma, *Sur les pas des saints au Liban* ([Beirut]: FMA, c1994), 415.

38 David Urquhart, *The Lebanon (Mount Souria); A History and a Diary*, vol. 2 (London, 1860), 175.

the monasteries. But the monasteries' archives show only a small number of donations. Regarding Balamand, 500 plots were acquired over three centuries. Fifty of them were waqfs, the majority of which were given by some members of the clergy.[39] For St. Ilyās of Shwayyah monastery, for a period exceeding two centuries, we have 112 deeds, only four of which are donations.[40] It is in fact inside the Maronite community that most donations were made to constitute waqf.

III. 1.5: Monasteries of Other Christian Communities

The notables of this community were essentially rural and tax farmers. So, Dayr Mār Shallīṭā monastery in Ghūsṭā in the Kisrawān was the first Maronite monastery of the mountain that was built at night by lantern light. During this period, Shīᶜīs represented the majority there. This monastery was one of the few to remain mixed (monks & nuns) following the Lwayzah council of 1738. For three centuries, the monastery, which was a family waqf, finalized 165 acquisitions, of which 47 were donations and 118 purchases. Among the 47 donations, 39 plots were given by peasants and eight by the Khāzin family. The Khāzins were hoping that these lands would become productive enough to allow them to pay their taxes. As for the peasants, the donations granted to the monastery were a kind of social guarantee and an old age security allowing couples to spend their last days in the monastery after having donated their lands.[41]

Added to donations and purchases, sharecropper's deeds with emirs were another means of land expansion. Greek Catholics whose community and religious orders started during the 18th century, also count only a few donations among their agricultural estates. The largest part of their notables belonged to the urban bourgeoisie, working in trade and finance. The monastery of St. John of Shwayr introduced an interesting new agreement formula with Druze emirs and the Abīllamaᶜ family. These were *mughārasah* contracts concerning sandstone lands of the Matn region that were leased by the Abīllamaᶜ.[42] These lands were entrusted for a period of twenty years to the Greek Catholic monks of St. John monastery. They had to be planted with pine trees. Then, twenty years later, when they lands became productive, they were divided between emirs and monks.[43]

---

39 Register of Balamand.

40 "Al-Maḥfūẓāt al-ᶜarabiyyah," deeds of Mār Elias Eli 1 to Eli 154.

41 Mohasseb, 45-6.

42 André Latron, *La vie rurale en Syrie et au Liban: étude d'économie sociale* (Beirut: Mémoires de l'Institut Français de Damas, 1936), 66-67.

43 Slim, "Métayage et l'impot," 46-47.

So, Christian monasteries were, at first, sharecroppers of the emirs and of Druze and Sunnī *muqāṭaʿjīs* on *mīrī* lands. And when, as provided in these *mughārasah* contracts, the monastery became owner or responsible of the waqfs, the monks hired sharecropper peasants to exploit the lands and estates, which had become quite large by then. Monks, who were farmers at first, moved towards different functions, religious, administrative and especially educational.[44]

Donations of *mīrī* lands to the monasteries and *mughārasah* contracts with them spread over the 18th century. The Talhūqs, *muqāṭaʿjīs* of the region of ʿĀlayy, gave lands to the Greek Catholic order of Aleppine monks in the region of Qumāṭiyyah. The Druze Junbalāts gave the lands of Jūn village in the Shūf to the Salvatorian monks of the same community. The Abī Nakad Druze tax farmers gave the lands of St. Georges of Naʿamah monastery to the monks of the Lebanese Maronite Order. The Sunnī Shihāb gave this same order the lands of the Ḥamādah, Shīʿīs who had been driven out from the region of Jubayl and Batrūn towards the Biqāʿ.[45]

The monks' initiative to hire peasant sharecroppers in order to exploit the land did not represent a threat to the acquisitions of the monastery since sharecropping contracts concluded with the peasants were not of the *mughārasah* type. In the case of waqf lands, the transfer of property was not possible. According to the law, waqf lands are inalienable. If the acquisition of lands through the *mughārasah* sharecropping contracts was possible with the *muqāṭaʿjīs*, there was no reciprocity regarding the monks. Transfer of *muqāṭaʿjī* lands to the monasteries turned the sharecropping contracts, from *mughārasah* to *musāqāt*. [46]

The *mughārasah* contract is a contract through which the owner concedes a land fund against an obligation to plant it with trees. After an agreement upon a time limit of several years, the sharecropper becomes owner of one-quarter or one-half of the cultivated lands or planted trees. The *mughārasah* is always a long-term contract. Its time limit depends on the nature of the plantation: the plantation is shared after three to five years for mulberry trees, four to six years for vineyards, seven to eight years for fig trees and ten to twelve years for olive trees. During the contract period, the fruit crops and intercalary culture products were shared as if they were part of a simple sharecropping.[47]

This type of contract could not be carried out by the monks because their waqf estate could not be divided. But it seems that the Abīllamaʿ

44 Karam, 226-227.

45 al-Maʿlūf, "Zaḥlah," 123.

46 Slim, "Métayage et l'impot," 217.

47 Latron, 66-67.

emirs applied this type of contract with the inhabitants of the Matn district. On the other hand, regarding the monks, the *mughārasah* contracts were a means of new land acquisition.

In the classical *musāqāt* contract, the owner provided either the soil or the plantation. The sharecropper had to provide the work, the seeds, and the draught cattle, and pay his share of taxes. The division of crops depended on the nature of the soil, irrigation and plantation. In fertile areas with abundant rainfall, the sharecropper was entitled to one-half of the crop regarding olive and mulberry trees. Where land was less fertile and rainfall less abundant, the sharecroppers' share increased up to seventy percent.[48]

Doc 4 - Deed of Share Cropping between the Greek Catholic Monastery of St. John at Khinshāra and the Abīllamaᶜ Muqāṭaᶜjī, XVIIIth century

[48] Ibid., 49-50.

When the contract is drawn, the owner requires from the sharecropper a cash guarantee, the amount of which depends on the condition of the parcel. According to this same agreement, the sharecropper should pay, in advance, a quarter of the estimated production price in order to get half of it later on.

At the end of the association agreement, the sharecropper takes back the guarantee and is entitled to an indemnity corresponding to the land development and its added value.[49]

The payment of this guarantee, called *shilsh* is problematic: at the beginning of the contract, the peasant, who is now a sharecropper, has to pay a quarter of the production of mulberry trees in order to obtain half of it annually, and one third of the vineyards so that he could get two-thirds of it. This was done for the purpose of inciting the peasant to take care of the land entrusted to him. Misunderstanding occurred easily in this case. Two words were used to designate the production, *shilsh* (root) and *hawā* (fruits). This led the peasant to believe that, with the payment of the guarantee, he became owner of part of the land.[50] Starting in the first half of the 19th century, several legal actions, claiming a quarter of the lands, were taken by the peasants against the monasteries. Either these peasants or their fathers were sharecroppers, of the emirs, or *muqāṭaʿjīs* in the Matn region. Appropriation of land, at the end of the contract, was possible for *mulk* lands owned by emirs or for *mīrī* lands they administered. This was not possible for waqf lands depending of the monastery. Most verdicts sentenced by Islamic *sharīʿah* courts of law were favourable to the monasteries. These courts dismissed the peasants and specified that they (the peasants) knew the lands were no longer owned by the *muqāṭaʿjīs*, but were now waqf lands belonging to one monastery or the other.[51] In this matter, it is important to know whether the sharecroppers were, in fact, aware of the laws and status controlling their lands and functions.

In northern Lebanon, monasteries and peasants were confronted with similar situations. In Balamand monastery, most legal actions dealt with contract cancellations and property limits. These proceedings confirmed the inalienability of waqf lands and made reference to antecedents and to practices in the central regions of the emirate of Mount Lebanon, regarding its Christian population.[52] The problems of the region were often solved by the Islamic court of Tripoli. However, in matters regarding the Christian

---

49 Chevallier, "Société du Mont-Liban," 138.

50 Guys, "Beyrouth et le Liban," vol. 2, 144-145; Aouad, 259.

51 Slim, "Métayage et l'impot," 68-9.

52 Balamand Archives.

population, this court would take into consideration decisions in agreement with the standards of the emirate.

III. 2: Expansion of Monastic Waqfs and their Land Policy

The study of the land policy of the monasteries in the Lebanese mountain could lead to a generalization of the information we already have concerning the economic growth of the waqf in Mount Lebanon. Could such a study confirm the stages of land policy previously registered and analyzed?

In fact, in a broad sense, both theoretically and practically, we can identify three main periods in policy development. The first period extended throughout the 17th century with its political upheavals, wars, etc. During this period, *mīrī* land and *mawāt* were converted to waqf lands not only in the narrow limits of Mount Lebanon, but also throughout the whole Ottoman Empire. This transformation coincided with administrative and fiscal changes in the Empire. As we have seen, the transition of the *timar* system into *iltizām* was very favorable to the development of waqf as far as administration and tax collection were concerned.

The second period, the 18th century, was the period of expansion. Many methods were employed to set up and extend the estates. Massive purchases were made. Acquisitions through association with the emirs and farmers of the districts increased. Donations of waqfs were not frequent in the Greek Orthodox communities, however, as the notables of these communities dedicated their assets mainly to finance and trade.

At the level of the waqfs, this expansion started with the beginning of the decline of the Empire's central authority, as several governors tried to split off and organize their provinces in accordance with local interests.

The 18th century was also the period when foreign interference, which started with the granting of the Capitulations in the 17th century, realized several military, economic and religious victories. European powers, aiming to gain priority for their interests in the empire, assumed the right to protect the Christian minorities in the empire.

The third period, the 19th century, was the period of the constitution and centralization of land estates. In this aspect, documents provide us with a large number of acts of delimitation, termination of partnerships, agreements, trials, etc. The monasteries were concerned with the legalization of their rights over the acquired property and with the centralization of their acquisitions.

This period, in fact, is that of the peasant uprisings provoked by fiscal extortion. They reached their highest level because the bids on the lease farming of the mountain tribute were constantly increasing. But it is also the period during which Ottoman reforms specifically affected the constitution of the cadastral register and the reinforcement of private property. Driven by their financial needs, the Ottomans forced the people to declare and to register their properties, thus making them easier to tax.[53]

This outline of the general evolution of the situation makes it necessary for us to point out that, in spite of everything, each region had its own specific waqf development. Religious, administrative, fiscal or political measures could sometimes disrupt ancestral patterns that seemed final. Political or economic situations, proper to certain regions, could lead the waqfs to follow different policies of expansion and management. Kinship and personal ambitions also could not be ignored in this process. In this frame of economic history and material analysis, one should also seriously take into account the evolution of personal and communal religious piety, which had enormous influence on the replenishment or depletion of the coffers of these institutions.

Another major point to consider concerns the representativeness of these documents. With the lapse of time, have we received them in their full integrity? Are there any important or significant gaps due to loss or destruction? In fact, the number of purchase deeds is quite important and can, at least, represent a major trend of the policy at that time.

This last point did not conflict with Islamic *sharīʿah* laws relating to non-Islamic waqfs that were in force during the Ottoman period. The absence of written documents did not constitute legal proof against the continuity of the waqfs. The *sharīʿah* acknowledged that these waqfs went back to immemorial times. In fact, these laws stipulated that the impossibility of finding anyone who could remember times when these lands were not waqfs was in itself was sufficient proof of the existence of these waqfs.[54] Thus, in those times, and according to the laws in force, an essential value was granted to oral testimony and to memory. This also explains the simplicity and briefness of written documents; the importance of the scrupulously accounted for testimonies in the trials, and the

---

[53] Much research has been done on this subject:
1. Rafic Chikhani, *Etude d'histoire rurale libanaise, édition, traduction et commentaire de quelques actes du couvent St. Jean de Choueir, 1684-1738* (M.A. thesis, Beirut, 1974).
2. Joseph Abou Nohra, *Etude d'histoire rurale libanaise, édition, traduction et commentaire de quelques actes du couvent St. Jean de Choueir, 1815-1836* (M.A. thesis, Beirut, 1975).
3. Souad Abou El Rousse Slim, *Etude d'histoire rurale libanaise, édition, traduction et commentaire de quelques actes du couvent St. Jean de Choueir, 1780-1815* (M.A. thesis, Beirut 1978).
4. Nohra,"Rôle des monastères."
5. Mohasseb.

[54] Harīz, 26, 53.

reports of disputes treated and judged by the Islamic courts of justice in the Ottoman cities.

The documents available for the monastery of St. Elie Shwayyah have been studied in a serial and quantitative manner, even though not all the data is numbered. The records of this data have been processed by computer in order to reveal the evolution of each element and to understand the different policies undertaken by the monastic superiors in the expansion of the monastery's waqfs. These policies naturally corresponded to the different political and economic situations in the region, but also to the different local conditions of supply and demand.

In the documents of this monastery, there are homogeneous series of prices, names of buyers and sellers, names of places, etc. over a long period. This data illustrates the varying local conditions which determined strategies of expansion or of crisis-survival. These documents, though often not numerical, have been fully transcribed in a serial manner; they provide a better understanding of the stages of social and economic history that overshadowed the policies of territorial expansion undertaken by different ecclesiastical hierarchies.

III. 2.1: The Land Expansion Policy of Mār Ilyās Monastery

The 112 documents concerning the expansion of Mār Ilyās Shwayyah are all acts of purchase dated either by the Christian era, the hegira era, or both. These documents give us information on sellers and buyers, on the type of the land acquired and their surrounding regions, on prices and boundaries. The transcription of these documents allows us to study and analyze data on regions, crops, and prices, in addition to the internal correspondence of this data.

We have no data concerning the area of the land. Price alone is not a good criterion for providing us with information about the dimensions of the lands concerned. Prices are only a measure of the importance of the crop yielded by that land. Trends towards crop specialization and variation and efforts in view of autarky or to promote investments are identifiable according to periods. Policies of expansion could be the result either of individual initiatives taken by monks and priests, or of well-planned projects, executed and achieved by the monastery superiors.

These policies, according to years and initiatives, could also be the result of opportunities occurring in accordance with the sequence of historical events. This can be clearly demonstrated by the dating and the choice of the used calendar.

Some of the deeds seem to have nothing to do with the monastery. Sellers and buyers were lay persons. Transfer of property did not seem to concern the monks in any way. But information gathered in the region assures us that the transfer of property did not always involve the execution and draft of a new deed. The drawing up of the document to prove the ownership of the seller was sufficient. Since the land boundaries, location, crops and prices was the same, the drawing up of a new deed was not mandatory.

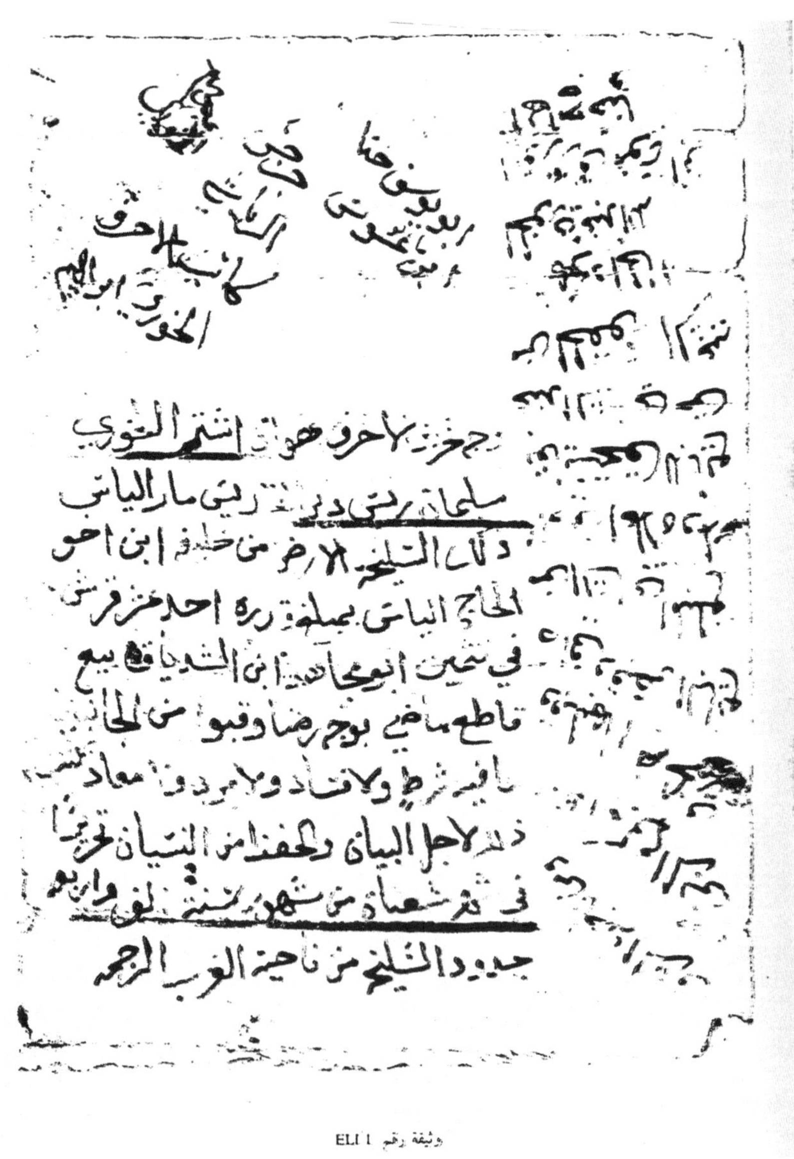

وثيقة رقم ELI 1

Doc 5 - First Deed of Acquisition of the Waqf of St. Ilyās Shwayyah

III. 2.2: Chronology and Time Sequence of Land Policy

As we have already specified, the dating of these documents follows both the Christian era and the Hegira era. Monks were well aware of the rules for official dating used throughout the Ottoman Empire. The argument over the autonomy of Mount Lebanon, claimed by contemporary historians more than by the emirs and governors to whom it was attributed, may be reviewed later. Of the 112 deeds dated from 1596 to 1912, 66 were dated according to the hegira year. However this observation needs to be clarified. Between 1596 and 1686, there is only one purchase act. Therefore, it would be more accurate to set the start of this land policy almost one century (90 years) later, namely in 1686, at the time of the first purchase.

On the other hand, the use of the Hegira calendar seemed to stop completely during 1838 A.D., which corresponds to the year 1253 A.H. This coincidence seems striking and curiously corresponds to the context of the period. This date marked the beginning of the Ottoman reforms introduced by the sulṭān in his Khaṭṭ-i-Sharif of Gulkhané in the year 1839. These reforms, partly suggested by the West and partly by the ruling Ottoman elite's wish for modernization, gave the Christian subjects of the empire citizenship equal status equal with the Muslims. It marked the end of the humiliating differentiation deriving from their status as inferior subjects.[55]

The use of the Hegira calendar by Christians did not effectively stop in 1839. Cities continued to use Muslim dating until the end of the Ottoman period. As for the mountain, the year 1840 marked the return of the Ottoman authority after the forced departure of the Egyptian armies of Muḥammad ʿAlī.[56]

Therefore, leaving out the first deed, and taking into account the year 1838, we have 66 deeds out of 91 (from 1686 to 1838), that is, more than two-thirds, dated according to the Muslim calendar.

During this period there were two intervals when this calendar was not used; in both periods, from 1772 to 1778 and from 1793 to 1807, intensive acquisitions were made. Chronologically and according to actual historical events, these two periods coincided with the rule of the Shihāb emirs, Yūsuf and Bashīr II. The first one was known to have openly converted to Christianity and to have led several military campaigns against the Ḥamādah, Shīʿah tax-farmers of the Jubayl and Batrūn regions. The second emir ruled Mount Lebanon for more than half a century and his conversion to Christianity remained a secret. He started a policy of centralization that materialized in the expropriation and exile of several Druze tax-collecting

---

55 "Al-Maḥfūẓāt al-ʿarabiyyah," Nos. ELI 155.

56 Salibi, 40-41.

families. Their lands were redistributed to partisans of the Shihāb emirs and entrusted in sharecropping to Christian peasants.[57]

So in both periods it seems that Mount Lebanon was ruled by governors whose policy suggested a favorable disposition towards Christian communities. For a short period of time, leaders of these communities thought they were exempted from using the Hegira date. Paradoxically, the same Emir Bashīr II, always aiming at centralization, obliged the Christian courts of the mountain to apply the Islamic law of the *sharīʿah.* This explains the revival of the use of the Hegira for dating between 1808 and 1832.[58]

The rate of purchasing over the different centuries was as follows: one act in the 16th century; six acts in the 17th, 67 acts in the 18th, 36 acts in the 19th and two acts in the 20th. The policy of land expansion, which had begun at the end of the 17th century in almost all of the monasteries in the mountain, brought about a crucial change in the monks' way of life. The monks' acquisition of waqf land property turned the spiritual life of the monastic institutions upside down.[59] Initially formed by groups of cenobites, living inside caves or caverns cut into the rock, old monasteries had only one constructed external facade. Whole partitions were constituted by the rock itself. Regarding the Eastern communities in communion with Rome, the development of monasticism prompted an official initiative to establish religious orders whose rules were established through contacts with the West and officially registered by the Council of Catholic Churches held at Lwayzah in 1738.[60]

These changes took place in a progressive and informal way inside the Orthodox community. This community has never recognized religious orders independent of the authority of the patriarch or bishop. Monastic communities were, and indeed still are, contemplative orders commonly known as *faqīr* and *haqīr (*poor and modest). However, these monks, within half a century, managed to become administrators of large agricultural estates.[61]

As for the monastery of Mār Ilyās, here also we can detect, in the land policy of this institution, three main periods corresponding to the general chronology of waqf development in the Ottoman Empire and Mount-Lebanon.

---

57 Salibi, 22.

58 Aouad, 59-61.

59 Michel Kaplan, "Les moines et le clergé séculier à Byzance," in *Moines et monastères dans les sociétés de rite grec et latin*, ed. Jean Loup Lemaitre (Geneva: Droz, 1996), 293-312.

60 Youakim Moubarac, *Pentalogie antiochienne, domaine maronite*, vol. 1 (Synodes maronites sous l'égide de Rome) (Beirut: Cénacle Libanais, 1984), 513-565.

61 Kaplan, 301.

Purchases that began at the end of the seventeenth century went on regularly, although less frequently, during the first half of the eighteenth century. Only ten purchases were made between 1700 and 1770, while there were 65 between 1770 and 1810.

III. 2.2a: The First Period

This period was not an easy one. Several difficulties, political and religious, hindered the land development of this monastery. In addition to the already bad situation, a natural catastrophe worsened the impasse in which the monastery was struggling. A major earthquake occurred in 1759 and destroyed the church and a large part of the ancient monastery of the prophet Ilyās.

The repercussions of the battle of ʿAyn Dārā and the redistribution of the districts of the mountain among the victors of the Qaysī party affected the beginning of the eighteenth century. The destruction of villages, emigration of populations, and fiscal problems were momentarily stabilized by the Emir Milḥim Shihāb, who was able to impose his authority on the different local parties as well as on the Ottoman Porte.[62]

The rivalry between the Qaysī and Yamanī parties had been settled militarily, but it persisted in the form of internal conflicts between Druze families of the Janbalāṭī and Yazbakī parties. These family divisions, inherited from Arab tribal affiliations, also divided the Shihāb family. The struggle for power among the members of this family was marked by battles and resulted in the rise of bidding for the mountain tribute.

Each emir, member of this family, and candidate to the emirate, tried to gain favor and support from the Ottoman *wālī* by increasing the fiscal sums due from Mount Lebanon and by sending valuable gifts to these officials in order to receive the *faramān* of investiture.[63]

It was mainly the religious conflicts that affected the land expansion of the monasteries at the beginning of the eighteenth century. In the Greek Orthodox Church, schism had already begun around the end of the seventeenth century and was confirmed in 1724.

After a difficult period of adjustment, the separated communities dispersed in the different Lebanese regions. A painful process of division of property and places of religious worship occurred.[64] Churches, convents, monasteries, graveyards, and agricultural lands were divided according to each community's size or relative power, affected by the pressure and influence of the *muqāṭaʿjī*.

---

[62] William Polk, *The Opening of South Lebanon 1788-1840* (Cambridge: Harvard University Press, 1963), 461.

[63] Ibid., 40.

[64] Paul Bacel, "La congrégation des basiliens choueirites," *Echos d'Orient* 4 (1903), 177-9.

These Druze or Sunnī sheikhs and emirs pronounced themselves in favor of one or another community, according either to the cash money each party offered to donate, or the sum of taxes and extortion each one of the fighting parties proposed to pay. In the first half of the eighteenth century, conflicts and wars between convents sometimes degenerated into elimination of superiors and even into defenestrations.

The Catholic monks of Saint John monastery tried to extend their proselytism to the monasteries of Mār Ilyās Shwayyah and Mār Shāʾyā in Brummānā. Thus, these monasteries switched several times from the Orthodox to the Catholics, paying each time an extra tribute to the Abīllamaᶜ, the Druze emirs of the region.[65] This conflict dragged on until 1749, when one of the orthodox notables of Beirut, Yūnis Niqūla al-Jubaylī, commonly known as Abū ᶜAskar, who was close to Emir Milḥim Shihāb, governor of Mount Lebanon at that time, interceded with him in order to recuperate Mār Ilyās monastery. The document certifying the return of this monastery to the Orthodox points out that the emirs Ismāᶜīl and Ḥaṣan Abīllamaᶜ received 1,500 piastres for the transfer of the monastery and its lands to sheikh Yūnis. He in turn entrusted them to the monks of his community – "their monks," as the text says.

This notable sheikh took it upon himself to install the hard-working and active monks to rehabilitate the monastery and maintain the lands as their predecessors had done. In counterpart, the emirs promised to protect and respect these monks, respect their security and listen to their complaints. "Their word would be listened to," as was the case for their neighbours, the Maronite monks.[66]

These emirs would not claim any increase or accept any bribe, They also agreed that in case they would one day ask the monks to leave the premises, they would have to pay the sum of 1,500 piastres, considered as a debt to the governor, Emir Milḥim Shihāb. A specific term ended this text, stating that it was to conform to God's opinion *(raʾy)* and the opinion of his prophet Shuᶜayb.[67]

Thus, even though this document was late, it showed the precariousness of the status of waqfs and *mulk* lands at that time. It also revealed that the essential aim of land donations and their conversion to waqfs was to fructify the productivity of these lands after their improvement by the monks. These lands, with their improved productivity, would give more profitable revenue to the monastery and, in the form of increased taxes, to the Ottoman treasury.

---

65 Slim, "Métayage et l'impôt," 46.

66 Asad Rustum, "Dayr Mār Ilyās wa-l-kathlakah," *al-Nūr*, no. 6 (1962), 168-170.

67 Ibid., 169.

Besides this difficult political and religious situation, the monastery of Mār Ilyās the prophet endured even worse circumstances; earthquakes shook the region between 1750 and 1760. Ten years after they had returned to the monastery, the Greek Orthodox monks had to leave it again.

On October 18th, 1759, an earthquake occurring in the middle of the night destroyed the church and the first floor of the buildings. The cellars and vaulted rooms remained intact. At this time, Yuwānīkus the Cypriote was the bishop of Beirut and Sufrūniyūs, son of Būlus al-Ṣayqalī of Beirut was the superior of the monastery.

Once more sheikh Yūnis al-Jubaylī worked for the reconstruction of the church and monastery. To commemorate this happy event, two inscriptions were engraved above the north and west doors in the church. The inscription on the west door, dated 1760, informs us that due to the laws forbidding the celebration of mass outside the church, bishop Yuwānīkus and superior Sufrūniyūs would rebuild, the monastery destroyed by the earthquake with the help of the Christians. The second inscription was not dated, but the letter count at last verse letters relating this episode are for the same year as that mentioned on the west door. This inscription mentions neither the name of the superior nor that of the bishop

However, the name of the notable was not mentioned on these steles. It was the historian ᶜĪsā Iskandar al-Maᶜlūf who attributed the rehabilitation of the monastery to the Beirut notable, Yūnis al-Jubaylī, known as Abū ᶜAskar.[68]

III. 2.2b: The Second Period

This was a long period of expansion extending from 1770 to 1810. In addition to reconstruction of the church, there was an increase of purchases lasting about forty years. During this period, Mār Ilyās monastery acquired 65 plots. In spite of the armed conflicts between the emirs of the Lebanese mountains and the regional *wālīs,* this period was also marked by the expulsion of the Shīᶜah tax farmers from Jubayl and Batrūn towards the Biqāᶜ. The regions abandoned by the Ḥamādah and their Shīᶜa supporters were rapidly occupied by peasant families coming from the north of the country and from Syria.

Important fiscal changes accompanied these demographic upheavals. New taxes were imposed. Did the increasing burden of heavy taxation push the peasants to sell their properties? Indeed, between 1770 and 1780, 28 plots were purchased by the monastery in nearby towns and villages. Between 1780 and 1790, 19 plots were purchased, all in the

---

68 al-Maᶜlūf, "Dawānī al-Quṭūf," 493.

village of Qinnābah close to the town of Brummānā. However, from 1790 to 1800, land purchasing slowed down, and the monastery acquired only ten plots scattered in different nearby towns. Between 1800 and 1810, the monastery purchased eight non-irrigated plots intended for wheat cultivation and commonly called *ṣalīkh.* Some of these were in a region called *qalᶜah*, meaning quarry.

This period of half a century was marked by higher and higher bids by tax farmers in the Mountain. Commotion, which at times led to armed conflicts among the *muqāṭaᶜjī* families, constantly increased the amount of taxes paid by Mount Lebanon's inhabitants. This tribute depended on the balance of forces between the mountain emirs and the Ottoman Porte. At the beginning of the century, under Emir Ḥaydar Shihāb, who feared the Ottomans, the tribute paid by the mountain amounted to 80,000 piastres; while under Emir Milḥim, who was feared even by the Turks, the mountain tribute amounted to 35,000 piastres only.[69]

In 1775, following the repression of the revolt of Ḍāhir al-ᶜUmar in Palestine, al-Jazzār, *wālī* of ᶜAkkā, began his long mandate over Syria. He claimed the payment of the *mīrī* six years in advance. He finally accepted 100,000 piastres from Emir Ḥaydar Shihāb in return for the right to rule Mount Lebanon. In 1810, Emir Bashīr had to pay 530 purses (265,000 piastres)[70] for the same right.

Over a quarter of a century, the official tribute paid by the Mountain more than doubled. During the last quarter of the eighteenth century, eight emirs from the Shihāb family aspired to govern the mountain; these were Yūsuf, Bashīr, Sayyid, Aḥmad, Efendi, Ḥaydar, Qaᶜdān and Ismāᶜīl.

Yet this official tribute was minimal by comparison with extortion, the award imposed by the Porte, and the *jizyah* imposed by *wālīs* and local governors in each district. The monasteries were exempted from the *jizyah* personal tax (locally called *jāliyah, shāshiyyah, fardah* or *farīdah,* according to the period). But they had to pay other taxes and donate gifts claimed by the *muqāṭaᶜjī* sheikhs of the region.[71]

These payments, constantly increased and claimed on several occasions per year, would result in a double and even a triple tax collection. Texts from the end of the eighteenth century mention *māl wa niṣf* or *mālayn* depending on the year.[72]

---

69 Carsten Niebuhr, *Voyages en Arabie et en d'autres pays circonvoisins* (Amsterdam: Baalde, 1780), vol.2, 362.

70 Volney, vol. 2, 68.

71 al-Maᶜlūf, "Dawānī al-Quṭūf," 252-253.

72 Ibid.

Bids on the amount of the mountain tributes progressively pauperized the mountain inhabitants. Even the privileged *muqāṭaʿjīs* were affected by the difficulties due to fiscal collection. The Matn region, and specially the Mār Ilyās Monastery (located in this region), which depended on the Abīllamaᶜ emirs, were also affected by these successive bids on the mountain tribute.

In 1776, Emir Yūsuf's insistent demands provoked the Abīllamaᶜ family into revolt. The struggle between the two factions ended in a costly repression for the Matn region, which had to endure the injustice and extortion of the Maghribī soldiers sent against the Abīllamaᶜ. Was this one of the reasons for the prosperity of the monastery and the frequency of its land acquisitions during this period?[73]

The inhabitants of the Matn, harassed by the *ḥawālī* (soldiers charged to collect taxes) and by the *muqāṭaʿjī* emirs, who were themselves in difficulty, responded by selling their land to the monastery, which was on the way to becoming a growing social and economic entity in the region. This would explain the acquisition of 28 parcels by Mār Ilyās monastery between 1770 and 1780.

From 1790 to 1792, there was a renewal of the competition between emirs Ḥaydar and Qaᶜdān on one side, and Emir Bashīr on the other. Bids continued to increase.

These years were also years of climatic crisis – drought was followed by food shortages, which led to more deterioration. Moreover Emir Bashīr advised Jazzār to close the access to the harbours of Beirut and Sidon, thus preventing the entry of imported foodstuffs to the mountain and increasing the devastating effects of the crisis. A song tells us that during this period, the Abīllamaᶜ emirs were exiled to the island of Arwād.[74] Although the closest to the Shihāb family in social rank, the Abīllamaᶜ was not at all favoured by the government of the Shihāb family. After a quarrel with Emir Bashīr II Shihāb, Emir Haṣan Abīllamaᶜ of Salīma took refugee in Bikfayyā and could not return to his *muqāṭaᶜah* until he paid 50 purses (2,500 piastres) to the ruling emir.[75] All of these difficulties endured by the Abīllamaᶜ family probably led them to sell to Mār Ilyās monastery the lands they had acquired between 1779 and 1796 in Qinnābah.

In spite of its land expansion, the monastery's prosperity was hampered by several difficulties. In fact, during the two periods of conflicts

---

73 al-Maᶜlūf, "Zajaliyyāt," 339.

74 Ibid.

75 Mīkhāʾīl al-Dimashqī, *Tārīkh ḥawādith al-Shām wa Lubnān, aw, tārīkh Mīkhāʾīl al-Dimashqī* (Damascus: Dār Qutaybah, 1982), 90.

and armed confrontations between the notables over lease farming of the mountain tribute, competition was not limited to the members of the Shihāb family, but it was extended to other Lebanese regions, particularly Beirut and the Biqāᶜ. The siege of the city of Beirut in 1792 was preceded by a fierce struggle between the two notables who farmed the town's taxes and customs, the Greek Catholic Fāris al-Dahhān and the Greek Orthodox Yūnis Niqūlā al-Jubaylī.[76] As we know the latter was the principal protector of the monks for Mār Ilyās monastery, who owed him their settlement in this monastery to the detriment of the Greek Catholic monks of Saint John monastery. In the meantime, lack of security and successive conflicts in the Biqāᶜ led the rich inhabitants of the region to deposit their money in the mountain monasteries, thought to be sheltered from the battle areas and the raids of the Ottoman soldiers and fighters paid by the emirs and the local *muqāṭaᶜjīs*.

Thus, the Greek Catholic notables of the city of Zaḥlah deposited their wealth in the convents of Saint John in Shwayr and Our Lady in Kfārtāy, while the Greek Orthodox notables deposited theirs in Mār Ilyās monastery. This did not prevent Emir Bashīr from robbing these monasteries in 1795 and taking possession of these deposits.[77] The difficulties and aggressions endured by Mār Ilyās monastery and its main protector slowed down the frequency of its acquisitions. In fact, the two decades between 1790 and 1800 and between 1800 and 1810 registered only eight and ten acquisitions respectively.

III. 2.2c: The Third Period

The third period of land expansion covers the nineteenth century and the beginning of the twentieth. Acquisitions were scarce but more regular. The following list shows the fluctuations in the purchases between 1810 and 1912:

1810	to	1819	4	purchases
1820	to	1829	2	purchases
1830	to	1839	5	purchases
1840	to	1849	3	purchases
1850	to	1859	5	purchases
1860	to	1869	3	purchases
1870	to	1879	3	purchases
1880	to	1889	2	purchases
1890	to	1899	1	purchase
1900	to	1909	0	purchase
1912			2	purchases

76 al-Maᶜlūf, "Zajaliyyāt," 339.

77 Ibid., 135.

Several factors affected land policy during this century: These were: the tax system, which was linked to local and Ottoman policies; the market economy into which Mount Lebanon was integrated; and foreign interference. Was the acquisition of 30 plots over one century a way to ensure property consolidation? Or was it instead a tendency towards more fragmentation, aiming to ensure a larger variety of production and thereby economic self-sufficiency, at least in foodstuffs? During this century, the rhythm of acquisitions remained very closely linked to the political and economical context of the country and the whole region.

The pressure of official tax-collection and extortion increased and reached such high rates that it went even beyond agricultural revenues. Additional collections, multiple contributions, and expensive capitations were turned into official taxes. Competition between local emirs and conflicts opposing governors in the Ottoman provinces pushed the bids on Mount Lebanon's tribute to the limit. From 1810 to 1820, the main reason for the wars between Emir Bashīr and the *wālī* of Damascus was the control over the cereal crops of the fertile Biqāᶜ valley, which were vital to the alimentary supply of the mountain.[78]

Twice, these struggles forced Emir Bashīr into exile, in order to avoid retaliation from his opponents. Nevertheless, misappropriations and fiscal insufficiency accelerated his return to his emirate and to his functions as the main tax farmer in the mountain.

This troubled period impoverished the peasantry and perhaps also facilitated the transfer of lands to the monastery: four plots between 1810 and 1820 and five between 1830 and 1840. This second period, influenced by the Egyptian occupation of Palestine, Lebanon and Syria, saw fiscal collection increase to its peak.[79]

This oppressive fiscal policy and Emir Bashīr II's centralization, added to the constantly increasing population, gradually made obsolete the role of the traditional landlord in the management of the affairs of the country. In the nineteenth century, new social categories established their power in the society of the Mountain.

The middle class became tax collectors. Through their merchandise, their wealth, their exchange channels and their network of customers, they could safeguard the remittance of taxes to the governor's treasury. In case the *muqāṭaᶜjīs*, emirs or *wālīs*, pressured by the demands of the Ottoman

---

78 John Lewis Burckhardt, *Travels in Syria and the Holy Land* (London: Kessinger Publishing, 1822), 194.

79 Ferdinand Perrier, *La Syrie sous le gouvernement de Méhémet-Ali jusqu'en 1840* (Paris, 1842), 52.

Porte, were short on cash and had to borrow,[80] the middle class themselves made funds available. This cash, usually scarce among traditional agricultural societies, was secured in Mount Lebanon thanks to commercial arboriculture. From the seventeenth century, Mount Lebanon's inhabitants had access to genuine European currencies, as a result of the export of silk, oil, wine, and soap. The other cereal-producing regions still depended on barter exchange to ensure a certain variety in food. Even taxes were paid in kind. Collectors' agents used to come to the fields and threshing grounds to deduct the state's share on the spot.[81]

The second category, favored by the traditional *muqāṭaᶜjīs*, was the clergy.

Competition between rural notables and the clergy was already felt at the beginning of the seventeenth century, and was basically concerned with the management of waqfs. In 1736 the Maronite Synod forbade the notables to interfere in monastery business, i.e. in the management of the waqfs.[82]

Concerning the Mār Ilyās monastery, we can outline two periods during which purchases resumed. The first one was under the Egyptian occupation from 1832 to 1840 when five plots were purchased. Favorable measures towards Christians were applied by Muḥammad ᶜAlī's government, along with a heavy increase in fiscal collection. Official taxes were collected up to 16 times a year in addition to the *fardah* (exorbitant individual tax), which was set at 35 piastres at a minimum, payable by all males aged 15 to 70 years.

Both confessional and fiscal conditions helped the land expansion of Mār Ilyās monastery. Following the Egyptian occupation, the state granted this monastery judicial responsibilities. Through its superior, the monastery acquired the status of a judge.[83]

Conflicts and trials were solved and judged according to either the Islamic *sharīᶜah,* or the Church's Canon Laws as set down in the Namūs al-Sharīf books. The Maronites too had their own law abstract, written by Bishop Būlus Qaraᵓlī, and enforced in the Maronite villages and monasteries in the mountains.

The autonomy of the Ottoman Empire's Christian communities, guaranteed by the *millet* system that allowed non-Muslim communities to administer their own affairs, was interrupted by the centralising measures

80 al-Maᶜlūf, "Zaḥlah," 146.

81 Ibid., 145.

82 Van Leeuwen, 606.

83 Rustum, "Kanīsat," 205-206.

implemented by Emir Bashīr II. In order to unify the judicial system, the latter imposed the Islamic *sharīʿah*[84] on non-Muslims.

The general situation was therefore favorable to the monasteries. Although the period that followed the Egyptian occupation and the *qāʾimaqāmiyyah* regime was marked by fiscal, political and confessional difficulties, the prosperity of Mār Ilyās monastery was not affected. From 1843 to 1858, eight plots were purchased by Makāriyūs, the superior of the monastery. Were these good opportunities to buy land from peasants affected by the crisis, or were they mainly aimed at new acquisitions? The second possibility is more likely, at least regarding the acquisition of the six mulberry parcels.

The prices of these mulberry orchards, definitely higher than those of the other plots, varied between 250 and 500 piastres. Nevertheless, during the difficult period of the *qāʾimaqāmiyyah*, the monastery could invest in their acquisition, so necessary to the expansion of its silk production.

Silkworm breeding, already flourishing in Mount Lebanon for several centuries, achieved a new expansion in the nineteenth century. Eighty-eight percent of the Lebanese silk production was exported to France, mainly to the city of Lyon, and the remaining twelve percent to England.[85] Through its silk production and exports Lebanon was integrated in the international market as far back as the eighteenth century. The economic condition of the mountain peasants was now dependent on the changes of silk prices in the world market. More particularly, researchers have observed the tendency of international trade to gather silk production through the waqfs, which by now had become large entities.[86]

Another witness to the prosperity of Mār Ilyās monastery under the *qāʾimaqāmiyyah,* has reached us through the diary of David Urquhart, the British traveller sent by the British Parliament to try and settle conflicts in the mountains. This politician/traveller visited the monastery in 1850. He reported that the monastery's superior, with whom he did not sympathize, took advantage of the good silk crop and its profits to rehabilitate and extend the monastery[87].

Under the *mutaṣarrifiyyah* system from 1860 onwards, the effects of the tax system on the impoverishment of the peasantry started to be neutralized. Property fragmentation, a fall in silk prices, the absence of an outlet to the sea, and the narrowness of the *mutaṣarrifiyyah*'s territory, requiring

84 Aouad, 59-61.

85 Boutros Labaki, *Introduction à l'histoire économique du Liban* (Beirut: Lebanese University, 1984), 213.

86 Van Leeuwen, 601.

87 Urquhart, vol. 2, 10.

the import of most of its foodstuffs, were the principal factors affecting both the peasants and the monastery in the second half of the 19th century. Acquisitions were scarce, but prices sometimes quintupled.

Around the end of the nineteenth century and the beginning of the twentieth, lands purchased at very high prices yielded a large variety of products. There was an alternation in the purchase of mulberry orchards, vineyards, pine-groves, and *ṣalīkh* lands planted with wheat. At the beginning of the twentieth century, the monastery made an innovation and acquired two parcels in Bṭurrām, a village in the north of the country. Were these olive groves, located far from the monastery and purchased at a very high price, intended to replace silk, which was already in jeopardy? We can see here the initiative of the monasteries in cultivating new products when others ceased to be profitable.[88]

III. 2.3: Land Categories and Production

Only two of the 112 land purchases made during the three centuries mentioned the type of soil or the nature of the crops usually grown. Different terms describing the kind of soil suggest the type of crops. Thus the word *ṣalīkh* refers to rocky non-irrigated lands, while *būr* are fallow lands. Both were often assigned to wheat farming. Sandy lands planted with pine trees were referred to as *smīt.*[89]

Some plots simply referred to as "land" were reserved for wheat or other leguminous crops. Other deeds mentioned several kinds of crops in the same plot. Thus, ten *ṣalīkh* plots were recorded as being planted with both vines and mulberries. From this we can get information about the administration of the lands. Purchased lands could either be fertilized and irrigated or terraced.

In some of the deeds, the boundary of the acquired land was marked by a *rujmah*, which means a mound of rocks. These mounds, brought from quarries cut in the cliffs, were used to build terraces. Rural sites are full of these rock collections, attesting to the fact that the terraces were not always completed.[90]

The production, exploitation and transformation of crops grown on these lands was diversified. Each crop could produce a variety of goods, which were fructified, consumed, sold or preserved. Wheat, vine, olive, mulberry and pine-tree farming was carried on according to the distribution of plots in the different localities, regions, and neighboring villages. The

---

88 Georges Khuḍr, "L'activité et la réflexion sociale chez les orthodoxes arabes de 1800 à 1920," in *L'église et les pauvres*, ed. J.S. Anna (Suisse: Lausanne, 1982), 168.

89 Latron, 54.

90 Mohasseb, 26.

crops depended on the specialisation of the region, as well as on its relief, climate, altitude, irrigation and soil.

The division and fragmentation of the lands reduced total production but was, nevertheless, an economic necessity in a traditional economy based on agriculture. Crops cultivated on monastery lands were not restricted to mulberry monoculture for silk production but included the traditional Mediterranean triculture – wheat, vines and olives.[91] We will try to determine the growing regions and average prices of each of these crops.

III. 2.3a: Wheat

Wheat was essentially grown on *ṣalīkh* lands, which included other lands whose product was not mentioned. Wheat was considered of little importance during this period, when only silk ensured money revenues. However, wheat was the basic staple food of the Lebanese mountain peasant. Converted into flour or *burghul*, this wheat was easy to cook in winter. Being a nourishing substance, it was either mixed with vegetables for *tabbūlah*, with dairy products for *kishk*, or with meat for *kibbah*. These dishes were quite refined and sophisticated. Everyday meals were made with *burghul* and oil, cooked with water and chick peas.[92]

Twenty-seven plots were mentioned as *ṣalīkh* and 27 others had no specific crops mentioned. Most of these lands were located in the immediate neighborhood. Only seven plots were located in Qinnābah and Nābāy near the village of Brummānā.

As we may see on Graph 2, showing lands whose yields are not mentioned, the plots are very small and their price is usually not more than 25 to 50 piastres. On the other hand, the price of *ṣalīkh*-land in Graph 1 sometimes exceeds 100 piastres. Also in Graph 1 are nine deeds of purchase in which members of the Ṣāfī or Bou Ṣāfī family are cited as sellers. Graph 2 shows that four plots were acquired between 1773 and 1776 in the village of Shrīn, which is the heart of the monastery's landed domain.

These *ṣalīkh* lands, whose crops were not mentioned (Graph 2), constituted the basic nucleus around which the monastery established its agricultural property. Out of the 17 plots purchased between 1596 and 1765 (Graph 1), only three were not used for wheat crops; two were mulberry orchards, and one a vineyard. Therefore, for a century-and-a-half the monastery seems not to have had any ambitions for land expansion. The areas planted with wheat or vegetables were sufficient for the consumption of the

---

91 Fernand Braudel, *The Mediterranean and the Mediterranean World in the Age of Philip II* (Berkeley, CA: University of California Press, 1995).

92 Guys, "Beyrouth et le Liban," vol. 2, 289.

monks and the peasants who worked with them. The amount of money dedicated to the purchase of these lands was rather small. Sometimes, nominal prices of four, eight, or nine piastres were paid for small plots.

During the total period of three centuries, the value of the *ṣalīkh* lands purchased by the monastery was 1,500 piastres, while lands for which crops are not mentioned cost 4,685 piastres. Included under this heading, however, were two plots purchased in Nābāy in 1912 for 1,500 piastres each. Apart from these two late acquisitions, the average value of *ṣalīkh* lands fluctuated between 55.5 piastres and 67.5 piastres for lands whose crops were not mentioned.

Putting together the two categories, small plots and *ṣalīkh*-land, we notice that 54 plots were acquired over a period of three centuries. This suggests that a preference for wheat cultivation and a subsistence economy persisted: although a market economy was developing, it was not yet present in all sectors of the economy of Mount Lebanon.

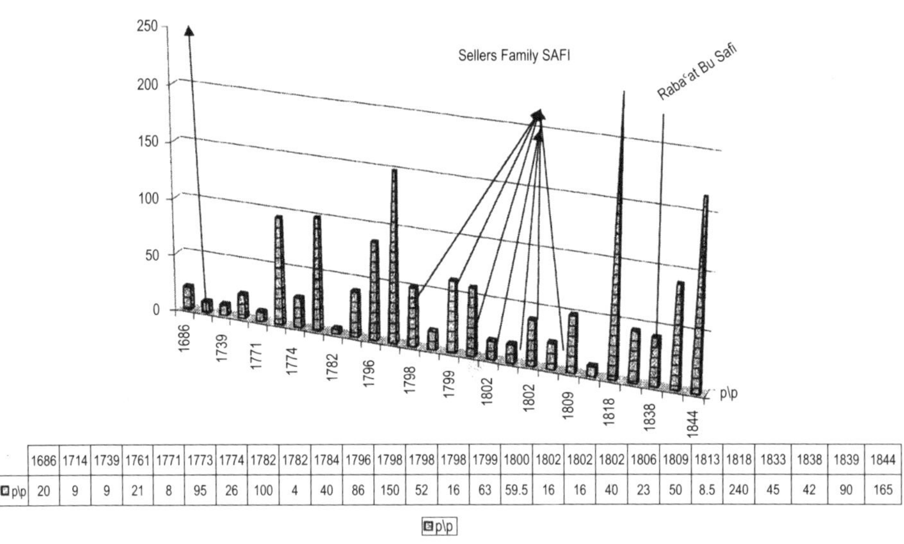

	1686	1714	1739	1761	1771	1773	1774	1782	1782	1784	1796	1798	1798	1798	1799	1800	1802	1802	1802	1806	1809	1813	1818	1833	1838	1839	1844
p\p	20	9	9	21	8	95	26	100	4	40	86	150	52	16	63	59.5	16	16	40	23	50	8.5	240	45	42	90	165

p\p

Graph 1 - Chronology of Acquisition / Category: Ṣalīkh

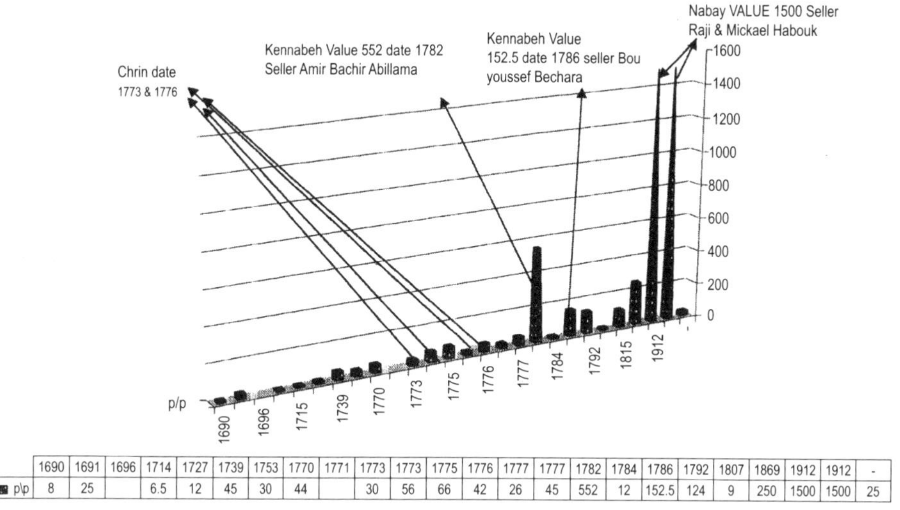

	1690	1691	1696	1714	1727	1739	1753	1770	1771	1773	1773	1775	1776	1777	1777	1782	1784	1786	1792	1807	1869	1912	1912	-
p\p	8	25		6.5	12	45	30	44		30	56	66	42	26	45	552	12	152.5	124	9	250	1500	1500	25

Graph 2 - Chronology of Acquisition / Category: Land

III. 2.3b: Vineyards

Vineyards were clearly less important than lands dedicated to wheat or mulberry. Ten plots were planted with vines. Vineyards were essentially purchased during the period of expansion and land acquisition from 1765 to 1800. They were mainly located in the neighbouring villages, except for two plots in Qinnābah. Graph 3, representing the chronology of vineyard acquisition, shows a gap of 50 years in purchasing. From 1800 to 1850, no vineyard was acquired. The decade 1850-1860 saw a revival of interest in viniculture: four vineyards were acquired in this decade, which was, besides, a period of political and confessional troubles. One vineyard was bought in 1854 for 100 piastres, two in 1860 for 100 piastres, and, most importantly, one in 1852 for 500 piastres. The value of these lands was not very important and reached 3,101.5 piastres, of which 2,056 piastres were paid in 1882 to acquire a single vineyard. It is not clear whether this price was due to the enormous increase in land prices that occurred at the end of the nineteenth century or due to the size of the land and the importance of its crop.

Viticulture in the Lebanese mountain yielded a variety of by-products that necessitated long and hard work. The different varieties of grapes were used to produce vinegar, wine, arak, raisin molasses (*dibs*), etc. Mār Ilyās monastery did not seem to have given much importance to the production and export of alcohol, for which some Lebanese and Syrian monasteries were famous.[93]

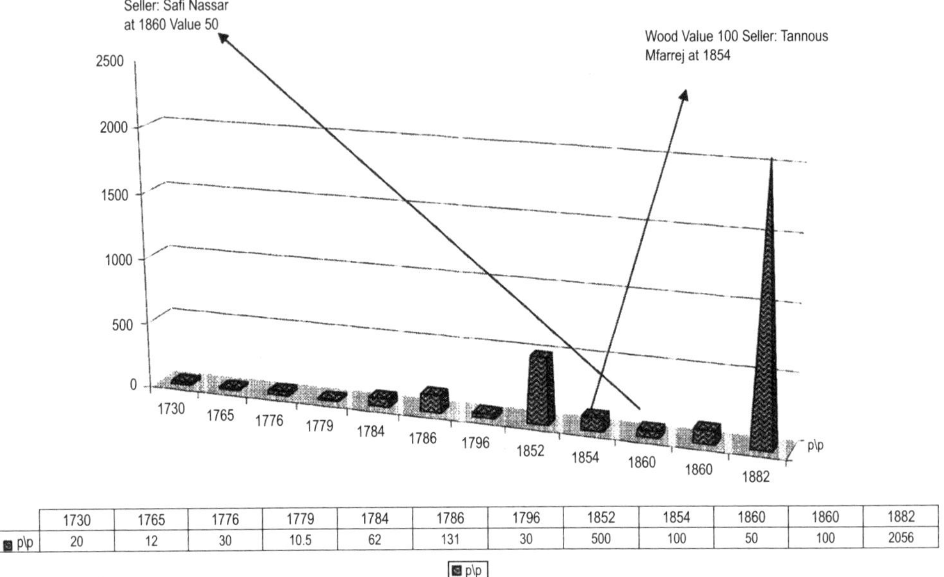

	1730	1765	1776	1779	1784	1786	1796	1852	1854	1860	1860	1882
p\p	20	12	30	10.5	62	131	30	500	100	50	100	2056

Graph 3 - Chronology of Acquisition / Category: Vine Yard

III. 2.3c: Mulberry Orchards

The monastery purchased 24 mulberry plots, of which 15 were acquired during the expansion period. Two mulberry orchards were purchased during the establishment period. One was acquired in Abū Mīzān for 300 piastres. This price was high for that time (1687), suggesting that the plot purchased was very large. For the period of expansion from 1770 to 1800, graph 4 shows a multitude of small mulberry plots acquired very cheaply. The price of each of these plots does not exceed 50 to 100 piastres. Graph 4 also shows that from the first half of the 19th century, prices for such plots began to rise progressively towards a peak in the second half of the century, reaching, for example, 900 and 1,038 piastres in the village of Btighrīn in 1871 and 1872 respectively.

---

93 Henri Guys, *Esquisse de l'état politique et commercial de la Syrie* (Marseille: [s.p.], 1863), 266-7.

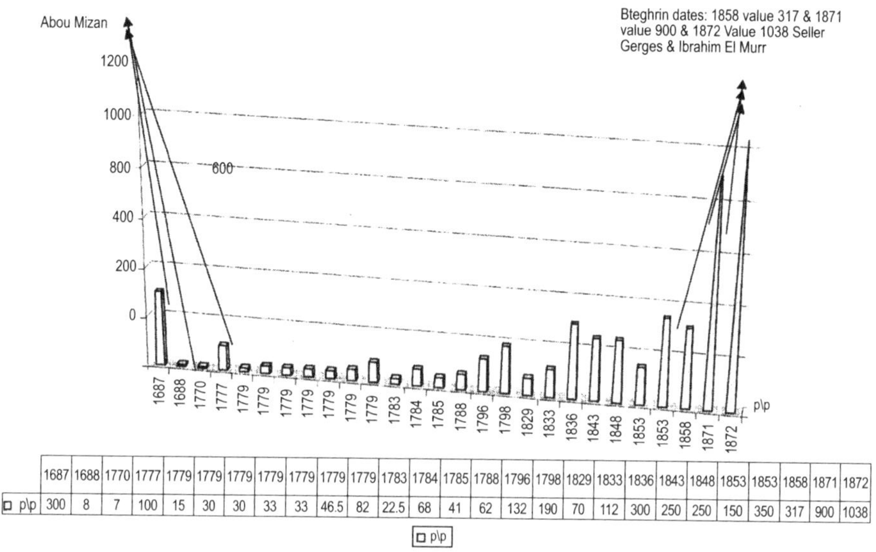

	1687	1688	1770	1777	1779	1779	1779	1779	1779	1779	1779	1783	1784	1785	1788	1796	1798	1829	1833	1836	1843	1848	1853	1853	1858	1871	1872
□ p\p	300	8	7	100	15	30	30	33	33	46.5	82	22.5	68	41	62	132	190	70	112	300	250	250	150	350	317	900	1038

□ p\p

Graph 4 - Chronology of Acquisition / Category: Mulberries

The locality in which this plot was located became the main estate in which the monastery had its properties. The mulberry trees were the main crops that ensured the peasants the necessary cash to purchase food that could not be grown locally. This crop was necessary for feeding the silk worms that in turn produced the silk thread that integrated the mountain in the international trade system. Lyon, the first European city to produce silk, became the first city to import silk from Lebanon via Marseilles harbor.[94]

Until the end of the eighteenth century, this trade between Marseilles and Syria resulted in a credit to the Syrian side. But during the nineteenth century the trade balance for the whole Ottoman Empire, and especially Syria, was in deficit.

With regard to peasants and silk, conditions were radically changed. Peasants in the mountain provided several silk by-products such as hanks, good quality silk, seeds, and cocoons. They became skilled at converting cocoons into silk thread and even sometimes at weaving it. Peasants were farmers and craftsmen at the same time. But with the establishment of European spinning factories and their new machines in the nineteenth century, peasants reverted to being cocoon providers. Their double professional experience was, again, confined to agriculture.

---

94 Labaki, 60-61.

Labour in the new spinning factories was essentially female. During this second period, the peasants' economic conditions depended essentially on silk prices on the international market. Since the *mutaṣarrifiyyah* regime had stabilized fiscal deductions up to a point, it was mainly the fluctuations of the silk market that affected Mount Lebanon's rural and industrial economy. Industrial activity, neglected by research, was prospering in the second half of the nineteenth century. Mount Lebanon possessed about a hundred spinning factories belonging to Europeans or Lebanese and run along modern Western lines.[95]

During the nineteenth century, the monastery purchased ten plots, some of them at rather high prices. Silk investments seemed profitable enough to justify such important purchases.

The total value of the 27 plots purchased between 1687 and 1872 amounted to 4,937 piastres. The average value of one plot was 183 piastres, which was, approximately, three times the price of lands used to grow wheat and twice the price of those used to grow vineyards.

The multiple croplands show the same pattern. Out of the twenty-seven parcels, nine mentioned other crops and plantations besides the mulberry orchards. Lands, *salīkhs,* olive groves, or vineyards were associated to mulberry orchards in nine deeds. There is no mention either of the areas reserved for each, or of the importance of the various crops.

Is this multiplicity of crops grown on one plot (indicating a self-sufficient economy) the result of the conversion of crops into more profitable plantations? Or is it rather due to the steep relief allowing several levels in the same plot? Cliffs, faults, and valley bottoms could have different soils and be of different altitudes, allowing different crops to be grown. It was not unusual for a single village to cover up to 400 metres of altitude difference.

It is in the localities reserved for mulberry orchards that we can observe specialization of certain regions. Thus in Qinnābah there were 13 mulberry orchards, purchased by the monastery through Emir Bashīr Abīllamaʿ. There were also three mulberry orchards in Abū Mīzān and three in Btighrīn. So, in the neighborhood of the monastery, it was essentially the Abū Mīzān plot, purchased during the establishment period, which gave the monastery the most important push regarding investment policy in this essential production. This plot was acquired in 1687 for 300 piastres, according to its purchase sharecroppers in charge of the administration and the care of the worms.

III. 2.3d: Olive Groves

Olive groves seemed to be the least appreciated plantation in the monastery's land policy. The altitude of Mār Ilyās monastery was not favourable to the

95 Gaston Ducousso, *L'Industrie de la soie au Liban* (Paris: N.p., 1913), 216.

olive tree. Even the lower lands in Abū Mīzān were not planted with olive trees. Widespread throughout the Mediterranean area, this crop was very important in the diet of Mount Lebanon's inhabitants. Olive groves ensured, oil, olives, soap. The seeds were essential for heating. Poorer quality oil was used for lighting.[96] During one century, between 1784 and 1894, Mār Ilyās monastery acquired four plots planted with olive trees. All were located far from the monastery: one parcel was in Qinnābah, and three in Bṭurrām. These two plots were the last ones to be purchased in a village in the north of the country, in Kūrah. The acquisition of these plots for 300 and 1,500 piastres respectively indicate the monastery's concern to ensure essential foodstuffs. The total value of these four plots was 2,215 piastres, giving an average of 553.7 piastres per plot this was the highest average price for one plot. Graph 5 shows that in the last quarter of the 19th century, the monastery turned towards the acquisition of olive-growing lands. This may have reflected a regional need for a substitute crop with which to replace mulberry-culture. Alternatively, the monastery may simply have taken advantage of a lucrative offer. The last quarter of the century marked the start of widespread emigration, and those who intended to leave needed to amass as much money as possible; they did not hesitate to sell their lands before leaving the country.

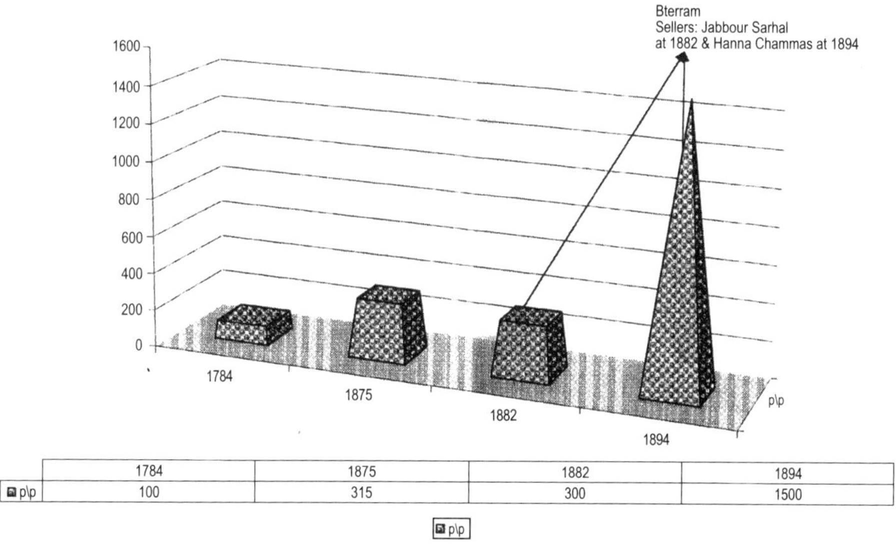

	1784	1875	1882	1894
p\p	100	315	300	1500

p\p

Graph 5 - Chronology of Acquisition / Category: Olives

[96] Guys, "Beyrouth et le Liban," vol. 1, 289.

III. 2.3e: Pine-Groves

Pine groves provided the essential green scenery surrounding the monastery. Nine plots planted with pine trees were purchased mainly during the land expansion period.

Four of these plots were located in the region of Mirḥāta (the former name of the contemporary summer village of Ḍhūr al-Shwayr). Several products essential to rural life were provided by the pine groves. Pine nuts obtained from cones were used in refined and rich cooking. The trunks were essential for building roofs. Pine trees were cut annually; their wood and dried cones were used for heating.[97]

Three deeds regarding the acquisition of pine groves, do not mention their location. One does not mention the price. Graph 6 shows the extent of pine-groves acquired and the prices paid for them from the end of the 18th century. Substantial sums were allocated for the acquisition of such plots. These pine-groves, which were common in the sandstone hills of the region, were the object of several sharecropping contracts between the monks of the monastery and the Abīllamaᶜ emirs, who were tax-farmers for the Matn district.

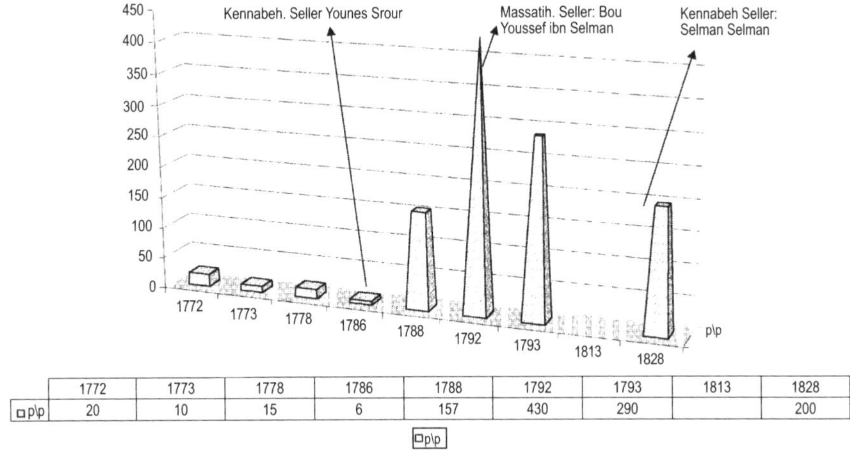

	1772	1773	1778	1786	1788	1792	1793	1813	1828
□p\p	20	10	15	6	157	430	290		200

□p\p

Graph 6 - Chronology of Acquisition / Category: Pine Land

[97] Toufic Touma, *Paysans et institutions féodales chez les Druzes et les Maronites du Liban du XVIIème siècle à 1914* (Beirut: Lebanese University, 1996), vol. 2, 610.

The sums spent on the purchase of the eight pine groves amounted to 1,128 piastres, with an average value of 141 piastres per plot. This was three times the price of a wheat-producing plot. It was only later, with the failure of the silk economy, that lands overlooking the village of Ḍhūr al-Shwayr, and those of Qinnābah in the valley below the village of Brummānā, were planted with pine groves.

III. 2.3f: Miscellaneous

The monastery also acquired three *būr* (uncultivated) plots. The location of only one of them, in Qinnābah, is mentioned. The prices of these lands were quite low at seven, eleven, and twelve piastres. Two houses were also purchased in 1779 and 1783 (expansion period) for 26 and 46 piastres, in Shwayr and Qinnābah.

III. 2.4: Fluctuations of Land Prices

Land prices were not based on surface area. The sale or lease evaluation of a plot or the finalization of a sharecropping or lease-farming contract took into consideration several elements. These included: relief, soil quality, irrigation, number of plants or quantity of seeds, weight of leaves (in the case of mulberry trees), number of bowls (*ṭast*) of grape molasses or wine, etc.

It was logical that lands providing marketable products were more expensive than *ṣalīkh* lands producing wheat. During the establishment period in 1687, a mulberry orchard was purchased in Abū Mīzān for 300 piastres, while another plot (with no crop mentioned) was acquired in 1714 in the same village for 6.5 piastres. Land value was also affected by varying economic and political conditions.

Successive monetary devaluation, made by the Ottoman State in an attempt to improve its finances, was the direct cause of the price increase in agricultural products.[98]

As the main source of production prior to industrialization, land was the most important element in the economy and prosperity of the country. Changes in the amounts dedicated to the acquisition of land plots seemed to correspond to the periods of land expansion by the monastery. But the acquisition by the monastery, in 1792, of a pine grove for 430 piastres indicates a significant rise in prices and is proof of changing economic conditions.

Between 1802 and 1833, prices tended to decrease. But subsequently, due to the Egyptian occupation, prices went up in a decisive way. During

---

98 Robert Mantran, *Istanbul dans la seconde moitié du XVIIème siècle à 1914: essai d'histoire institutionelle, économique et sociale* (Paris: Maisonneuve, 1962), 262.

this period private property seems to have been more secure.[99] Towards the end of the nineteenth century and the beginning of the twentieth, prices went beyond 1000 piastres. In 1871 and 1872, for example, mulberry orchards were purchased in Btighrīn for 900 and 1,038 piastres respectively. Two olive groves were acquired in 1882 and 1894 in Btighrīn and Bṭurrām for 2,056 and 1,500 piastres respectively. In 1912, two plots whose crops are not mentioned were purchased for 1,500 piastres each in the village of Nābāy near Qinnābah.

During this later period, property investments in mulberry groves were less important than before. Other traditional crops were replacing silk production, which led to a great decrease from the 1860-1870 prices.

On the other hand, this period marked the influx of capital sent by the first emigrants to Egypt and America. For many, land was no longer considered only as a source of productive wealth. It was now an object of commerce whose trading value fluctuated according to supply and demand.[100] During this period, the supply of land was favored due to the increased poverty and the fragmentation and scattering of estates. Property sales were necessary to relieve the worries and necessities of the subsistence economy, but they did not suit the market economy, which promoted specialisation and monoculture of commercial crops.

Demand, however, was also strong. It was encouraged by the return of emigrants anxious to acquire properties in their native villages and by the new middle-class, enriched by trade, which reinvested its fortune in large agricultural estates, coastal orchards, and olive or mulberry groves in the mountain. This increase in the supply of landed property was reinforced by the sale of several waqfs during the first half of the twentieth century. Land therefore became a commodity in addition to being a means of production.

Faced with a decline in agricultural revenues, the monasteries sold remote plots and invested in the purchase of land and real estate inside the cities, where leases on buildings were more profitable than incomes from agricultural land.

III. 2.5: Sellers & Buyers

The list of the different bidders on the purchase acts of Mār Ilyās monastery gives us an overview of the different social stratification in the mountain over two centuries. Lack of information prevents us from studying

---

[99] Asad Rustum, *Bashīr II: bayn al-sulṭān wa-l-ʿAzīz* (Beirut, 1988), 80.

[100] N. Verney and G. Dambman, *Les puissances étrangères dans le Levant, en Syrie, et en Palestine* (Paris: N. p., 1900), 192.

the different families who negotiated with the monastery. The seller is often named after his son, his father, or both, as for example Bū Yūsuf Ibn Silmān or Ibn Mikhāyil Bū Brāhīm. The patriarchal line of descent was very important in the social structure and the rural economy of the Lebanese Mountain in particular and the Arab world in general.[101] These nicknames or surnames, which mean almost nothing to us, seemed very familiar to the village inhabitants. Some first names or jubb were proper to particular families and others avoided using them. Often the enlarged family, after leaving its neighborhood or native village, took as a new patronym the first name of the person who initiated the new establishment. It was the start of a new lineage (*jubb*), still acknowledged by its clan or original family.[102] Names and surnames were often.

There was another problem concerning acts of sale between two individuals independent of the monastery. Since the act of sale was the essential document, its possession was proof enough of the acquisition of the said plot by the monastery. As we have already mentioned, it was not necessary to draw up a new document. The problem concerns dating, for there is no way for us to know exactly when the plot mentioned in the deed became a waqf of the monastery. Fifteen deeds out of 112 were made between known personalities, six of them in 1779 by Emir Bashīr Abīllamaᶜ alone. The remaining deeds were drawn up in different periods and did not concern very important lands. They were mainly *ṣalīkh* lands, aside from the three olive groves purchased in Bṭurrām and the six mulberry orchards acquired in Qinnābah through Emir Bashīr Abīllamaᶜ.

III. 2.5a: The Sellers

The sellers were essentially peasants coming from a wide range of villages. Although the purchases tended to be made in one region over a certain period, the establishment of the monastery and its expansion in the region did not seem to have been detrimental to a particular family or region. Nevertheless, two cases were important enough to be mentioned in the villages of Shrīn and Qinnābah. Here it seems that the sellers were concentrated among some particular families. In the village of Shrīn it was the Ṣāfī family, who, at different times and through several of its members, provided the monastery with 13 parcels.[103]

---

101 Robert Creswell, "Parenté et propriété foncière dans la montagne libanaise," *Etudes Rurales* 40 (1970), 48.

102 Toufic Touma, *Un village de montagne au Liban: Hadeth el-Jobbé* (Paris: Mouton, 1958), 100.

103 "Al-Maḥfūẓāt al-ᶜarabiyya."

Eleven of these plots were *ṣalīkh* lands sold at derisory prices. It has been reported that each seller of this family referred to as Abū Ṣāfī or Ibn Ṣāfī sold two or three plots. Thus we have Bashshūr (3), Anṭūn (3), Buṭrus (3), Mikhāyil (3), and Naṣṣār (2). The lands sold by this family were located in a region called *qalᶜa*, meaning quarry, one of which was named after this family. In 1829 Naṣṣār Ṣāfī sold the monastery a mulberry orchard for 70 piastres and later in 1860 a vineyard for 50 piastres. Both plots were located in two spots named after the monastery, *Maᶜṣarat al-Dayr* and *Karm al-Dayr*, which must have been close to the monastery's estate. Thus, by its right of preemption, the monastery must have had no difficulty in acquiring them.[104] This right was established in the Koran; it permitted an owner, especially a moral entity, to develop its properties.

The second case concerns two families of the village of Qinnābah who sold their properties, essentially mulberry groves, to the monastery: The Bishārah family sold 11 plots and the Kanᶜān family sold eight plots at different times. These two families are known to be from Brummānā, and originally from Qinnābah. The name Kanᶜān was once related to Bishārah as in the case of Jirjī ibn Kanᶜān Bishārah. All these lands were acquired during the period of the monastery's land expansion in the eighteenth century, except for two plots, one in 1828 and the other in 1869. These latter were not mulberry orchards. Was this already a sign of a lack of interest in mulberry trees? In the meantime, the monastery had already bought a pine grove for 200 piastres and a plot for 250 piastres in a region where the monastery had previously owned the bulk of its mulberry orchards.

No information whatsoever in these deeds mentioned the reasons for these massive sales. The causes could shed light on the socio-economic situation of these former landowners-become-peasants. We can learn from other documents that most of these sellers were former landowners reduced to the status of sharecropping tenants of the monastery.

These transfers of properties did not exclude the fact that sellers could still own other plots. As we already know, the economy of subsistence involved ownership of several plots in different places. Thus the peasants could be sharecropping tenants and landowners at the same time. If the lands were large and productive enough, the situation of the sharecropping tenants could be better than the situation of landlords who owned scattered and very small plots. The different political and fiscal contexts existing in the Mountain, together with demographic growth and the monopolization of lands by *muqāṭaᶜjī* sheikhs and waqfs, made the peasants' situation more and more difficult. Among the sellers, there is also the name of Emir

104 Rustum, "Bashīr II," 69.

Bashīr Abīllamaᶜ, mentioned only twice as seller and six times as buyer. The lands he bought from the peasants were probably sold to the monastery at the same prices since the deeds kept in the monastery do not mention any change in price.

We have no evidence that lands purchased from the peasants were regrouped and sold to the monastery at higher prices. Plots acquired in 1779 by the emir were all planted with mulberry trees; they were worth 254.5 piastres. In 1782 and 1784 the emir sold a plot of land and an olive grove at 652 piastres. It does not seem logical that lands planted with mulberry trees would be turned into olive-groves in a period during which mulberry trees were most appreciated and valued.[105]

This practice of transferring lands owned by emirs into waqf lands falling under the jurisdiction of the monastery anteceded the decline of the mountain *muqāṭaᶜjīs.* We can only venture a guess at the reason for this. Was it due to conflicts related to the Shihāb family, which led to their exile and the sale of a part of their properties? Or were these sales part of the *muqāṭaᶜjīs'* plan to fructify the lands they were entrusted with in order to increase fiscal earnings? Both suppositions seem plausible. The decline of the *muqāṭaᶜjī* class, a common phenomenon in Mount Lebanon during the second half of the nineteenth century, seems to have occurred at the end of the eighteenth century in the Matn for the Abīllamaᶜ who ruled this region. In spite of their title of emir (prince), this family was the first to be affected by the social changes that occurred. Following the battle of ᶜAyn Dārā, in which they distinguished themselves by their bravery fighting for Emir Ḥaydar Shihāb, two *muqāṭaᶜas*, or districts, were entrusted to this family. At the beginning of the nineteenth century these had become nineteen districts. Inheritance divisions over one century reduced the revenues from those districts to insignificant levels. But the moral and political position of this family does not seem to have been seriously affected.[106] It quickly adapted itself to political and administrative duties. Moreover this family, originally belonging to the Druze *muqāṭaᶜjī* class, was one of the first to embrace Christianity.

Under the influence of women, wet-nurses and household maids, the Abillamaᶜ emirs progressively changed their conviction and adopted, at first, the esoteric attitude allowed by the Druze which permitted the hiding of one's true faith. As soon as the Christian demographic evolution was well established in the mountain, the majority of sharecropping tenants working for this family embraced Christianity. Even the Abīllamaᶜ

---

105 Verney and Dambman, 187.

106 Chevallier, "*Société du Mont-Liban*," 147.

emirs got rid of their Druze tax inspectors and agents, who were too bold, unfair and authoritarian. Thus local Christian agents replaced the Mundhir of Brummānā and the Ḥāṭūm of Kfar Silwān.[107] In 1843, Emir Ḥaydar Abīllamaᶜ of the Bikfayyā lineage acted as the governor (*qāʾimaqām*) of Mount Lebanon's northern region, which was ruled by Christians, while Emir Arslan governed the southern region, ruled by the Druze. During the Egyptian occupations, Emir Bashīr Shihāb exiled Emir Ḥaydar, who had also converted to Christianity.[108]

During the emir's absence his family was protected and supported by the superior of Mār Ilyās monastery, the *hygoumené* Makāriyūs, who was of Greek origin. When the Maronite emir came back home, he granted his protection to the superior of the Greek Orthodox monastery.[109]

III. 2.5b: The Buyers

The buyers were monks from Mār Ilyās monastery, whose rank (superior, priest, bishop, deacon, monk) was stated in several title deeds of property transfer. We do not know if the lay individuals who bought lands were *wakīls*, i.e. managers of the monastery charged with making these purchases. The buyers' list shows a wide range of purchasers. The crisis raging throughout the country was not the only influencing factor in the land policy of the monastery.

The two centuries that favoured the growth of waqf property was a period of great difficulty for the Orthodox Church on which the monastery depended. The Orthodox had to face successive conflicts with the Greek Catholic community, Ottoman fiscal exertions, interference from the Greek Hellenistic church of Constantinople, and struggles for influence between Greeks and Russians.

Calm periods are indicated in the deeds by the presence of the same superior for many years. During periods of difficulties the names of many individuals, clergy and lay, are mentioned as intervening in the acquisition of lands. Three important superiors seem to have had a decisive influence in the management of the monastery's land policy. Since we do not know their dates of birth and death, or the dates of their nomination to the monastery, we will indicate beside the name of each one the date of the first and the last purchase they made together with the number of purchased plots.

---

107 al-Dimashqī, 73.

108 al-Mashriq.

109 Rustum, "Kanīsat."

1. al-Khūrī Sufrūniyūs al-Ṣayqalī (1761-1786):
   He was born in Beirut and was charged by the bishop of Beirut and supported by Yūnis Niqūlā al-Jubaylī, notable of the city, with rebuilding the church after the earthquake and with taking in hand the management of the lands after the resolution of the conflict with the Greek Catholics. During his administration, which lasted 25 years, he acquired 47 plots.[110]
2. al-Khūrī Wākīm (1798-1808):
   We know nothing about the ten years of his nomination as superior. He might have bought nine plots, all of them *ṣalīkh* lands.
3. al-Khūrī Makāriyūs (1833-1872):
   He was of Greek origin. His alliance with Emir Ḥaydar Abīllamaᶜ was very beneficial to the prosperity of the monastery. He had an important role in the region's judicial life. He affixed his seal on all agreements and reconciliations that took place in the region.[111] He purchased 15 plots over 39 years.

The responsibility of the monastery's superior was very important at both the spiritual and economic levels. This did not mean that nepotism was a general rule. Sometimes the superior was the nephew of either the patriarch or the bishop on whom the monastery depended. The responsibility of the superior or *hygoumené* remained spiritual as long as the monasteries were dedicated to prayer and kept away from material life. But as soon as these monasteries acquired land properties, things became completely different.

In the case of Mār Ilyās monastery, there seems to have been no land policy during the first period. The 16 plots acquired over 84 years, from 1686 to 1770, were purchased through several persons, twelve of whom were members of the clergy and four secular persons. Among the clergy, the name of monk Sulaymān was mentioned four times. The same name is recorded in the first deed kept in the monastery, which might date from 1596. This priest was once referred to as al-Amyūnī (from the village of Amyūn).

Two other priests were each mentioned twice. Their names were Ḥannā and Neophitos. During the second period, when there was no superior to administer the monastery, these two priests were mentioned as having concluded land purchases. Also there are six deeds in which no name, but only the title of the superior or the monks is mentioned. Whatever may have

---

110 ᶜĪsā Iskandar al-Maᶜlūf, "al-Shaikh Abū ᶜAskaryūnis Niqūlā al-Lubnānī," in *al-Niʾma,* February (1911), 539.

111 Rustum, "Kanīsat," 205-206.

been its cause, the absence of religious authority did not hinder land expansion. Unknown or anonymous superiors and monks signed nine deeds over ten years. A similar period occurred between 1808 and 1833, and during the last period after the death of the *hygoumené*, when five clergymen and three laymen signed the deeds.

A bishop, a priest and three laymen acquired lands for the monastery without being directly involved in its affairs. Did they acquire these plots for their own use and then left them to the monastery after their deaths? The fact that such important acquisitions were made in the absence of an *hygoumené* or without his initiative is proof enough that there must have been a higher authority that, with or without the help of a local authority, effectively controlled the administration of the monastery's affairs. For a very long time this monastery was dependent on the authority of the bishop of Beirut. Indeed, from the end of the nineteenth century, it was placed under the patriarch's authority and was considered as one of his residences.

"Sharecropper house"

III. 2.6: Regions and Boundaries

The region where the monastery was built has changed through the centuries. Since its establishment, it was acknowledged in the property documents and in popular tradition as dependent on the village of Muhaydsah, considered a simple district of Bikfayyā. The colophons of the oldest manuscripts in the monastery mention that it was linked to the Qatiᶜin *muqāṭaᵓah* of the Shūf near Kisrawān.[112] But after the battle of ᶜAyn Dāra, the Abīllamaᶜ were elevated to the rank of emirs and their district extended over the region known today as North Matn[113] in which the monastery is located. Since 1814 this monastery has been known as Mār Ilyās Shwayyah (the small cliff), Shwayyah being a small village located below the monastery. Today the monastery is listed in the land registry of the village of Zighrīn, part of the municipality of the village of Ḍhūr al-Shwayr.

III. 2.6a: Abū Mīzān-Shrīn

The expansion of the monastery's waqfs in different geographical regions evolved chronologically in line with the evolution of its land policy. It seems that the monastery concentrated its efforts until it could constitute an estate specialized in one specific crop. Thus, if we follow the different periods chronologically, we notice the persistence of purchases in some particular regions. The monastery began its acquisitions in the region of Abū Mīzān and continued to purchase land until 1770. Graph 7 shows that the monastery's interest in the region of Abū Mīzān was most apparent during the period when its territorial domain was initially founded. A mulberry plantation, acquired in 1678 for 300 piastres, was the first and principal step in the development of the territory of the monastery of St. Elie. The plots acquired later, even in the second half of the 18th century, seem insignificant by comparison; their value does not exceed 50 piastres each. The graph shows that two plots acquired in 1775 and 1777 were bought very cheaply, their price not exceeding 100 piastres. Part of these stony chalklands, which had been originally sown with wheat, were terraced and converted into mulberry-plantations.

---

112 Mār Elias Manuscript, No. 23.

113 Isṭfān al-Bishᶜalānī, *Tārīkh Bishāᶜlī wa Ṣalīmā* (Beirut: N.p., 1948), 261.

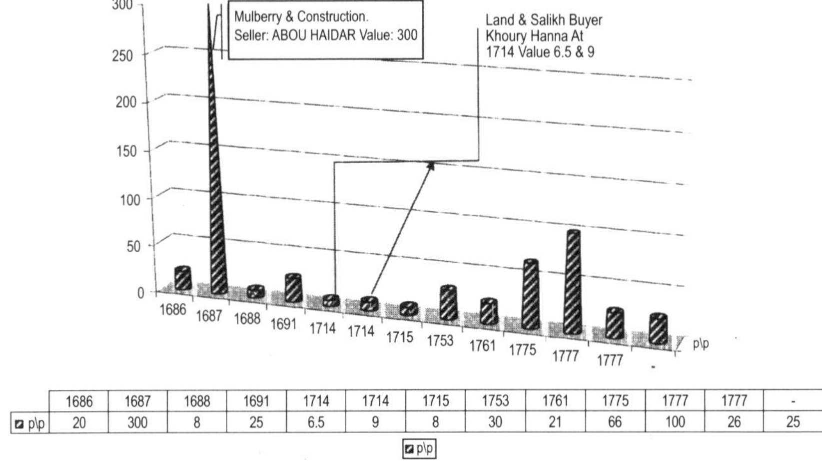

	1686	1687	1688	1691	1714	1714	1715	1753	1761	1775	1777	1777	-
p\p	20	300	8	25	6.5	9	8	30	21	66	100	26	25

Graph 7 - Chronology of Acquisition: Region Abū Mīzān

During the second period, while continuing its purchases in Abū Mīzān, the monastery also acquired lands in the village of Shrīn. From 1779 to 1788, it started purchasing mulberry orchards, almost exclusively in Qinnābah. Then between 1788 and 1810, new acquisitions complemented the properties in the two regions mentioned. These later purchases comprised both *ṣalīkh* lands and mulberry orchards. From 1810, and for the next century, the attention of the monastery moved to regions in its close neighborhood. Here too, we notice a variety to which were added important plots of olive groves and vineyards. In studying the land policy of the monastery with regard to the regions, we notice, with a few exceptions a specialisation at the local level. Thus both places, Shrīn and Abū Mīzān, together with those called Shīr and Qalᶜa, were steep limestone regions mainly dedicated to wheat crops. All the plots purchased in these regions were designated as *ṣalīkh*. Shrīn and Abū Mīzān were "twin villages," a phenomenon, quite frequent in Lebanon and the Mediterranean world, in which the same population and families lived and worked on both sites. According to Fernand Braudel this practice was a form of seasonal migration forced by the requirements of animal breeding.

However, in the deeds there is no mention of breeding, although it was an essential activity in this region; this phenomenon is still deep-rooted in North Lebanon and springs from the need for diversification in a subsistence economy. It is possible that the lands in Abū Mīzān and Shrīn were reorganized and irrigated for the purpose of conversion into mulberry orchards. The valley of Abū Mīzān still has a spring that irrigates gardens and orchards. The sharecroppers' accounts book mentions the presence of 35 sharecroppers in the villages of Shrīn and Abū Mīzān.

The plantations cultivated by these sharecroppers were mulberry orchards. The crop was divided between peasants and monasteries. In this region, 13 plots were acquired in Abū Mīzān, 13 in Shrīn and five in Qal^ca. Each of the 35 sharecroppers had exploitation rights. We may suppose that the refitting affected not only the production but also the constitution of the plots. When the monastery attempted to terminate the sharecroppers' agreements in the region of Abū Mīzān in the 1960s, the peasants entrenched themselves in their houses in the village of Shrīn, where they remain today.

Agriculture was not the only source of revenues. This region also contained an exploited quarry and is crossed by very high and steep cliffs. The word *qal^ca*, designating this area, suggests that its stone quarries were exploited for building houses and terraces. Traditional exploitation was manual and was done in a progressive and slow rhythm.

III. 2.6b: The Qinnābah Region

This region, where the monastery purchased 26 plots, eight of them through Emir Bashīr Abīllama^c, is specialized in the mulberry crop. Thirteen plots were initially purchased and planted with mulberry trees. Other plots purchased in the neighborhood of this village were added to the lot, especially if they had common boundaries with the properties of the monastery in this village. This concerned especially an olive grove and a *ṣalīkh* purchased in Brummānā near Qinnābah in 1782 for 100 piastres, a mulberry grove with olive trees purchased in 1798 for 190 piastres, and two olive groves in Nābāy purchased in 1912 for 1,500 piastres each. Graph 8 shows a typical region specialising in mulberry cultivation. Despite the importance of this crop during this period, the price of plots in this region did not exceed 100 piastres each. The lands of Qinnābah were mostly acquired during the period of expansion. This region, located on the western side of Brummānā village, is sandy and planted mainly with pine trees. The difference in levels is very important. Here too the monastery's acquisitions must have been regrouped and restructured. Ten sharecroppers working for the monastery on waqf lands were mentioned in the accounts books of 1905. Although the number of purchased plots in this region was equal or superior to the number of plots purchased in Abū Mīzān and Shrīn, the type of crops planted here did not require material or human investments for land development.

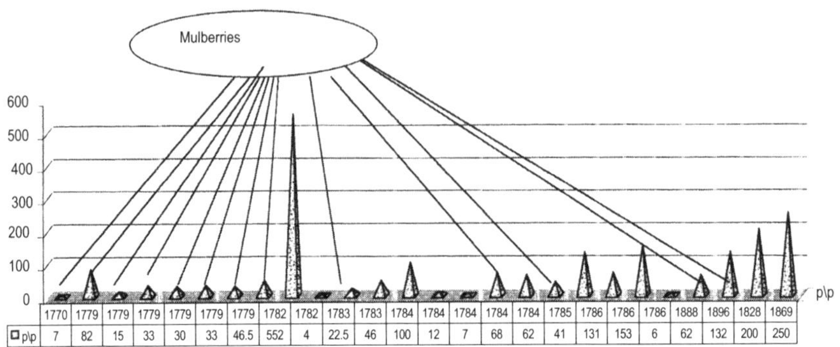

Graph 8 - Chronology of Acquisition: Region Qinnābah

Although the amounts initially dedicated to the acquisition of lands in Qinnābah, exceeded the amounts spent in Abū Mīzān and Shrīn, the revenues from the second estate are three times as great as those of Qinnābah.

III. 2.6c: Mirḥātā and Shwayr, Btighrīn, Muhaydsah

These are the main villages around the monastery. Although it belonged to the village of Muhaydsah, the monastery owned only two plots in it, one of them *ṣalīkh* and the other a vineyard and a mulberry orchard. The monastery owned five plots in Btighrīn, which were purchased towards the end of the nineteenth century at rather high prices – 315, 900, 1,038, 317 and 2,056 piastres for three mulberry orchards, an olive grove and a vineyard respectively. In the village of Shwayr the monastery owned three plots, two *salīkhs*, and a house, but they were not very expensive. The village of Shwayr was very important and densely inhabited; its inhabitants were considered to own the best lands. In Mirḥāta (known today as Ḍhūr al-Shwayr), the monastery had four plots on the sandy lands overlooking the village of Shwayr. These comprised three pine groves and a vineyard. The lands of the villages surrounding the monastery were not purchased for a high price. Their acquisition was made especially during the period of expansion. Graph 9 shows that the lands of these neighbouring districts were not at all specialised: instead, they grew various crops to supply the needs of the local village population.

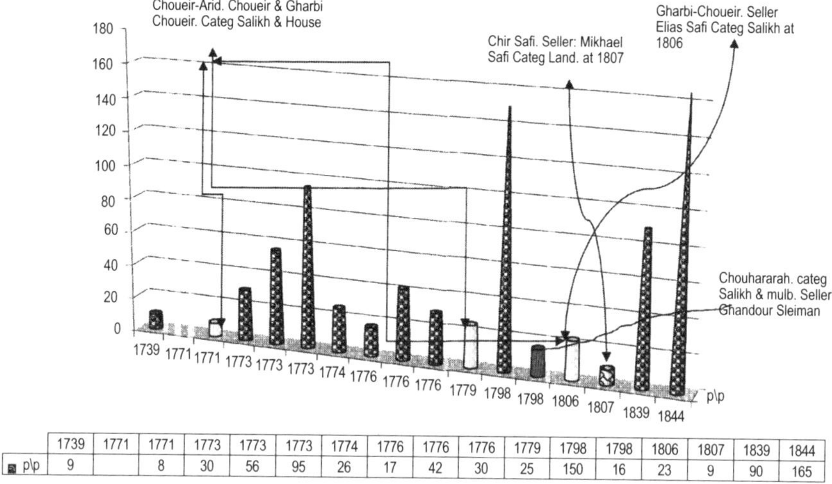

	1739	1771	1771	1773	1773	1773	1774	1776	1776	1776	1779	1798	1798	1806	1807	1839	1844
p\p	9		8	30	56	95	26	17	42	30	25	150	16	23	9	90	165

Graph 9 - Chronology of Acquisition: Shrīn and Shwayyah

III. 2.6d: Lands with no Location Mentioned

There are 14 purchase deeds finalized with the monastery that do not mention the location of the acquired plot.

III. 2.7: Limits and Boundaries

In the old deeds, it was essential to record the limits of the land that was sold, bought, given or exchanged. These limits were to confirm the proof of property and also to help acknowledgment and identification of the concerned land. Boundaries were stated according to the four cardinal points, beginning generally with the south, called *qiblah* (the direction of Mecca). The data used to indicate the limits was various. It was sometimes geographical or material, but often it was merely limited to the name of the neighboring landowner. The limits might be indicated by cliffs, rivers, heaps of stone (*rujmah*), a terrace wall, a tree, a road, a path, a forest, a ditch, or a planted cross. The limits of the landholdings of Mār Ilyās monastery were not mentioned in most of the documents. Of the 112 deeds signed over two centuries, only 35 specified the limits of the purchased plots. Of these 35 deeds, 22 specified the monastery's lands as one or more of the limits. In these cases, it does not appear that the monastery was trying to concentrate or centralise its properties. The trend to centralization was apparent only in the regions of Shrīn-Abū Mīzān and Qalᶜa.

During the two periods 1730-1778 and 1796-1806, all the land limits mentioned are for *ṣalīkh* plots. Price was not taken into consideration for delineation of these limits. Even when the lands were very expensive, it was not mandatory to specify their boundaries. Was it because of the large area of the *ṣalīkh* lands involved that the contractors preferred to state their limits officially? These stony and steep lands were often undistinguishable from one another, and so it may have been necessary to insist on specifying their boundaries. In contrast, shrubbery and especially mulberry groves in terraced areas were limited by walls, bramble hedges, or clumps of reeds, and they surrounded the houses of the peasants cultivating them. Therefore the extent of these Faramān of St. Mary of the Anounciation in al-Daḥdāḥ quarter 1913-1914 properties was commonly recognised and did not always need boundary statements.

In the case of this monastery, there was an insistence on self-sufficiency, which lay behind the scattering of its properties. On the other hand, since its land expansion began late, and since it was surrounded by prosperous and populous villages as Shwayr and Bikfayyā, this monastery had no central domain.

Thus, along with the tendency to self-sufficiency and the scattering of lands, there was also a specialisation of regions in a particular crop. For example, Qinnābah became the main producer of mulberry leaves, Abū Mīzān grew wheat above all (later its salih-lands were terraced and produced vines, olives and mulberries), and the heights of Mirḥāta, Qinnābah and Shwaya were planted with pine-groves.

Although the documents provide no data on the exploitation and management of lands, several travellers' accounts give a negative witness to the state of the monastery's lands at the end of the 19th century, compared with those of the region's Maronite or Greek Catholic monasteries.

The remoteness of the patriarchal authority on which this monastery depended, the indifference of monastic superiors, and the remoteness of waqf lands from the principal domain – all these factors may have hindered the exploitation of the estate. Possibly the neighbouring villages, very flourishing and densely populated, blocked the expansion of the monastery in this region, which besides is mainly sandstone, not ideal for mulberry monoculture. If all this is so, then how can we explain the extent of the purchases made by the monastery's superiors during this period? Perhaps the answer is that this expansion was linked to a fairly precise phenomenon in the modern history of Mount Lebanon and the Ottoman Empire – namely, the rise of waqfs; the Greek Orthodox too joined in this phenomenon, if somewhat tardily. It should not be forgotten that monks departed from this monastery to "restart" the monastery of Dūmā. The territorial growth was not the fruit of the labour of monks alone, but also the fruit of the organised labour of sharecropping peasants. It was also the work of notables, who through their contacts and relations were able to create a centre of production and growth for their community.

This monastery, whose prosperity in the late 18th and early 19th centuries permitted it to act as a bank, nevertheless suffered reverses: the schism of the Greek Catholics in the first half of the 18th century and the Arabisation of the patriarchate at the end of the 19th century. However, it let premises to a Russian school in the 19th century and to a local school in the 20th. Contacts between the two Orthodox churches of Russia and Antioch brought Russian monks to the monastery at the start of the 20th century; their task was to revive the dwindling number of local vocations. Certain innovations, visible on the premises and remembered by the local people, were undertaken by these Russian monks. An irrigation system, a heating system, a new building, new icons and iconostasis – all were completed in the very short time that the monks stayed at St. Ilyās Shwayyah.

Despite the difficulties of exploitation, the lands of this monastery were cultivated by sharecroppers longer than any other; only in the 1960s were the sharecropping contracts wound up. The lands were entrusted to entrepreneurs and converted into stone quarries under new terms of land redevelopment.

This kind of contract is also well known in the archives of Muslim lawcourts relating to waqfs, where it is known as murṣād.

CHAPTER IV

EXPANSION OF URBAN ORTHODOX WAQFS IN BEIRUT DURING THE NINETEENTH CENTURY

The situation of waqfs in Beirut during the nineteenth century was quite different from that in other regions. There is a wide range of issues that can be studied, although archives and documents that are available for this bishopric are more limited than those of other convents or monasteries. There are many aspects that we will examine in this chapter. In Beirut the fundamental problem was how to reconcile and adapt the original Islamic aspect of waqf institutions to urban conditions. In terms of population size, construction activity, artisanal production, and trade, the cities of Sidon and Tripoli were probably more important historically. Yet in the short span of one generation, Beirut surpassed her rivals. The city became the leading port of a new *wilāyah* hearing its name, which encompassed, in addition to the Lebanese coastal regions, the northern half of Palestine, including the ports of Haifa and Acre and a considerable stretch of Syria's coastline and hinterland including the port of Latakia.[1] The position of Beirut as a coastal city and after 1888 as the capital of a new province (*wilāyah*) of the Ottoman Empire, the presence of official public authorities represented by the Sunnī law court, and the political, economic, and social evolution of the city and of the Ottoman Empire generally all bear directly on the development of Orthodox waqf in the city. The nineteenth century witnessed some major changes in the development of the Ottoman Empire and, consequently, in the province of Beirut. We can note those transformations in the economic, social, and cultural developments of this period as well as in the evolution of Beirut Orthodox waqfs. The city grew rapidly at both the geographical and the administrative levels. What was for a long period a little city inside its walls, belonging to the province of Sidon or Damascus, expanded onto new lands and became the capital of several coastal cities and districts of the Eastern Mediterranean seaboard.

---

[1] Marwan Buheiry, *Beirut's Role in the Political Economy of the French Mandate* (Oxford: Center for Lebanese Studies, 1986), 1.

The expansion of the city began with the military campaigns of Ibrāhīm Pāshā in Syria. The intervention of several European powers to check Egyptian expansion in the late 1830's stimulated the economy and attracted an influx of money, goods and consumers. Beirut served as a quarantine station and a military headquarters and garrison during the decade of the Egyptian occupation. Following Ibrāhīm Pāshā's defeat and his return to Egypt in 1841, the city's growing stratum of traders and entrepreneurs took full advantage of events.[2]

Beirut's population grew mainly through the immigration of refugees fleeing the mountains and the interior after 1860.

It was less than 10,000 in 1830, but it had grown to about 50,000 early in the 1860's[3] and reached 100,000 in 1900.

This demographic expansion was contemporary with the general expansion of Beirut's trade. Three factors contributed directly to the revival of the economic situation of the city:

1. The Anglo-Turkish commercial convention (Balta Liman) of 1838 produced favorable effects on exports and imports.
2. The development of steam navigation due to the growth of security on the Syrian coast, so that in 1864, for example, 204 European steamers called into Beirut.
3. A strong impetus to silk production was given by French capital and technology. The first modern machinery for reeling was introduced by a Frenchman in 1836 and the first steam plant by an Englishman in 1848.[4]

A branch of the Ottoman Bank was established in Beirut in the 1850's and the Beirut-Damascus carriageway was constructed by a French company in 1858. It was rapidly followed by a railway line serving the Syrian interior.

With a newly constructed port, an ever expanding market place, and a sophisticated network of economic, cultural and political relations with Europe and America, Beirut became the proud capital of a prospering *wilāyah* which dominated all the eastern coast of the Mediterranean Sea.[5]

In a parallel development, the bishopric left its former seat inside the walls near St. Georges's Cathedral in the ancient *sūqs* and moved in 1890 to the hill of Ashrafiyyah in the suburb of the city.[6] We will

---

2 Ibid., 2.

3 Issawi, "British Trade," 91-101.

4 Ibid., 100.

5 Buheiry, 3.

6 May Davie, *La millat grecque orthodoxe de Beyrouth, 1800-1940* (Ph.D. thesis, Paris IV, Paris 1993), 99.

begin, as a first step, to localize, to define and to evaluate approximately the waqfs of different Orthodox institutions by studying different lists and inventories of lands, houses and shops that were established by the ecclesiastical authority at the end of the nineteenth and the beginning of the twentieth centuries. Then we will study available land deeds to understand the politics of land expansion during this period of revival. Finally, we will study the role of the community in the development and urbanization of the city by creating new streets and *sūqs*, by offering medical assistance, and education through the creation of new schools and hospital, and by helping in social relief and emergency situations. At the personal level, all these changes, in addition to political reforms in the Ottoman Empire, converted Orthodox minorities into Ottoman citizens. Minorities who were *dhimmīs* and were personally taxed by *jizyah* became full citizens and called on to participate in military service. Because of their high degree of economic evolution and social emancipation, the new Orthodox citizens preferred to be exempted from this new obligation by paying a new tax called *badal ᶜaskariyyah*, which could indeed be identified with the ancient *jizyah*.[7] The documents of the waqf of Beirut, which consist essentially of acts of waqf, sale and purchase, or of inventories, have also been studied according to the method of serial history. Like the documents of St. Elie Shwayyah, these acts contain little numerical data. Moreover, since they were drawn up and decreed by the sharīᶜah court of Beirut, their style is very elaborate and the obligatory legal formulas extremely long; this reduces the numerical data to a small fraction of the complete text. Yet here too it has been possible to draw up series of names of sellers, buyers, and donators, and series of places where property was transferred (quarters, streets, places named, etc.), along with dates and time-limits. These series show how waqf expansion strategies changed from one period to another, and how much they determined the development of the city's shape and appearance during a very important era in its history. However, before exploring those different issues it is important to have through inventories of waqf, an overview of the evolution of the city and its impact on our subject.

---

[7] Mitri Jurdāq, *Awdāᶜ al-rūm al-urthūdhuks fī madīnat Bayrūt wa ᶜalā qātuhum bi-l-dawlah al ᶜUthmāniyyah (1876-1906)* (M.A. thesis, Lebanese University, Beirut 1999), 44.

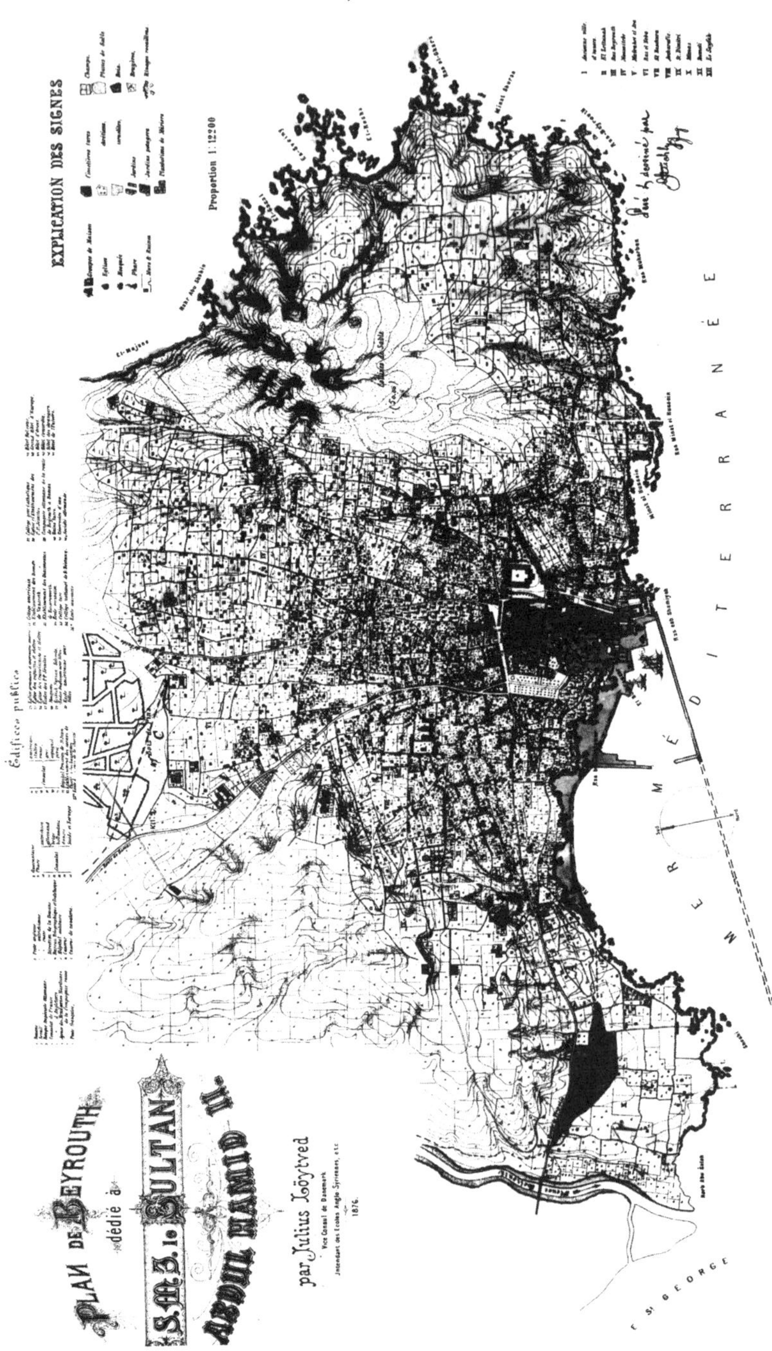

Map 4 - Beirut – 1875

IV. 1: Inventories of Waqf

These inventories seem to have been made at the end of the nineteenth century. At this period different local governors decided to undertake land registration. This was the case especially in the Mutaṣarrifiyyah of Mount Lebanon, where problems of land properties had been the cause of many clashes and social revolts, culminating in religious conflicts in 1841 and 1860. But it is more probable that we can date these inventories to the beginning of the twentieth century, because we have no references to Mount Lebanon waqfs. It is important to point out that the diocese of Beirut and of Mount Lebanon was separated in 1901. Prior to this date, the Greek Orthodox diocese of Beirut included all the monasteries and churches of Mount Lebanon. We have a note addressed to Luṭfallah Ḥabīb by Iskandar Ṭrād asking him to rearrange limits and to specify the area of the waqf of Mār Ilyās Btīnah with the aim of having the title deeds of all lands related to Greek Orthodox waqf. Most of those lands as indicated in the inventory had no titles, which were considered from this period as legal proof of ownership.

This note is dated July, 22nd, 1914, but we can not be sure that the inventories and the note are from the same period. It is likely that inventories preceded this note for at least one or two years.

Those land registrations aim essentially at defining a new sort of private land estate related to individual possession. Until this period the traditional status of land estate was very common. But during the nineteenth century the economic situation and political reforms made those traditional forms of property status obsolete and inadequate to the new situation. By means of land reform, the Ottoman authorities tried to transform *mīrī* land into *mulk* and to lease *mawāt* land to large companies that would fructify them.[8]

Besides the modernization of land status and registration of private property, the statistical information aimed specially at increasing state income through taxes. These statistical lists show the extent to which the ancient norms of land property were inadequate. The lists mark the beginning of the use of acreage. Previously, land was evaluated by quantity of production to fix the taxes that each one had to pay. The use of acreage was not adopted for all lands. It was used only sometimes for rural properties. Lands, plots and constructions inside the city were evaluated by the number of doors they had. The use of those constructions for commercial reasons could explain why real estate was valued in this way. Even here we do not have equal information for all waqfs and plots.

---

8 Padel and Steeg, 31.

These lists give us the survey of eight groups of waqf: Waqf Fuqarāʾ al- Rūm, Waqf Fuqarāʾ St. Georges, Waqf St. Dimitri, Waqf St. Elie, Waqf Zahrat al-Iḥsān, Waqf St. Georges's Hospital, Waqf Ittiḥād al-Birr, and Waqf St. Mary of Dormition.

The largest, richest and oldest are the Waqf Fuqarāʾ (poor) of the Greek Orthodox Community, and the St. Georges's poor waqf with 29 and 27 plots respectively. We notice that all these waqfs are placed under the name of the "community poor" that fall within the concerned parish. The word "poor" precedes every waqf donation, whether it be a church like St. Georges, St. Dimitri, St. Elie, or Our Lady of Dormition; or an institution like St. Georges's Hospital or Zahrat al-Iḥsān School; or a charitable institution. As stipulated by Islamic law, it was a main condition for Christians in constituting waqf endowments to dedicate them to the poor.[9] The concern for the needy and the destitute is stressed even in the naming of the waqfs. The name *fuqarāʾ* (the poor) could be justified by the fact that it was legally accepted by Islamic law as *qurbah*, which means it corresponds to both the Muslim and Christian faiths.[10] These inventories of waqf properties include several types of data:

1. The nature of the property: field, building, house, shop, *khānah, khān* (commercial building), *ḥārah*, etc.
2. Expanse or content: number of floors, rooms, appendages like kitchens or cellars. In the case of agricultural estates the area is sometimes given in *pics* and in the case of shops and commercial exploitation the number of doors is mentioned.
3. Location: in a *sūq*, in a *khān*, etc.
4. Limits: marked either in relation to neighboring owners or to a known building or to a street. Several of these waqf properties are catalogued as being in association with other owners, whether religious institutions (waqf) or Greek Orthodox or Sunnī Muslim individuals.[11]

We shall proceed with a quick description of each inventory before drawing together a synthesis of the whole of the Orthodox waqf in Beirut.

IV. 1.1: St. Georges's Poor Waqf

This is the waqf related to the community's main church, St. Georges's Cathedral. Its chief aim was the maintenance of the cathedral and of the

[9] Zaydan, 486.

[10] Ḥasan al-Zayn, *al-Awḍāʿ al-qānūniyyah li-l-naṣārā wa-l-yahūd fī-l-diyār al-islāmiyyah ḥattā al-fatḥ al-ʿUthmānī* (Beirut: Dār al-Fikr al-Ḥadīth, 1988), 171.

[11] Inventories of Waqf, held in the archives of the Greek Orthodox Bishopric of Beirut under the numbers Bey 1380, Bey 1389, Bey 1417, Bey 1418.

liturgical life that took place in it.[12] It also had to take care of the needy parishioners who resorted to the charity of well-to-do community members.

Its waqfs were distributed as follows:

1. Farming lands considered as profitable since they contained mulberry trees that were essential to the production of silk. There were 190,000 *pics* of mulberry trees in the orchards at Mazraᶜah, and another 2,300 *pics* at Ḥayy al-Ghābah near the hospital. The agricultural lands were managed by sharecropping contracts that we shall examine when we come to discuss waqf exploitation practices.

"St. George Cathedral"

2. Another type of waqf described in these inventories was commercial urban real estate, which was divided into shops and *khānāt* (commercial property usually situated on the upper floors of buildings). Some of these *khānāt* include several rooms, a kitchen or a cellar; here we may presume the existence of a dwelling whose ground floors were entirely converted into commercial property. The *khānah* may vary from two to five rooms, as shown in the inventories. Thus in St. Georges's waqf we have 63 shops and 17 *khānāt*. The two types of commercial

---

[12] May Davie, "Le Couvent St Georges de Beyroûth al Qadîmat," *Chronos*, no. 1 (1998), 7-31.

properties are evaluated in the inventory as 145 doors. This evaluation is probably due to the payment of a fixed land-tax commonly called *wirko*. St. Georges's Poor appears to have been the most important waqf, for it was related to the most ancient church in the city and other churches and institutions were based on it. Two institutions were later built on waqf lands related to St. Georges Cathedral: al-Salām School and St. Georges Hospital. Moreover we know from the waqf documents that Zahrat al-Iḥsān School also benefited from the waqf funds of St. Georges, and that Bishop Ghifrāʾīl Shātīlā transferred to it the new orphanage school for young girls. It was mostly lands and *khānāt* outside the city centre that were handed over to the new institution. In 1898 the Bishop of Beirut gave a plot to the poor of the community.[13]

In fact, the most important plots depending on St. Georges were those located at Birkat al-Muṭrān and adjoining the cathedral. These are two large buildings, bounded by the Catholic and Armenian waqfs, and forming a block completely surrounded by roads. These two buildings, evaluated at 28 and 54 doors, seem to have been very profitable commercial properties whose rents constituted the waqf's main source of income. Like Birkat al Muṭrān, the district of Ṣayfī appears to have been just as important; a number of educational and medical institutions began there before they were transferred to the Ashrafiyyah quarter. These were St. Georges's Hospital, the Three Doctors School, and Zahrat al-Iḥsān School. In the inventory this locality was given the name of "Maḥallat." Previous waqf documents designated it as "Mazraʿah." The same remark can be made about the district of Rmayl, where this waqf owned three important plots. The properties at Rmayl and Ṣayfī were *khānāt*: 24 and 18 doors at Ṣayfī and 10 and 2 doors at Rmayl.

It seems that these *khānāt* differed from the others because this inventory specifies the presence of annexes, rooms, or kitchens, and one of these plots was surrounded by an enclosure wall. This leads us to suppose that these *khānāt* were used more for habitation than for commerce.

The remaining plots belonging to St. Georges's waqf are scattered in various districts of the old town. The *sūqs* that are mentioned included a shop each, except for Sūq al-Quṭun: this waqf owned four shops and twelve *qīrāṭs* of a shop. As for their location, these shops seem to be all in the same block, bounded by the road to the east and by the Ayyās family estates to the west.

The other *sūqs* mentioned in this inventory bear the name of the crafts that were exercised in them. Industry, craft and commerce seemed to be closely linked up to this period. In spite of all that has been said about the ruin of Lebanese and Syrian handicrafts and the annihilation of local pro-

---

13 Kustī, 75, 220; Document: Bey 67.

duction in the country resulting from the expansion of foreign European trade,[14] traditional and local merchandise continued to have their place in the market. It seems that all these plots were well situated, bounded by a street on at least one side. Christian and Muslim families are cited in these limits but here we find a completely confessional distribution: the 29 Muslim family owners are cited in plots inside the old city, whereas the 16 Christian ones are found in quarters immediately outside the old town: Ṣayfī, Rmayl and Ashrafiyyah. The tendency of the waqf to centralise real estate is not very common. It can be seen on twelve of the Greek Orthodox-owned plots, and on seven of those belonging to the other Christian communities – two Catholic and two Armenian waqfs inside the old town boundaries and three Maronite waqfs outside them.

IV. 1.2: The Rūm Poor Waqf

This seems to have been the oldest. It was directly connected to the bishopric, and before the end of the 19th century it was located in the old town next to the cathedral. This waqf contained the buildings in Rmayl's upper district where the new bishopric was established. It also included Our Lady of Annunciation Church in Maḥallat al-Darkah, a church that was later transferred to the Qirāt neighborhood near Ashrafiyyah.

This waqf held 29 plots, all located inside the old town, except for one in Ṣayfī and two in Rmayl. These lots, though numerous and well situated in the commercial area, seem to have been less important and more scattered than those of St. Georges's Poor waqf. The Rūm Poor waqf included approximately 19 shops and 19 *khānāt*. From the description of the number of rooms and outhouses (kitchens and cellars), these *khānāt* seem less important than those of the preceding waqf. They often comprised two rooms with kitchen or three rooms with cellar. This waqf also included a number of lots owned in association with individuals. The *khānāt* are described in quarters, varying between six *qīrāṭs* of an estate (i.e. one-fourth of the whole) and one-and-a-half *qīrāṭs* of a building, or 23 and a half *qīrāṭs* on a *khānah*. The importance of the proportion in the association means that the sale took place in two phases so as to influence the price of the land and to avoid preemption of the sale. This practice aimed to prevent the neighbor of the estate from exercising any right he might have to buy the land.[15] The associates of the Waqf al-Fuqarāʾ al-Rūm in these plots and buildings are various. They are either the Muslim families Ayyās or Beyhum; or the Ṣaydnāyā convent waqf, which owned land in Beirut; or Orthodox families

14 Issawi, "British Trade," 100.

15 Perrier, 70.

such as Ṭrād, Shamlāṭī, Jubaylī, and Karkabī (notably al-Ḥajjah Catherina, founder of al-Ṣaydah monastery).

The plots belonging to this waqf were concentrated in four main regions: Sūq al-Khamāmīr, Ḥayy al-Ghalgūl, Sūq al-Arwām and Maḥallat al-Rmayl (the seven lots in Sūq al-Khamāmīr are very small *khānāt*, buildings, or property shares. These shares are sometimes limited to some *qīrāṭs* or one room and a kitchen located on the upper level. Three of these properties were surrounded by buildings and had no access to the road. The seven- and-a-half *qīrāṭs* held in association with Julia Jubaylī were bounded by a private road. The use of the term *khānah*, the entanglement of shares, and the number of parties involved in such an apparently limited space all tend to indicate that these buildings were devoted almost exclusively to commercial exploitation.

The three Sūq al-Arwām and Bāb Khān al-Arwām plots are likewise parts of a real estate. They included a *khānah*, shops, and a cellar. They had the same particularities as the Sūq al-Khamāmīr plots except that they seemed to be better situated, since streets ran along two sides for each lot.

The three Ḥayy al-Ghalghūl plots constituted an estate of 10 rooms, a ten-room *khānah*, and four rooms plus five *qīrāṭs* held in association with al-Ḥajjah Catherine Karkabī. Located within the convent and the Lazarist Hospital boundaries, these plots seem to have been more concentrated and better situated than the preceding ones.

The plots that seem most widely spread were the two called Maḥallat al-Rmayl. These were established as waqfs by individuals at different dates. The first, the present seat of the bishopric, was given as waqf partly by Ibrāhīm Sursuq and his brothers and partly by the bishop Gerasimos Faraḥ. The waqf deed for this land specifies that it is located in Rmayl outside the city of Beirut and that it contains seven houses with a water well, a kitchen and outhouses, in addition to several trees and plants. The second plot, in the same district of Rmayl but in the lower part, was donated by Ḥannā al-Jammāl. It also seems large, since it contained four properties with a total of 56 rooms and five shops.

The other plots belonging to Fuqarāʾ al-Rūm waqf are scattered inside the old city in the traditional *sūqs* devoted to the trades for smiths and cotton-weavers. In these we find chiefly *ḥārāt* or *khānāt* of only average importance. The other plots consisted of shops distributed in the town's old *khānāt*: three at Janh al-Nawfarah, one at Khān al-Tūtī, one at Khān al-Amīr Manṣūr, and one at Khān al-Ṣāghah. Like the *sūqs*, these *khānāt* were also specialized. They grouped wholesale dealers and small traders.[16]

[16] Abdel Nour, "Introduction," 227.

Concerning the boundaries of these plots belonging to the poor of the Greek Orthodox community, we note that the environment of this waqf was inhabited mainly by Christian families. Yet we can also find many Muslim families living inside the so-called Christian quarter. These were families long installed in the traditional quarters of the city, the old *sūqs* and *khānāt*. The confessional entanglement in business was gradually replaced by an exodus of Christian dwellings towards rural districts that rapidly became urbanized. These came to form city-villages organized around their respective institutions and professionally linked to the city centre.

This movement was first manifested in the migration of the institutions, which could no longer be assimilated in an urban context that had become too restricting. The bishopric first took the initiative of settling outside the walls in Rmayl district. The reason for this move was that the apartments joining St. Georges's Cathedral had become too narrow to shelter the various associations encouraged by Ottoman reforms at the end of the 19th century.

IV. 1.3: St. Dimitri's Poor Waqf

This was composed of six plots. It was the most representative of the new districts located outside the old city. It essentially included the church and the adjoining cemetery and also the rooms turned into servants' dwellings. Beirut's Greek Orthodox cemeteries had been situated near St. Georges's Cathedral, but they had to be moved to make room for St. Elie Greek Catholic Cathedral after the 1725 schism. St. Dimitri's monastery was a promenade site often mentioned by 18th and 19th century travellers.

This waqf includes two lots whose use shows the rural character of this region. Indeed 15,000 *pics* planted with mulberry trees and 7,000 *pics* planted with olive trees must have constituted an interesting source of income for this institution, which was basically linked to the religious life of the city dwellers. The inventory of the waqf also lists plots comprising two buildings, one with three rooms, and the other with only one room. The most important plot containing constructions was that of Ashrafiyyah: four *khānāt* of 13 rooms and their appendages.

The rural plots were surrounded by roads, whereas plots of urban real estate all belonged to Christian owners. Some of these owners are designated as being heirs to this or that member of the Ṭubājī, Bekhᶜāzī or Twaynī families. This reflects two essential realities. Firstly, there was the difficulty of distributing inheritance shares, which caused some lands to be administered in association with these families. Secondly, as rural district were transformed into residential areas, plots tended to be more and more divided.

IV. 1.4: St. Georges's Hospital Poor Waqf

This is divided into five plots, essentially located in Ashrafiyyah and Maḥallat al-Ghābah. This waqf was established from property which belonged to the St. Georges Cathedral waqf. Another plot was part of Ṣaydnāyā Monastery waqf and was exploited by the hospital waqf with the agreement of the Patriarch according to a deed of *ḥikr* (deed of exploitation in urban zones). All these plots were built-up, but they were surrounded by wide estates of 2,500 *pics* and 1,340 *pics*. Here again in the description of the buildings we find mention of the number of doors. It seems that this number corresponded to the number of rooms in every *khānah* and building. In this waqf there were a total of 45 doors.

The hospital buildings were described as being under construction at Maḥallat al-Ghābah on a large plot surrounded by roads on four sides. The construction was legalised by a *faramān* of the Sulṭān that stipulated, in addition to the hospital, the building of an asylum for the old and also a hospital for contagious diseases.

This waqf, established initially on plots belonging to other waqfs, was also surrounded by lands depending on it. It seems to have been the least divided waqf. Because of its vocation, the buildings of this waqf tended to be concentrated in the same area, so that it could better fulfill its mission.

The building of the hospital by the Greek Orthodox community in Beirut was an answer to the needs arising from the new changes occurring in the city. The economic boom led to the influx of the rural population into a town that was not ready to receive it. Hygiene was far from satisfactory, and in the second half of the 19th century several epidemics fell on the city.[17] The experiment of the hospital institution in Beirut must have been successful enough for the Greek Orthodox to consider seriously the establishment of hospitals in their Tripoli and Damascus dioceses.

IV. 1.5: St. Ilyās Btīnah Poor Waqf

This was composed of six plots whose use was entirely rural. These lands were planted with mulberry trees. Orchards, forests and *ṣalīkh* lands planted with cereals were all in the same area and four of them had common borders with the community waqf estate. These agricultural lands covered an area of 19,900 *pics*. Land whose use is not mentioned was designated as *ṣalīkh* and was bounded to the south by the road that divided the Beirut *wilāyah* from the Mount Lebanon *mutaṣarrifiyyah*, to the west by the road that led to Sidon, and to the north and east by several plots. This

---

[17] Marlène Ḥaydar, *Mustashfā al-Qiddīs Jirjis 1877-1934* (D.E.A. thesis, Lebanese University, Beirut, 1992), Monograph, 39.

meant that this planted land was probably not very productive, and rather too spread out. The two other plots were surrounded on all sides by roads. These lands, which had not yet been divided, became the basis for the establishment of several schools, churches and a cemetery. When the income from the city centre plots was devalued, these plots constituted a considerable source of revenue. As for the confessional occupancy of the area, most of the neighboring estate owners were either Greek Orthodox families or Orthodox waqf institutions. One Muslim (al-Bawwāb) and one Druze (al-Zuhayrī) family are mentioned.

The buildings on these lands were few in relation to the areas: three rooms on 9,000 *pics*, two rooms and a kitchen on 17,500 *pics* and twelve rooms in four *khānāt* on 72,500 *pics*. These constructions were simple housings for the sharecroppers living and working on the lands.

IV. 1.6: Zahrat al-Iḥsān School Waqf

This was composed of three lots, mainly occupied by the nuns' convent buildings with a church and four rooms for their habitation. The school was built on land donated by Yūsuf and Emilie Sursuq, the latter being the president of the association that administered and controlled the school. The third plot comprised a three-floor *khānah* containing two shops and a bakery, whose rent income helped to finance the school.

These lands, located in Ashrafiyyah, were surrounded by plots owned by Greek Orthodox families and also encircled on several sides by the road. We also find here a rather compact nucleus that was progressively transformed into an important pedagogical and charitable institution.

IV. 1.7: Sayyidat al-Niyāḥ Waqf in Rās Bayrūt

The inventory here is very succinct. It specifies the presence of the church, to which two rooms for the servants' dwellings and five rooms used as a school were adjoined. In this same plot, it is specified that the cemetery occupies 14,000 *pics*. The church also owns half a shop located in the same quarter.

IV. 1.8: Ittiḥād al-Birr Association Waqf

This charity association owned only two plots situated at Ṣayfī and at Rmayl. Work in pedagogical, social and hospitable fields began with this association. The buildings in these plots were rented and thus constituted an important source of income for charitable work. This was also the beginning of the establishment of waqfs specifically devoted to these associations, which were now usually located in the city's new districts.

These inventories, which were recorded at the beginning of the 20th century, allow us to describe the location of the new waqfs, their expansion and the kind of real property and its value.

IV. 2: Localization of the Waqf and Expansion of the City

In the localization of waqf real estate we can point out three main regions that were situated concentrically around the old town. These areas were unequally inhabited and differently utilised. They corresponded to different stages of urban and economic development. Urban expansion can be perceived differently in those three regions at the levels of both architecture and professional specialization. Beirut waqfs followed the expansion of the city. Initially concentrated in the commercial center, they spread over the ancient community waqf and benefited from the waqfs' income.

IV. 2.1: The City Centre or Old City

Situated inside the walls, it included the most divided plots. The quarters of this downtown were relatively homogeneous and self-sufficient units.[18] Gradually the traditional, old-style buildings were replaced by multi-floored buildings. The *khānāt*, which used to shelter foreign traders and travellers, specialised and became annexes to the *sūqs* in which they were located. Five *khānāt* are mentioned. Khān Janh al-Nawfara, Khān al-Amīr Manṣūr, Khān al-Tūtī, Khān al-Ṣāghā and Khān al-Arwām. These *khānāt* are cited as including shops or shares of shops: eight shops belonging to the waqf are situated there. The oldest existing waqf foundations were established in these *khānāh*.

A greater number of sūqs are mentioned in the inventories. They were merely narrow lanes specialized in a certain type of production or trade. The streets of the *sūqs* were organized by profession and not by religious affiliation. While there was probably some correlation between the two, it was still profession and not religion that determined location.[19] On either sides of these alleys, the small shops were surmounted either by places of work or by living quarters for artisans and traders. Workshops, warehouses, shops and houses succeeded each other, were intercalated or superimposed according to their varying associations. Family alliances, legacies, business and family affairs mingled intimately. It may well be that this type of building went by the name of *khānah*.

These *sūqs* were very often named after the type of activity they sheltered: Sūq al-Ḥaddādīn (smiths), Sūq al-ʿAttārīn (perfumeries), Sūq al-Khayyāṭīn (tailors), Sūq al-Warrāqīn (paper or construction workers). They were also named after the merchandise that could be bought from them: Sūq al-Khamāmīr (*khimār*, plural for veil) or Sūq al-Quṭun (cotton) and Sūq al-

---

18 Leyla Tarazi Fawaz, *Merchants and Migrants in the Nineteenth-Century Beirut* (Cambridge Mass, London: Harvard University Press, 1983), 103.

19 Ibid., 106.

Makhāzin (warehouses). The *sūqs* can also be designated by the name of their tenants or their owners; thus we find Sūq Mār Jirjis, so called for it depended on the Cathedral waqf, and Sūq al-Arwām, because it was held by the Greeks (or Orthodox Greeks). The number of shops in a *sūq* is not relevant to the importance of the waqf; the eight shops in Sūq al-Khamāmīr are less important than the two *ḥārāt* (buildings) in Birkat al-Muṭrān, evaluated at 28 and 54 doors respectively. What gave value to those buildings was that they were surrounded by streets and by waqf real estate, and they were situated near the cathedral. We can infer from these inventories that the shops facing the street and the flats on the upper floor were called *khānāt.*

The *khānah*, whose rooms number from two to eight, was intended either for work or for habitation. The word *khānah* may derive from *khān* – it may mean a little *khān* – and also from *khānah*, designating all the families whose names were under the same mark, number or division in the official registers. The word *khānah* seems to unite two notions, one referring to architecture, and the other to family. Similarly, the word *bayt* later on came to designate both house and family.

The very same problem is found with the word *ḥārah*, which could mean either the quarter as a whole or a building. In the villages, the district where owners of a same family lived was called *ḥārah* and it bore the name of this family. The two *ḥārāt* designated in St. Georges's waqf seem to refer to a quarter, since they were composed of five *khānāt* and 27 shops and three *khānāt* and 15 shops respectively, and they were surrounded by roads or waqfs and constituted a large block in the urban environment. In the Greek Orthodox poor waqf, the word *ḥārah* seems to mean a more modest type of construction: it could be 15 rooms adjoined by two shops in Sūq al-Arwām, five rooms and a kitchen on two floors in Sūq al-Khamāmīr, and ten rooms at Ḥayy al-Ghalghūl. This ambivalence between *ḥārah*-quarter and *ḥārah*-building preceded the advent both in the old city and the new district of a new type of building. This covered an area of 800 to 1000 square metres and was built as one block with carefully worked facades and profuse wrought-iron decorations on windows and balconies.[20]

The renewal of streets and buildings that took in the waqfs at the end of the 19th and the beginning of the 20th centuries did not compensate for the fragmentation of plots and the reduction of shares. In time the process of division reduced waqf income to insignificant proportions, forcing the institutions that needed more space to leave the old city for the new quarters outside the walls.

---

20 Souad Slim, "Khané et Hara dans le patrimoine architectural de la ville de Beyrouth," in *Patrimoine Urbain au Liban*, ed. Michael Davie (Balamand: Alba, 2000), 229.

These quarters offer an example of intercommunal mixing in the centre of the town that was greater than is usually assumed. They formed the heart of the city, where people from all regions would come to transact their business, earn their living, and deal with others. They remain in the forefront of the country's collective memory and pose a difficult challenge in the reconstruction of the city after the end of the civil war.[21]

IV. 2.2: The New Quarters

The new quarters are essentially Ṣayfī, Rmayl, Ashrafiyyah, Mazraᶜah and Ḥayy al-Ghābah.

The transfer of institutions was made gradually towards the nearer quarters – Rmayl and Ṣayfī – before settling down ultimately in the Ḥayy al-Ghābah or Ashrafiyyah localities in the hills overlooking the old city of Beirut.

These new quarters were the residences of a class of merchants that had grown up as a result of the expansion of trade with Europe. In their new Italianate houses in the Rmayl quarter, this new bourgeoisie was living a life similar to that of the cities of Mediterranean Europe.[22]

Apart from the waqfs belonging to St. Dimitri and St. Georges's hospital, waqfs of these new areas were plots depending on the two main waqfs, Fuqarāʾ al-Rūm, and St. Georges's cathedral. These plots were granted by the bishop to the newly formed associations in order to help them start the institutions founded for various purposes. The churches built in these regions – St. Mary of the Dormition in Rās Bayrūt, St. Michael in Mazraᶜah, St. Elie in Muṣaytbah, and Saydah in Ashrafiyyah – thus became the nuclei around which new parishes and institutions were formed. St. Dimitri and the Virgin of the Dormition are typical of the traditional churches around which were grouped a cemetery, presbytery and school. At the end of the 19th century these schools existed at all Orthodox churches in Beirut. The Russian Imperial Association of Palestine undertook the task of establishing a primary school close to each church, in addition to the schools founded by the diocese inside the Beirut city walls – Zahrat al-Iḥsān and the Three Doctors School. These small schools were the rather unassuming basis for the propagation of education among the common classes of the newly arrived inhabitants.[23] After fleeing the massacres in their original

---

21 Aḥmad Baiḍūn, "Bayn arkhabīl al-aḥyāʾ wa-l-majāl al-ᶜumūmī," *al-Marqab*, no. 1 (1997), 179-214.

22 Albert Hourani, *Political Society in Lebanon: A Historical Introduction* (Oxford: Center for Lebanese Studies, 1982), 11.

23 Dāghir.

regions of Damascus, Ḥāṣbayyā, and Rāshayyā, the refugees looked for the benefits of the booming economy in the port and city. They settled in the semi-rural environs of the new capital,[24] the quarters of Rmayl, Ashrafiyyah and Mazraᶜah. Although populated and built up, these areas still included large plots planted with trees. Unlike the commercial and business areas, mulberry and olive orchards were a common sight in the landscape of these suburbs that were rapidly becoming areas of residence and associated activities. Plots of 190,000 *pics* in Mazraᶜah, 7,000 *pics* of olive-trees in Ashrafiyyah, and 15,000 *pics* of mulberry-trees in Maḥallat Nabᶜat al-Muṭrān, for example, were not uncommon. The plantations in use yielded an important income from rent and sharecropping indentures.

In these regions the buildings were distant from each other. *Khānāt*, *ḥārāt* and *dukkāns* (shops) are present, but they are not dense except at Rmayl, where plots depending on Fuqarāʾ al-Rūm held four buildings including 56 rooms and 15 shops. The *khānāt* were smaller in these areas: they averaged three rooms with their annexes, whereas the old city *khānāt* had five to eight rooms. The constructions were sometimes limited to only one, two, or three rooms surrounded by farming land. The large extramural plots owned by the city centre waqf progressively gave way to other institutions whose foundation required more space. The St. Georges's hospital waqf inherited the name of the Cathedral waqf and the greater part of its lands. Likewise, al-Salām School was founded on the lands of this waqf, whereas Zahrat al-Iḥsān School benefited from the lands of Fuqarāʾ al-Rūm waqf. Other plots situated in these regions were also yielded later to the new churches in these quarters and to charitable associations established by these parishes.

IV. 2.3: The Suburbs

These comprised the new quarters of Waṭā al-Mazraᶜah, Ashrafiyyah, and Waṭā al-Tīnah. The waqfs established here, which were attached to St. Elie Bṭīnah and St. Georges, were noted for their large areas. They were essentially wide rural estates whose areas spread beyond the limits of the new quarters.

At Mazraᶜah there were 190,000 *pics*, at Waṭā al-Tīnah 100,000 *dhirāᶜ* (about 70 cm), and at Nabᶜat al-Muṭrān 15,000 *dhirāᶜ*.

The rural districts situated on the sparsely inhabited hills were resorts during the summer months, when the heat and humidity became unbearable in the lower quarters. These extramural estates were appendages to the exiguous city plots. They remained attached to the Beirut Greek Orthodox

---

24 Tarazi Fawaz, 24.

waqf because they were part of the city territory. In 1901, other plots in adjoining areas but outside the administrative limits of Beirut were attached to the newly founded Mount Lebanon waqf. This followed the division of the diocese of Beirut into two sees, one (called the diocese of Jubayl and Batrūn) for Mount Lebanon, whose seat was at Ḥadath, and the other for Beirut. Before 1901, the rural zones adjoining churches and monasteries were attached to the bishopric of Beirut. They annexed to the new Mount Lebanon diocese after the crisis related to bishop Ghifrāʾīl Shātīlā's succession in October 1900.

These rural districts were initially used for quarrying stone for construction and plastering. Ashrafiyyah was called the quarter of Ḥawwārah, and Mazraʿah and Muṣaytbah were called the quarter of al-Dabsh.

These districts received refugees from the mountain and from Damascus after the events of 1840 and 1860. Armenians and Syrians also arrived in the city after the difficult period of 1895. The genocide of the Armenians brought a large refugee community to these suburban districts after 1917. The collapse of the Ottoman Empire was a disaster for the Greek Orthodox inhabitants of eastern Anatolia, Cilicia, and Adana. From 1920 to 1923, many of them came to Ḷebanon, especially to Beirut, settling on most of the hills near the church and cemetery of Mār Mitr and in the still unfinished buildings of Madrasat al-Salām behind the Zahrat al-Iḥsān girls' school.[25]

The rural estates that were established as waqfs over the centuries were an important source of income. Farmlands around the parish churches or around the monasteries (six monasteries were attached to the new diocese of Mount Lebanon) were scattered in the mountains. These waqfs formed solid material elements that facilitated the division of the old diocese and have assisted in the development of the Mount Lebanon bishopric.

IV. 3: Growth and Development of Waqf Landholdings

We do not know the exact date of the foundation of the Greek Orthodox waqf community of Beirut, but we know that it is a long-established community of this city and that the diocese of Beirut was founded in 70 A.D. by Quartus, one of the Seventy Apostles.[26] In spite of the fact that we have seen no documents or archives before the nineteenth century, waqf endowments and religious institutions related to this community did exist

---

[25] Rāʾid Juraydīnī and Dunyā al-Asmar ʿAllām, *Awḍāʿ al-Rūm al-Urthūdhuks al-wāfidīn ilā Bayrūt fī maṭlaʿ al-qarn al-ʿishrīn: dirāsah maydāniyyah fī ʿilm al-ijtimāʿ al-madīnī* (Balamand: University of Balamand, 2000), 38.

[26] Rustum, "Kanīsat," 299.

in a more or less continuous way since the Byzantine period. The proof of their existence need not be a legal written document. It is enough that no one can remember a period when those endowments did not exist as a waqf.[27]

In private archives belonging to the Jubaylī family there are ten deeds of waqf concerning the Greek Orthodox community of Beirut. Specifically, there are seven deeds of acquisition, one deed of exchange and one of loan recovery. In spite of the fact that these deeds are few and perhaps not representative of the foundation and expansion of waqf, they do illustrate the trend of land estate policy with measures that were practiced well into the nineteenth century.

All these deeds are dated in the second half of the eighteenth century 1766-1776 (1171-1179 A.H.). They all involve the *wakīl*-notable of the community, who was charged by the Ottoman governors and emirs of Mount Lebanon with the collection of the municipal taxes and the customs revenues of Beirut harbour. Seven of the deeds were issued by the Islamic court of justice in the city.

The deed for the loan recovery is signed by two emirs of the Shihāb family, Milḥim and Qāsim. It states that two shops shall be the property of Yūnus Niqūlā al-Jubaylī until the money (*darāhim*) is paid. The *darāhim* were owed by the sons of Bū Shadīd Ḥbaysh, part of a Maronite family of *muqāṭaʿjīs* in the region of Kisrawān. This may explain why it was necessary for the emirs to intervene in the recovery of the loan. This document is not dated, but it concerns the same Greek Orthodox notable during a period when Beirut depended on the Shihāb government.

Another interesting deed involves an exchange with the Maronite community. It begins by an act of donation (*wahabnā*) of a cave used as a cemetery to the Greek Orthodox waqf of St. Georges. In a second paragraph the Maronite bishop of Beirut, who signed the documents, writes that the *wakīl* Yūnus Niqūlā gave them the two shops near the door of the Maronite church as an indemnity (*ʿawwaḍa ʿalaynā*). This deed is dated 1756 (1171 A.H.). In theory, exchange is the only legal process that is allowed by *sharīʿah* law for the transfer of waqf endowments.[28]

Two of these documents were made for the acquisition of agricultural lands in the suburbs. One refers to the fourth part of an *ʿawda* plot in the region of al-Ghābah, and the second to three-quarters of a plot in Taḥwīṭat al-Ghadīr. Both of these estates were planted with mulberry-trees; 50 piastres and 300 piastres were paid for the two plots respectively. All the other deeds are concerned with the acquisitions of six shops, two caves, and a

27 Harīz, 26.

28 al-Maqdisī, 282.

group of houses. Most of them are near the church or in a quarter very close to it. In two of these deeds, the church is described as Melkite, which means "royal" or "the community of the roy (king)." We do not know if this adjective referred to the magnificence of the church or to the Greek Orthodox community. The word was later used by the Uniate Greek Catholics to designate their community.

The sum of money dedicated to these acquisitions and mentioned by these deeds is 1,320 Asadī piastres for seven acquisitions completed over a period of ten years. The average price of a plot of land in the city was about 200 piastres, which was regarded as very low. Those 10 years, 1756-66 (1170-1179 A.H.), were very difficult. The account of these years by the historian ʿĪsā al-Maʿlūf is one of many describing the harshness of the period. Following the conflict between the Ottoman Porte and the dissident governor Ḍāhir al-ʿUmar al-Zaydānī, Russian vessels intervene and shelled the city of Beirut in 1770. This period was also difficult for the city because of the internal religious conflict between the two Christian communities, Greek Orthodox and Greek Catholic. The conflict reached its climax in a struggle between the two notables of the city, the Greek Catholic Fāris al-Dahhān and the Greek Orthodox Yūnus al-Jubaylī. There was a bitter competition to control the farming of the city taxes and the customs revenues. The Christian population fled to the mountain and sold their land at half-price.[29] In these deeds, the transfer of property is made in the name of Yūnus al-Jubaylī. A little post scriptum at the end of the document mentions that the shops, houses, or lands have been given to the church of St. Georges or to the Melkite church.

These deeds show the continuous evolution of several aspects of the waqf and land policies from the eighteenth to the nineteenth century:

1. The importance of houses and shops in assuring direct revenues for the waqf.
2. The persistent acquisition of properties in rural areas; in the nineteenth century these would be dedicated to the creation of new institutions.
3. The *wakīl*-notable continued to act as an administrator, with full discretion in all procedures and formalities regarding waqf.
4. The acquisition of parts of land with the intention of acquiring the rest later.

The waqf expansion which took place around the monasteries of Mount Lebanon in the eighteenth and nineteenth centuries was paralleled in Beirut in the second half of the nineteenth century, although under very different conditions. There were again two means of increasing the size of the waqf:

---

[29] al-Maʿlūf, "Zajaliyyāt," Introduction.

the first was by donation, and the second by purchase and sale. The latter depended largely on the private initiative of the bishopric in buying land throughout the city and its suburbs, and in selling unwanted property. We shall separately consider both means before examining the social and urban roles of the waqf.

IV. 3.1: Acts of Donation

The act of waqf or donation is commonly seen as a simple act of piety. Yet, judging by the written text, they appear to have had more to do with family and financial matters. They often raised problems between the family of the donors and church administrators. These acts may be seen as rather unusual forms of social security or pension.

Fifteen acts of donation took place between 1860 and 1910, a high number compared to the 32 purchases made during the same period[30]. These donations were connected to family affairs and followed the traditional custom established in the Ottoman Empire.

Some of these acts gave money in cash. Others, more complicated, donated land. Most of them were made by individuals or families, and stipulated that the donations would become property of the church after the death of the donor.

Some donations were made under special conditions: one donor gave 5,000 piastres to the waqf of the Church of the Annunciation on condition that he would be appointed manager of this waqf during his lifetime. Other donors specified that money should be given after their death to religious and charitable institutions, and the introductions to these wills typically contain many allusions to death, eternal life and judgement. Most of the donations, however, were made by childless people. The income from the donation would go first to themselves, then to their wives, and after the death of their immediate heirs – brothers, sisters and their children – it would revert to the waqf. This was an effective way to provide for their old age and prevent the dissipation of their property by their heirs. Some acts of donation stipulate that income from the property should be administered by the bishopric until the donor's decease.[31]

Sometimes personal conditions were attached to donations, with the aim of attaining a higher social position, for to be director of a waqf was a highly respectable position in nineteenth century society.[32] Other dona-

[30] Archives of the Greek Orthodox Bishopric of Beirut under the numbers: Bey 902, 910, 914, 916, 936, 939, 942, 943, 948, 950, 952, 953, 1127. The two others are recorded in the registers.

[31] Harīz, 22.

[32] Encyclopédie de l'islam, Nov. ed., s.v. "Waqf."

tions were more altruistic; for instance, that of 1,000 French pounds to help poor clergymen and to construct a school. Yet the personal aspect was not completely absent here, for the donor appointed his brother to execute his will after his death. Again, Bishop Ghifrāʾīl Shātīlā donated a large estate, including 19 rooms, in 1893, on condition that the waqf build a school for girls on the land.

Most of these donations were made during the period 1873-1893, a period of religious renewal which led to the organisation of charity associations. The building of schools, hospitals and new churches encouraged people to participate in the revival of the Orthodox community's social and economic life. Ottoman reforms had introduced laymen into the adminstration of church affairs, and thereafter people felt themselves to be more involved in the life of the church and more concerned for its situation and future.[33]

All the donations except one were of land in the new quarters and suburbs. This corresponded to the general movement of waqf property and helped to create new institutions outside the old city.

The donors themselves were of diverse backgrounds. There were two bishops and eight laymen from different families; two women also participated in these donations. Separately, three women and one man donated land jointly inherited from a woman who had owned it in partnership with the waqf.

Land donated in most cases contained buildings, and when waqf was established in the countryside, the acts of donation state exactly how many houses or rooms were included. The kinds of trees were also specified. Donations were not always very substantial. They could be part of a larger estate, such as, for example, one third of a house or seven *qīrāṭs* of a holding inherited by a mother from her deceased son.

Not only was land donated; there were also four deeds mentioning money in cash, to a total of 16,000 piastres and 1,000 French pounds. European money was in circulation in Beirut by the end of the nineteenth century, and several currencies other than the Ottoman piastre were accepted as legal tender at the port.[34]

These acts of waqf donation are sometimes followed by court trials. Records exist of several court cases at the end of the 19th and beginning of the 20th centuries. The trials are brought by the heirs of the donator after the latter's death against the bishop or his representatives, the members of the community council. The demand is for the recuperation by the heirs of the land that has been established in waqf. There are several extant documents,

33 Davie, "Le Couvent St Georges," 7-33.

34 Alphonse Belin, *Essai sur l'histoire économique de la Turquie d'après les écrivains originaux* (Paris: N.p., 1865) 23.

which record judgements pronounced by the Islamic court of Beirut. These judgements are made in favour of the waqf. Waqfs were made for the benefit firstly of the donator, then of his wife, then of his family, then of the poor of his community; if there were no longer any poor in his community, the waqf should benefit the poor in general. These legal and official formulas, cited in the act of donation, suggest that these were in effect *dhurrī* family waqfs. Only after legal process does such a waqf become a *khayrī* waqf, and only then can the bishop exercise his authority over goods dedicated in this way to the poor. According to Islamic *sharīʿah* laws relating to waqf, it was essential from 1739 onwards to register waqfs with the judicial authorities. The waqf only then became properly effective after a legal process termed *al-daʿwāh al-jaʿliyyah*. Therefore these processes were really fictitious. They were merely judicial actions carried out by common agreement between the legal heirs and the *mutawallī*-administrators of the waqf under the aegis of the *muftī* or *qāḍī* of the Muslim court of justice, who applied the rules of Islamic *sharīʿah*. The practice became obsolete and fell into disuse after the adoption of the cadastral register. Henceforth all properties, and the legal formalities pertaining to them, came under the authority of the land register and the relevant authorities who were responsible for duly recording them.[35]

IV. 3.2: Purchases

There survive 32 deeds of purchase, by which the waqf of the community bought land, houses and shops, either in full or in part, through its agents.[36] Many of these deeds involved very small surface areas and extreme fragmentation of ownership. Only half of the deeds concerned an entire property. The rest dealt with very small parts of large properties. It seems that these purchases were intended to liquidate inheritances. The waqf progressively acquired small parts in order to help minor heirs or to gain control of a large property. Nine of these small part-properties belonged to women, who were always represented, either by official agents (*wakīls*) or by their male next-of-kin. In three other deeds, women of the Muslim community were mentioned as sellers of whole properties to the waqf. They were of the Drūbī, Jammāl and Yamūt families, and their properties within the city were adjacent to the properties of the waqf. They were mentioned by name, without any representation by *wakīls*.

35 Harīz, 54-5.

36 Archives of the Greek Orthodox Bishopric of Beirut under the numbers: Bey 901, 903, 905, 911, 912, 920, 922, 923, 935, 940, 941, 947, 953, 955, 956, 958, 959, 1009, 1010, 1011, 1034, 1058, 1059, 1060, 1061, 1062, 1063, 1064, 1067, 1069, 1071, 1072.

These three deeds were drawn up in the same year, 1906, and concerned very important landholdings within the city. Such purchases indicate that the waqf intended to centralise its properties inside the city. Evidence of this also appears in the purchase of a lot in al-Nūrīyah from the Maronite Jabbūr family. This lot was sold in two stages: in 1904 for 80 pounds sterling and in 1906 for 13,052 piastres.

In general, a certain complementarity between donations and purchases may be observed in the growth of the waqf's acquisitions.

Most of the deeds were drawn up and signed by directors or representatives of each waqf, and the purchases were made in their names. The waqf of the Orthodox Poor seems to have played the most active role. But other waqfs outside the city walls also made their own, more limited, purchases. The waqf of St. Dimitri in Ashrafiyyah and St. Michael in Mazraʿah each bought agricultural land in its own area. However, the policy of land purchase was generally supervised by the directors of the waqf of the Orthodox Poor and, to a lesser extent, by the directors of the waqf of St. Georges Cathedral. Bishop Masārrah directly managed the purchases made at Nūrīyah and Birkat al-Muṭrān; his name is mentioned six times in connection with property purchases in the first decade of the twentieth century.

The property acquired, in part or in whole, included houses, shops, gardens, and orchards. Many people of all classes continued to occupy these properties; gardens, yards, cellars, shops, houses and *khānat* were all exploited by families living and working in the same place. Traditional placenames, such as *khān*, *khānat*, *maḥallah*, *zuqāq*, *bāb* and *sūq*, remained unchanged, as did the buildings for the most part, although some were demolished to make way for new construction. For example, we know that the house at Maḥallat al-Darkah, bought in 1897, was in ruins; the shop and *khān* of the lot bought in 1901 were replaced by a narrow road; and the *khānat* bought in 1906 were demolished. The decline of traditional building and the rise of new architecture and urban planning accompanied the city's entry into the international market. New imported goods required new buildings for storage and trade. Old working and residential quarters became dwarfed as the city expanded, and were unable to absorb the surplus of immigrants; these settled in outlying areas that had once been reserved entirely for farming and vacationing.

But these developments in the city's expansion were not paralleled by the Greek Orthodox waqf's policy of land acquisition. Unlike the donations to waqfs, most of which were located in the suburbs, purchases were, for over 60 years, concentrated in the old city. Of 32 acquisitions, only six were made in the new quarters. The waqf's expansion was mostly limited to the labyrinthine confines of the old city. Most of the research made on late 19th century Islamic waqf emphasises the decay of traditional waqf buildings. Such research concludes that the Ottoman reform policy of entrusting waqf administration to laymen was responsible for the ruin of the waqf institution.[37] What was a positive measure for Christian communities appears to have been a disaster for Islamic waqf endowments.

Was this choice prompted simply by factors of supply and demand? Did the old city contain much ruined and abandoned property that could be cheaply and easily acquired? Was there a move to liquidate fragmented and uneconomical properties? Or was it the need to increase the value of property held by the community that prompted the *wakīls* to consolidate and renovate the traditional urban waqf?

These questions can be answered by examining the change in the amount of capital allocated to land purchase over a period of decades. Though the documents are incomplete and cannot give us a perfectly clear idea of the waqf's land purchase policy, we can nevertheless observe trends which are related to the general political and economic situation. In addition, internal factors, particularly the disorder within the Greek Orthodox community, also influenced the waqf's policy of land purchase within the city of Beirut.

Looking at the distribution of purchases over time, it can be seen that most of the highest value purchases were made between 1860 and 1870: ten lots were bought for 187,750 piastres. Was this a result of the religious conflict of 1860, or of the economic crisis that followed it? We cannot say anything except that the deeds allude to possible reasons for the purchases: first, the social position of an orphan at that time, and secondly, traditional patterns of landholdings in a country subject to the laws of Islamic waqf.

Later decades, by contrast, seem to have been of little importance in terms of funds allocated to land purchase: 1870-1880, 13,800 piastres for five lots; 1880-1890, 1,759 piastres for two lots; and 1890-1900, 5,777 piastres for three lots. During this last period there was an improvement in the price of land, which could be due to the increased security of private property. Certainly during this period the new Ottoman land code brought a greater stability to landed property. In Beirut many buildings were constructed to connect the new harbour with the city. These new urban developments yielded an average profit of 6% per annum.[38]

These decades saw no decline in either the city or the Orthodox community. On the contrary, they saw the development of lay associations that founded educational and health institutions. For 30 years, the policy of land expansion was virtually halted, in order to concentrate on assisting the

---

[37] Barnes, 118.

[38] Verney and Dambman, 192.

growing population. In particular, charity associations were established to meet the needs of a rapidly changing society.

This period of suspension did not last. In the first decade of the 20th century, 11 lots were acquired for 112,512 piastres. Two developments seem to have been at work here. First, there was the division in 1901 of Beirut and Mount Lebanon into two separate dioceses, and the subsequent division of waqfs, for the most part in favour of the new bishopric of Mount Lebanon. The waqf of Beirut felt itself obliged, it would seem, to recover its loss by a large-scale effort to improve, build and expand its remaining waqf properties. And secondly, there was the policy undertaken by the Christian bourgeoisie to improve the city by laying new roads and building shops and new commercial areas. This encouraged the director of the waqf and the bishop to concentrate the community's properties around the central location of St. Georges's Cathedral, in areas such as Birkat al-Muṭrān, Ḥayy al Nūrīyah, Sūq Mār Jirjis, Maḥallat Kanīsat al-Rūm, Maḥallat Rijāl al-Arbaʿīn (Forty Martyrs).

IV. 3.3: Deeds of Sale

A number of important deeds of sale have been found in the land registers.[39] The waqf rarely sold land, and indeed the very word "waqf" suggests that sales were in theory forbidden. These deeds of sale contained saving clauses which emphasised that the sales had been made in the waqf's interest, for the lands disposed of had yielded a meagre income, insufficient to cover maintenance costs. Even now the sale of waqf remains a very delicate and complex matter. Christian and Islamic laws require many conditions to be met before the sale of waqf can be regarded as legal.

The deeds also state that the proceeds of sale should go towards improvement of waqf lands. Of the 18 deeds of sale in question, 17 were made in the first decade of the twentieth century. Twelve lots are mentioned, with a total surface area of 10,696 square *pics*, which were sold in stages. The proceeds of these sales during the decade 1901-1910 amounted to 173,462 piastres and 770 French pounds (equal to 97,790 piastres), more than twice the amount paid for land purchases during the same period. In some cases, the deeds mentioned differing prices per square *pic* for land located in the same areas and sold during the same year. In 1906, for instance, four lots in Maḥallat al-Ḥusayniyyah were sold for four, six, seven and ten piastres per square *pic* respectively.

From the deeds, it seems that the waqfs selling land were more varied than those buying.

---

39 Archives of the Greek Orthodox Bishopric of Beirut under the numbers: Bey 913, 915, 919, 938, 949, 968, 970.

The purpose of the sales seems to have been, not to enable the purchase of new land, but rather to raise needed funds for the construction and improvement of large institutions. For example, St. Georges's Hospital was moved to Ḥayy al-Ghābah and the new premises were built between 1903 and 1905.[40] Similarly, seven shops were built in Sūq St. Georges Alley in 1911 and then rented for the waqf's benefit. The same went for the enlargement of Zahrat al-Iḥsān School and the construction of al-Salām School. Probably the bishop's immediate influence facilitated the use of sales income for projects that the small waqfs were unable to finance.

Throughout the period 1860-1910, it seems that, in spite of the bishopric's decision to establish itself outside the old city, much was done to improve the city centre waqf, in order to turn it into a profitable commercial zone. Donations and sales were made in the gardens and orchards around the city, while purchases were concentrated in the area of the old walled city.

IV. 4: The Role of the Waqf in the Life of the City

The waqf's role was manifold. The religious function of the church was supported by the establishment of many lay associations whose main purpose was charity and urgent assistance to the poor. But during the later nineteenth century, certain factors came to alter the behaviour of these associations. First, there was the Ottoman decision to introduce laymen into the direction of church affairs and to create community confessional boards in order to ensure popular representation. Then came the nomination of Midḥat Pasha as governor of Syria, following his failure as prime minister to establish a new reformed constitution for the Ottoman Empire and his dismissal by Sulṭān Abdul Ḥamid. This enlightened minister did his best to lay the foundations of a civil society. Newspapers, schools and cultural activities were then introducing a new way of life to all Ottoman cities. Freemasonry was already well established in the Middle East, and many if not most upper-middle class men were connected with Masonic orders. Midḥat Pasha encouraged local notables and members of the cultural elite to found non-political associations of all kinds – scientific, literary, religious, medical and charitable – in order to encourage civic life.[41]

Beirut, previously attached to the province of Damascus, became the capital of a separate province in 1888. The city was already modernising: European religious missions had established many schools for boys and girls, so helping to adapt tradition to the new age.

---

[40] Marlène Ḥaydar, 55.

[41] Nagib Saliba, "The Achievement of Midhat Basha as Governor of the Province of Syria 1878-1889," *International Journal of Middle Eastern Studies* 9 (1978).

Economically, the city's rise to become one of the main centres for trade between Europe and the Ottoman Empire promoted the rise of a class of Levantine merchants familiar with European ways of life. This commercial elite was drawn largely from the Orthodox community, long settled in the city and well-known for its business activity.

IV. 4.1: The Associations

Many associations were founded among the Greek Orthodox community of Beirut under the auspices of the bishop and the community council. Members of this council were themselves often founders of such associations, each of which owned and ran its own institutions. In his book on Lebanese historiography, Ahmad Beydoun says that "the Lebanese state was founded in a moment of 'community reticence'." For a while, that is, the communities made a tactical retreat, in order to allow for the establishment of the state.[42] But in the last quarter of the nineteenth century, the Lebanese state did not exist, whereas community influence was at its height. The needs of the community were as far as possible met by active members of the church. The principal aim of the associations they founded was to found and maintain specialised institutions for education, medical care and charity, and to replace the church in providing emergency help to the poor, as was required in many a difficult circumstance. Church revenue was modest, and the parish priest could usually do little more than distribute alms.

These institutions were established to facilitate social services. Community solidarity played a key role in renewing the life of the church in modern times.

The oldest association was *The Greek Orthodox Charity Association*, the first to work in the field of education. Its main aim was to administer the oldest school in Beirut, the School of the Three Doctors. The association undertook many works of charity, such as the distribution of food and clothes on various occasions. The school was used as a shelter for the refugees who escaped from Damascus after confessional conflicts.[43] Another charity association in Beirut was *The Association for Piety and Charity*.

Other associations were established in Beirut for the development of Mount Lebanon. *The Association of St. Paul the Apostle* was one example. Its work was directed mainly towards church restoration and renovation of liturgical books and sacramental vestments and vessels. It also paid salaries to priests and teachers in some poor villages where schools were attached to the local parish church. The activities of this association ceased in 1901

---

42 Beydoun, "L'identité confessionnelle," 334.

43 Dimitri Debbas, unpublished manuscript kept by his family.

when Beirut and Mount Lebanon were separated into two dioceses; more will be said of this later, as part of a discussion on the relations between city and countryside.[44]

A special association was also instituted for Christian education. Its activities give us a good impression of the cultural atmosphere of the period. It published a weekly magazine, al-Maḥabbah (1899-1907), containing stories with a religious and ethical message, articles on religious doctrine and church history, biographies of patriarchs and bishops, and reports on Orthodox communities worldwide.

The main aim of this publication was to promote solidarity among Orthodox believers and to act as the community's spokesman in its religious polemic with Catholic missions. It also aimed to provide news about Antiochian Greek Orthodox diocesan activities such as associations, schools, institutions, celebrations and journeys.

Other achievements of this association were the establishment of night schools and libraries for students to read literature, theology and cultural topics, and Sunday schools in each parish in order to teach children the catechism, the gospels and hymns from the Orthodox liturgy.[45]

No less important was the *Greek Orthodox Association to Bury the Dead and Repatriate Needy Travellers*. The existence of such an organisation was a clear indication of the poverty and misery that accompanied the city's social and economic progress like the other side of the coin. The rapid integration of Beirut into the international market, so profitable to the class of merchants and local notables, marginalised a large number of craftsmen and workers. Moreover, ethnic and confessional conflicts in the Ottoman Empire brought to Beirut refugees from many different regions. Armenians, Syrian Orthodox, Damascenes and Anatolian Greeks, facing difficulties in their own regions, were attracted by the city's promise of prosperity.

At the same time there began the emigration of Syrians and Lebanese to the New World, and Beirut, the chief port of the Levant, was the main point of departure. Pauperisation of some of these emigrants might lead to their death or an uncertain future at best. Some returned home, while others died far away, their hopes and dreams unrealised. Both categories were the responsibility of the association. After functioning for a period as an emergency centre, it managed to found a house for abandoned destitutes.

Each association was responsible for an institution. Two of these, Zahrat al-Iḥsān (the Flower of Charity) School and St. Georges Hospital continue their mission to this day.

---

44 Birbarī, 23.

45 *al-Maḥabba*, no.1 (1899), introduction.

"Zahrat al-Iḥsān School"

The school was founded in 1881 by the association of the same name, in order to teach girls, especially of the poorer classes. It was first located in a small house in Jummayzah, donated by a woman named Susan, the widow of Ḥannā ʿArab. Its aim at first was to educate girls in order to help them found good families and teach their own children; later a more ambitious aim was proclaimed – to give women more autonomy by providing them with the means to work and to feed themselves and their aged parents. The institution began as an orphanage for girls; later it admitted paying students and moved to larger premises in Ashrafiyyah, built and donated by the bishop, Ghifrāʾīl Shātīlā.

It is worth mentioning that the school's founder, Labībah Jahshān, decided seventeen years later to take vows and to establish a female religious order which would be responsible for all internal aspects of the school's running, including teaching, manual work and many other activites without remuneration. This was the only order in the Orthodox community that combined the religious life with social work. In this respect, the success of Catholic missions and schools set an example for the Orthodox which was recognised, if somewhat grudgingly, and followed. This may well be the reason for the school's continued thriving until now. Both the school and the order were linked to the bishopric in all matters concerning religion. For waqf formalities and fund raising, the school depended on the Orthodox community committee, whose members had family ties with the female members of the school association. The success of the Flower of Charity School was evidenced by the increasing number of pupils and orphans registered.[46]

"St. Geeorges Hospital"

St. Georges's Hospital began its activity in 1877 under the supervision of the Association to Help the Needy Sick. It began by helping patients at home, offering first aid to the poor and taking care of their families by giving food and clothing when necessary. The period before and after the hospital's institution had seen many epidemics – malaria in 1861, cholera in 1865, 1883 and 1897, influenza in 1874, Small Rose in 1896, plague in 1900 and typhoid fever in 1894 and 1914. The city could not cope with poor hygiene and overcrowding resulting from the stream of migrants.

In 1879, members of the association found a sick person in the street; he was a stranger with no home. They brought him to their meeting place in the quarter of Ṣayfī, where the association's cashier offered him two rooms in his home.

In 1881, St. Georges's Hospital began work, intending to provide free medical care. The association took care of 2,000 people at home during its first five years (1877-1882). In 1883, the hospital moved into a building

---

46 Kustī, 122.

of six rooms, four for medical care, one for examination and one for pharmacy. The new hospital, located in ʿAkkawī, was inaugurated in March 1884. It was the only national hospital to receive patients from the city's municipality.

In 1913, the hospital moved again, to the quieter area of al-Ghābah, near Ashrafiyyah. The new, large and handsome building was financed by the waqf of St. Georges. The hospital was taken over by the Ottoman authorities in the latter part of the First World War, and subsequently by the High Commissioner of the French Mandate from 1919 to 1923.

The hospital was called "national" to emphasise the fact that it was open to all, regardless of religious affiliation. The annual report published by the association shows the number of patients, classified by community and also as in-patients and out-patients.[47]

IV. 4.2: Urbanisation

The role of the waqf in the life of the city was not limited to creating associations and institutions whose impact was essential to the formation of a more modern mentality. The waqf also took some important direct initiatives concerning the urban plan of the city. These initiatives included the creation of a new street-plan, which aimed at improving the value of urban real estate, much of which was waqf owned by the different Christian communities. Secondly the waqf undertook to build seven shops in St. Georges Alley. There were several parties to this contract: the waqfs of the Greek Orthodox, the Greek Catholic, the Maronite, and the Armenian Catholic communities, and the Sursuq family, represented by two of its members. The main documents consist of separate agreements between the Greek Orthodox waqf and representatives of each of the other contracting parties.

The first agreement was dated 12 July, 1891. It was made with the sons of the late Mūsā Sursuq. This agreement specified the area and measurements of the land that was to be converted into a street. The land is described as extending from the orange tree to the door of the building, and covers two separate plots of 88 and 20 square *pics* respectively.

The second agreement was dated 29 April 1903 and was made between the Greek Orthodox bishop and the Armenian Catholic bishop, Bāsīl Kalyounjian. A plot belonging to the Greek Orthodox waqf was to be completely converted into a street between the Armenian *sūq* and the *sūq* of St. Georges. In compensation the Armenian Catholic waqf would give the Greek Orthodox waqf a triangular-shaped plot measuring approximately six metres by eleven metres. The Greek Orthodox have no right to contest

---

47 Marlène Ḥaydar, 73.

the width of the street belonging to the Armenians, set at five *pics*. For their part, immediately after signature of the agreement, the Armenians would begin enlarging the new street on Greek Orthodox land, as prescribed by the map drawn up at the law-court. This new street would be lengthened from the house of the porter as far as the door of the old Maronite church. The width of the new street would be ten *pics*.

"sūq St. Georges"

The third agreement, between the Greek Orthodox bishop and the Maronite bishop, consisted of three separate documents, signed on 6 March 1905, 21 January 1907, and 23 December 1909. The agreement with the Maronites aimed at opening a junction between Sūq al-Najjārīn and the new Maronite *sūq*. To do this, the Greek Orthodox waqf had to demolish a house it owned in the area. The agreement also affected a large plot of land measuring 200 metres by four *pics*. This was probably intended to be the new street. The price of this land, 34,000 piastres, would be paid by the Greek Orthodox. The document of 1907 dealt with the sale by the Maronites of two shops for 30,000 piastres, payable by the Greek Orthodox bishop, Jarāsimūs Masarrā. Both these documents were so complex that they had still not been acted upon in 1909. Consequently, the last document signed by Bishop Masarrā and the Maronite bishop, Buṭrus Shiblī, specified that any further delay in the demolition of the shop that blocked the junction between the two *sūqs* would lead to a fine of 200 French pounds per month, payable to the Maronite confessional council. This last document reveals that construction of the new Maronite sūq was approaching completion. Clauses in this document specified finishing work such as reinforcing the ceilings with iron beams, paving the street, fitting doors in party walls, plastering walls and ceilings, and reconstructing the dividing wall between the two waqfs.

The agreement made with the Maronites also mentions a shop whose ceiling seems to have been converted into a part of the stairs leading up to the door of the Greek Orthodox church.

The aim of this agreement, as specified in each document, is to improve the situation and increase the value of real estate belonging to the waqfs of the two communities.

The fourth agreement is dated 26 January 1907. It was made between the Greek Orthodox bishop of Beirut, Jarāsimūs Masarrā, and his Greek Catholic counterpart, Athanāsiyūs Ṣawāyā. This agreement does not deal with streets and town-planning, but is concerned with increasing the value of waqf real estate and partitioning properties held in common. The chief aim of the agreement with the Greek Catholics was to terminate their association with the Greek Orthodox community in the church of Nūrīyah. In exchange the Greek Catholic community would receive 25,000 Ottoman piastres and a plot of land that would allow them to restore the entrances of their principal church. The restoration of the first entrance had to take into account a plan to straighten the street beside the wall of the Greek Catholic church.

Taken together, these four agreements demonstrate a real town-planning policy that consisted of the following measures: creating new streets and lanes in the old market; enlarging existing lanes in the same area; clearing space around churches; and creating new passages of entry into the churches.

This new policy of improving urban infrastructure and increasing the value of the Church's real estate was made possible by Ottoman reforms that gave more freedom to Christian minorities within the empire. Churches and chapels had previously been hidden away behind buildings, *khānāt*, and shops. However, the Ottoman Khaṭṭ-i-Humayun reforms of 1856 proclaimed civil equality between Muslims and Christians, recognising the Christians as Ottoman citizens and no longer as protected *dhimmīs*. Christian architectural monuments could therefore now be openly displayed. Separately, the movement of residences and institutions outside the old city led to the clearance of some space, which could be used for laying out new streets and new entrances into churches and chapels.

In conclusion, the Greek Orthodox waqf of Beirut played a crucial role in the urban development of the city. The new reforms introduced by the Ottomans reveal some essential changes in both the waqf and the city.

First, the city of Beirut at this time offered an exemplary model of the administration of waqfs by laymen. Here a particular social category, the big business and financial bourgeoisie, which was closely linked to the newly created community council, came to administer both the city and the community waqf. These bourgeois notables were prominent in the chief businesses and markets of the city, the municipal council and the wilaya council. The role played by such laymen in the administration of church property was of course similar in all city diocesan centres (metropoles) in the Ottoman Empire generally (Istanbul, Alexandria, Izmir etc.) and in the patriarchate of Antioch in particular (Damascus, Tripoli, Aleppo, Hims). But this reform was most successful at Beirut. The role of the community council (*majlis al-millāt*) may better be studied in the chapter on waqf administration; it suffices to say that in the founding and running of associations, the expansion of waqfs and the influence of waqfs in urbanisation, lay notables were the decisive factor.

The waqf of Beirut had long been limited to the area around the church of St. Georges in the centre of the old town; however, under the weight of demographic growth and the impact of the city's economic prosperity, it began to spread outwards. Recently-founded institutions – hospitals, schools, and charities – began to move their premises into the new quarters and suburbs where more space was available for their establishment and development. Thus, in order to expand and to have a wider area of activity, the St. Georges Hospital, the Three Doctors School, and the Zahrat al-Iḥsān School all moved premises at least three times in less than 30 years

This expansion took place at the expense of the gardens, orchards and quarries on the hills around the city. These rural village areas were transformed into suburbs, fashionable or working-class, while professional activity was still concentrated in the city centre. This urban expansion was accompanied by a functional specialisation between residential and business quarters.

The growth of the city was matched by the decentralisation of waqfs. Previously limited to two main waqfs (St. Georges's and the Rūm Poor), the waqf property of the Greek Orthodox community disintegrated into a multitude of little waqfs intended to finance the newly founded associations and institutions. Farmlands whose revenues had been remitted to the central waqf to which they belonged now underwent development and construction; they became the seats of flourishing institutions, henceforth independent.

لائحة

اوقات الامتحانات والاحتفالات السنوية لمدارس الجمعية الخيرية الارثوذكسية في بيروت

وهي السنة الرابعة والاربعون لتأسيسها

مدرسة مار الياس – المصيطبة

الاربعاء في ١٢ حزيران فحص صفوفها عموماً

الاحد في ١٦ منه الساعة ١٠ (قبل الظهر) احتفالها فتمثيل رواية يوسف الصديق وتلقى خطب ادبية واناشيد ثم توزع الجوائز على مستحقيها

مدرسة مار ميخائيل – الزرعة

الجمعة في ١٤ حزيران فحص صفوفها عموماً

الاحد في ١٦ منه الساعة ٣ (بعد الظهر) احتفالها فتمثيل رواية جنفياف وتلقى خطب ادبية واناشيد ثم توزع الجوائز على مستحقيها

مدرسة السيدة – راس بيروت

الخميس في ٢٠ حزيران فحص صفوفها عموماً

الاحد في ٢٣ منه الساعة ١٠ (قبل الظهر) احتفالها فتمثيل رواية في سبيل الشهامة وتلقى خطب ادبية واناشيد ثم توزع الجوائز على مستحقيها

مدرسة مار نيقولا

الجمعة في ٢١ حزيران فحص صفوفها عموماً

الاحد في ٢٣ منه الساعة ٣ بعد الظهر) احتفالها فتجري محاورات وخطب ادبية وتلقى اناشيد ثم توزع الجوائز على مستحقيها

مدرسة البنات – الحي الصيفي

الخميس في ٢٧ حزيران فحص صفوفها عموماً

السبت في ٢٩ حزيران عيد الرسل احتفالها في منتدى المدرسة الكبرى الساعة ٣ (بعد الظهر) حيث تجري محاورات ادبية وتلقى خطب واناشيد ثم توزع الجوائز على مستحقاتها

المدرسة الكبرى – تلة الخياط

الاثنين في ٢٤ حزيران (قبل الظهر فحص التعليم المسيحي مع عموم التعاليم الدينية والموسيقى الكنسية مع اللغة الانكليزية لعموم الصفوف · وبعد الظهر فحص الدائرة الاستعدادية بكامل دروسها

الاربعاء في ٢٦ منه الرياضيات لعموم الصفوف والطبيعيات والجغرافيا باللغة الفرنساوية للصفوف الأُول

الخميس في ٢٧ منه العروض والمعاني والبيان والبديع للصفوف الأُول العربية مع تتمة الصفوف الثنوية الفرنساوية

الجمعة في ٢٨ منه فحص اللغة التركية · والموسيقى الآلية · وتتمة الصفوف العربية الثنوية

الاحد في ٣٠ حزيران الساعة الثالثة بعد الظهر تحتفل احتفالها في باحة منتداها الخلا لي. بآيات الشكر لباري العباد · والازدان بالاعلام العثمانية بسرور الدعاء لمليكنا الرشاد · الترنم باناشيد الترحاب بآل الاريحية من سراة القوم وادبائه · وعيونه ونبلائه · فيمثل فريق من نجبائها المعروفين بحسنات السيدة وثلاثة الاقمار وغرة الآداب المنشآت في المدرسة عام ١٩٠٠

رواية المروءة والوفاء

ويتخلل هذه الرواية ترنيم جوق المنشدين وعزف الموسيقى ويلي بكل فترة خطاب بإحدى لغات المدرسة الاربع · ومحاورة فرنساوية ادبية هزلية صغيرة ثم تختم الحفلة بمنح الأكاليل الفخرية وجوائز الشرف واخصها الساعات الذهبية والفضية وبعض آلات موسيقية وما شاكلها من التحف للتلامذة المنتهين الذين امتازوا بحسن السلوك والاجتهاد وفازوا بقصب السبق في حلبة ميدان العلوم والمعارف

تنبيه يبتدئ الفحص في الايام المعينة الساعة ٨ – ١٢ (قبل الظهر) ومن ٢ – ٥ ½ بعد الظهر)

رجاء لما كان اقدس فرض على الانسان نحو الله تعالى والقريب انما هو العمل والتعليم عملاً بآية الانجيل الشريف القائل طوبى لمن يعمل ويعلم · اصبح تهذيب الشبيبة وهدايتها الى الصراط المستقيم بنبراس المعارف ومصابيح العلوم ضربة لازب لكشف براثن الغباوة واجلاء غياهب الجهل وتقويض اركان السجون · فلذلك نشرت الجمعية لائحتها السنوية راجية نصراء العلم والفضل والادب مع والدي التلامذة ووكلاء الايتام الذين وكلت اليهم تربيتهم الحضور في الاحتفالات المذكورة تنشيطاً لناشئة العصر الحاضر المتوثب بنور (الرشاد) وساماً نشكر لهم الشكر الجزيل · ونعترف لهم بالفضل والجميل · فلا زالوا شموس الهداية في الوطن · وغرة فخر في جبين الزمن في ٨ حزيران شرقي سنة ١٩١٣

الجمعية الخيرية الارثوذكسية

لائحة لأوقات الامتحانات والاحتفالات في مدارس الجمعية الخيرية الارثوذكسية - Bey 1305

Doc 6 - List of Exams and Festivities of the Schools of the Greek Orthodox Association for Charity in its Fourty Years

CHAPTER V

ADMINISTRATION AND MANAGEMENT OF THE WAQFS

The estates acquired by the monasteries and dioceses had to be cultivated and developed in order to ensure the expenses necessary to their functioning and especially to cover charitable expenses. The management of the waqf estates created a clever and complicated book-keeping system which we encounter again in books and documents kept in the archives of other religious institutions. Daily expenses, sharecroppers' accounts, and fiscal invoices were accounted for on a yearly balance sheet stating revenues and expenses. In the cities, it was mainly through leasing houses and shops constituted in waqf that dioceses ensured sufficient income to cover the maintenance of parishes and the salaries of priests, deacons and servants of the church. In addition, urban dioceses owned lands in the neighboring countryside, which were cultivated by sharecropping peasants living in these regions. Supervision, management and book-keeping were under the responsibility of the monastery superior or bishop, usually referred to as *mutawallī*. During the 18th century, the Maronite and Catholic monasteries of Mount Lebanon were reorganized along the lines of Western religious orders. Monasteries entrusted their financial responsibilities to managers known as *mudabbirūn*, of whom there were usually four for each monastery. Towards the end of the 18th century, churches were brought under much closer patriarchal control. Until then, local communities had been practically autonomous, giving only nominal recognition to one or other of the patriarchs.[1] The authority of the churches grew, while the influence of the lay notables and the traditional patronage of Sunnī or Druze leaders weakened. In the Greek Orthodox community, however, similar reforms occurred only in the second half of the 19th century, with the beginning of the Ottoman reforms.[2] The tendency to adopt a more rural life and to accept the influence of the clergy, who were mostly monks, permitted great changes in the management of waqf estates.

---

1 Bernard Heyberger, "Les chrétiennetés d'Orient au XVIIIème siécle," vol. 10, in *Histoire du christianisme* (Paris: Desclée, 1995), 150-69.

2 Catherine Mayeur Jaouen, "Les chrétiens d'Orient au XIXème siécle: un renouveau lourd de menaces," vol. 11, in *Histoire du christianisme* (Paris: Desclée, 1995), 792-849.

Reforms initiated by the application of the Tanzimat introduced the laity into the management of the waqfs. Towards the end of the 19th century, in both the cities and in the countryside, the laity began to take over land management, rent collection, association activities, and the running of the new educational and charitable institutions.

Whether lay or religious, these administrators depended on the help of the managers who ran the estates and collected the rents. The documents usually name such managers *wakīls* or *khawlīs*.[3]

At the beginning of the Ottoman occupation, the urban religious/judicial authorities supervised the management of the waqfs. The Muslim *sharīʿah* law courts kept the account-books of the city waqfs. Christian waqfs were listed after mosques, *madrasahs,* and other Muslim institutions. Although Muslim waqfs were the direct concern of the *sharīʿah* courts, it appears that the accounts of Christian waqfs were kept in the *maḥkamah* registers simply to permit the payment of the *mīrī* tax by these waqfs and dioceses. Documents from the 16th to the 19th century designate those waqfs as being those of the poor of a particular community. Waqfs of the poor of the Rūm (Greek Orthodox) the Armenians, Maronites and Syrian Orthodox, for example, are listed in Aleppo registers of the 18th century.[4] Until the 19th century in Beirut, the term "poor" followed the word waqf, such as the Waqf of the poor of St. Georges, and the Waqf of the poor Rūm. Even Balamand, which depended on Mount Lebanon *mutaṣarrifiyyah*, kept the designation *fuqarāʾ dayr al-Balamand.* Book-keeping of this type is not available for Tripoli or Beirut. The only extant specimen is provided by the registers of Aleppo.

This chapter is devoted to the management and exploitation of the waqfs. We will study the transfer of authority from the clergy to the laity and we will examine two models of book-keeping. The first is the register of a mountain monastery 1,000 metres high in the village of Dūmā in Batrūn district, and the second is the register of revenues from rented waqf premises in Beirut and Aleppo.

V. 1: The Transfer of Religious Authority to the Laity

V. 1.1: The Responsibilities of the Superior of the Monastery

The responsibilities of the superior of the monastery, the *hygoumené,* are described in a document dated 20th September, 1880. This document was issued by the Bishop of Beirut, Ghifrāʾīl Shātīlā whose diocese also in-

[3] Barnes, 42.

[4] Damascus National Archives. Registers of Aleppo nos. 152-177.

cluded Mount Lebanon. Yuwānikūs Ibn Ḥāyik from the village of Ḥāmāt (Batrūn) was designated by the bishop as superior of Our Lady of Ḥāmaṭūrā monastery.[5] The *faramān* of investiture contains 16 articles clearly outlining the superior's religious and worldly responsibilities. Eight of these articles refer to the monastery estates and their management. In the first article, which appoints him to the position of superior, the bishop designates the objects given to him, among which are the deeds and proofs of property.

The second article refers to persons dependent on the superior, such as sharecroppers and servants living inside or outside the monastery.

The fifth article concerns the attention and care that must be given to furniture and other objects, such as books, registers and documents. They must be preserved from moths, dust, rust and mildew.

The sixth article deals with the care the superior should give to the food and clothing of the monastery's inhabitants, and especially to cleanliness. Cleanliness was essential and very difficult to maintain, which explains the importance given to both articles. Monasteries, besides being places of contemplation and prayer, were also centres of agricultural exploitation, wintering of herds and flocks, and gathering of crops, where it was often difficult to keep a high standard of hygiene. In addition to their religious and economic functions, they were havens for populations in difficult times. Wars, epidemics, and earthquakes displaced many families, who moved into the monasteries for long periods of time. Depending on the size of the catastrophe, the stay could last for up to several months. Manuscript pages are full of colophons where visitors recorded and dated the events that brought them to read those very pages in the monastery. In times when epidemics ravaged the population, cleanliness was the only means of effective prevention. The enforced residence of city-dwellers was often an occasion for them to grant generous donations to the monastery. Again, manuscript colophons describe measures taken to enlarge the monastery during or after such so-called difficult periods.[6]

Today it is difficult to attribute to the monastery of Ḥāmaṭūrā any importance in sheltering refugees. It is the last monastery that remains accessible only by a tortuous and very steep path. But in past centuries all the monasteries were in the same situation. Roads suitable for vehicles were built only at the end of the 19th century and in certain regions only in the mid-20th century.[7] The difficult access to the monasteries helped to provide

---

[5] Archives of Greek Orthodox Bishopric of Beirut, register Bey 15.

[6] Slim, "Balamand," 27-28.

[7] Ismāʿīl Bayk Ḥaqqī, *Lubnān: mabāḥith ʿilmiyyah wa ijtimāʿiyyah* (Beirut: Lebanese University Publications, 1970), 623-625.

the security and peace necessary to monastic life. The arrival of new guests at Ḥāmaṭūrā meant each time the digging into the rock of new cells more or less spacious depending on the importance of the newcomers.[8]

The other articles from 11 to 16 are all dedicated to waqf estates and their exploitation. Article 11 clearly states that the superior is in charge of the monastery's estate and its sharecroppers. He should do his utmost to foster the interests and prosperity of the monastery. Article 12 states that the superior should supervise the monastery's property with care in order to ensure its maintenance and development.

Article 13 states that the *hygoumené* had to gather the crops and harvests and collect the waqf revenues, which he should record in the books of the monastery. He should withdraw from these crops the necessary supplies and spend wisely and sparingly. He should also record his sales, specifying the weight, price and the name of the sharecropper to whom the land was leased as well as the expenses arising from the maintenance of these lands.

Article 14 stresses once again the importance of book-keeping and the obligation to register all revenues, including those coming from the church as well as cash donated by pilgrims or through vows. The superior should also mention the details of expenses dated as to the day, month and year in order to provide monthly and yearly balance sheets which may be referred to when needed.

Article 15 forbids the superior to sell, exchange or mortgage the lands of the monastery or its furniture and possessions. He should not lend or borrow goods or money, nor introduce any new obligation or habit which could involve the monastery or its estates in any operation or contract.

Article 16 specifies that the monastery should not bear any loss of objects, property or money. Should there be any loss, the superior in charge would himself refund it with his own money.

In conclusion, this document states that the superior, as a spiritual son, should accept all these conditions and commit himself once again to respect all the obligations of the *faramān* and to work to enhance the monastery's prosperity and development. He should also accept the responsibility for any transgression of the stated conditions. A copy of the *faramān* was written and remitted to the superior, so that he could execute the articles and show it as a proof, if necessary.

This document is of primary importance because it stipulates the rules for the management of all monasteries depending on the bishopric of Beirut in the 19th century and on the bishopric of Mount Lebanon in the 20th century.

---

8 "al-Makhṭūṭāt al-ʿarabiyyah," Manuscript of Ḥāmatūrā, nos. 14-31.

In the accounts register of the monastery of St. John of Dūmā, we can observe the practical application of the different articles of the *faramān* of investiture. This is one of the best-kept monastic registers in Lebanon, and it permits an overview of about thirty consecutive years. According to the *faramān*, the superior is designated as *hygoumené*, with all the religious responsibilities that this title implied, as well as managing *wakīl* by the *mutawallī*, who is effectively the bishop himself. Apart from the duplication of economic and religious functions, there were a number of temporal functions. In addition to his book-keeping obligations, the superior was responsible for the monastery's manuscripts and documents. Thus he had to be librarian, restorer and builder in one. He had to preserve liturgical objects and furniture and decide on the best use of agricultural profits. When available, such profits were usually invested in the restoration of old churches and the construction of new apartments to host visitors coming on pilgrimage or to fulfill their vows. These expressions of religious piety were accompanied by donations in cash, sometimes quite generous. The *faramān* of investiture defines the type of revenues to be registered in the books. Thus the investment generated interest, although indirectly.

Hosting pilgrims and believers was not the only aim of new construction. Starting from 1880, several monastic premises were transformed into schools. This was the case of Balamand, where, in 1901, an entire wing was built for the seminary school. Thanks to the assistance of the Russian monks and the Russian Imperial Association of Palestine, Mār Ilyās monastery got its school during the same period. The Dūmā school, established in St. John monastery, also benefited from the Russian help.[9]

The double presence of monasteries and schools did not occur without misunderstandings and friction. The superior of Our Lady of Ḥāmaṭūrā monastery since 1880 became superior of Balamand in 1899. During this period that Balamand reopened the seminary school in its premises. The superior's responsibilities and functions could sometime be opposed to those of a newly-appointed manager. In a letter addressed to the superior Yuwānikūs, the patriarch indicated the obligations required by the reopening of the school.[10] Certainly there would be important additional expenses to the monastery's normal functioning budget. In addition to the cost of premises, the monastery had to provide students and teachers with the necessary food and heating during their stay. The monastery also had to pro-

9 Ahatanhel Krymskyj, *Bayrūt wa Jabal Lubnān ʿalā mashārif al-qarn al-ʿishrīn: dirāsah fī taʾrīkh al-ijtimāʿī min khilāl mudhakkirāt al-ʿālim al-Rūsī al-kabīr A. Krīmskī: rasāʾil min Lubnān, 1896-1898*, trans. Yūsuf ʿAṭʾallāh (Beirut: Dār al-Madā, 1985), 262.

10 Beirut Archives, register no. 1562.

vide the students with mattresses and ensure domestic help. The letter also mentioned straw mattresses for the resident teachers. The school should have its own separate kitchen, but rules of fasting and Lent had to be applied according to the prescriptions of the Orthodox Church. Because of the expenses incurred by the monastery, the patriarch exempted the superior from paying the annual financial contributions that were usually given in cash by the monastic waqfs to the patriarchate. The urgent expenses had to be provided for by the monastery and recorded in its books as a debt to be reimbursed to the patriarchate.

In spite of the monastery's contribution to the school's expenses, the patriarch's letter ordered a kind of separation between the two institutions. Monks and visitors were not supposed to attend the school. The chapel of St. Georges was reserved for the daily services of the seminarians, while the liturgies would be celebrated in common in the chapel of Our Lady.

Another example of competition between religious and laity seems to have occurred 10 years after the opening of Balamand school. In 1908 the school, which had 36 students, unfortunately had to close its doors due to obscure administrative reasons. It should be pointed out that the closing of the school coincided with the death of the patriarch Malātiyūs and the nomination of his successor Ghrīghūriyūs IV. The resulting period of transition may have caused a deficit in the school budget, which would explain its closing down.[11]

Nevertheless, in the same year, the patriarch appointed the archimandrite Ighnātiyūs Abū Rūs as new school director. The latter started to look among the clergy for new teachers, although in the past most of the teachers had been laymen. In 1910, the school was once more the object of discussion at the Antiochian Synod. The bishop of Tripoli wanted to transfer the school to Damascus, while the bishop of Beirut proposed to relocate it in his city, in the monastery of Mār Ilyās Btīnah. In fact, the latter proposal was adopted, with the proviso that the school would remain under patriarchal jurisdiction. Its procurators would be the bishops of Beirut and Mount Lebanon Jirāsīmūs Masarrah and Būlus Abū ʿAḍal and its director Ighnātiyūs Abū Rūs. The number of students was limited to forty. However the transfer did not take place. It seems the inhabitants in the neighborhood of Mār Ilyās Btīnah monastery protested strongly and refused the establishment of the new school in their waqf. Several petitions were signed by the inhabitants of Muṣaytbah and Mazraʿah districts and sent to the Beirut bishopric, demanding the cancellation of the project. On the other hand, it seems that other parties and families approved this initiative because op-

---

11 Sanāʾ ʿAbbūd, *Dayr al-Balamand wa madrasatuhū al-iklīrīkiyyah* (B.A. thesis, Balamand Institute of Theology, 1978), 98.

posing petitions were also sent.[12] The whole matter reflected conflicts between laity and clergy. It also reflected the problem of partisan conflict within the Church and suggests one of the aspects of the conflict between cities and villages.

Finally, Balamand won. In 1911, Ghaṭṭās Qandalaft was again nominated director of the school. On the graduation day, a great number of Kūrah personalities were present, a fact confirming the importance of the school in the region.[13]

V. 1.2: The Secular Authority in the Management of the Waqf Estates

Secular authority inside the Church was not new. We have repeatedly seen the roles that the notables had during the 17th and 18th centuries. In the 19th century this role was structured and organized under the functions and reforms undertaken by the Ottoman Empire. During the 19th century, the civil and political emancipation of many Eastern Christians took place. The reorganization program (Tanzimat), which aimed to modernize the empire to enable it to resist disintegration, directly affected the situation of the non-Muslim minorities. The Khaṭṭ-i-Sharīf of Gulkhané, promulgated in 1839, established civic equality between Christians and Muslims. It stated: "The national institutions should, from now on, guarantee a perfect security to our subjects concerning their lives, honor and properties. These sovereign concessions are given to all with no discriminating as to their religion or sect." A more equitable fiscal reform was promised. In 1856, the Khaṭṭ-i-Humāyūn asserted the equality of *dhimmīs* and Muslims, with regard to justice, military recruitment, and taxes. Political rights were also granted to non-Muslim communities: Jews and Christians obtained voting rights for communal and provincial councils, freedom of religious worship, the ability to construct new churches or restore old ones, and access to public function. Nevertheless a contradiction arose. While the reforms advocated equality and the fragmentation was authorized in the *millets*, the 19th century witnessed the crumbling of the unity of the Christian communities and the consolidation of their individual particularities.[14] The traditional patriarchates remained loyal to the Ottoman Porte. However, the new elite, encouraged by the Western powers, tried to claim simultaneously the equality of all subjects in the Ottoman Empire and the maintenance of the old *millet* privileges. Some researchers consider that the notion of *millet* did not even

---

12 Beirut Archives, document nos. Bey 1280 to Bey 1297.

13 *al-Kalimah*, no. 16 (1907).

14 Catherine Mayeur Jaouen, "La renaissance dans les églises d'Orient à la fin de l'époque ottomane: les 18 et 19 siècles," in *Christianity Through its History in the Orient.* Not published yet.

exist before the 19th century and that the reforms undertaken by the Ottoman Porte introduced the tendency to fragmentation and the splitting of the communities into *millets*.[15] Others tried to prove that the *millet* system preceded these reforms and that the *millet* concept dated from immemorial times to designate minor communities and was even used in the Koran.[16]

According to the Khaṭṭ-i-Humāyūn of 1856, these *millets* kept on enjoying their traditional privileges, namely the internal organization of their churches, but the sulṭān requested them to reform their temporal administration. Assemblies, elected in each community, had to participate in its administration. These internal reforms were bound to improve the traditional and antiquated *millet* structures so as to adapt them to modernity and to the new Ottoman State under construction. In the second half of the 19th century the *millets* were reorganized under the pressure of the lay notables who wished to take over the administration of the communities' waqf revenues and, especially, their schools, which had by then acquired an unprecedented importance.[17] The cultural revival and the economic rise of the laity experienced by the elite of the upper middle class in the cities led the Greek Orthodox laity to be more demanding regarding their participation in the management of church business. In spite of ethnic and linguistic divisions, the conservatism of the Greek Orthodox church, the competition of the Latin and Protestant missions, and the proselytism of the Catholic Uniates, the Greek Orthodox of the empire undertook a reform of their church in 1860-62 that gave a small share in community decisions to the laity.[18] The main reform was the one that took place in 1876 when a lay council was elected to preside over church and community affairs. The Greek Orthodox of the city of Beirut were the first to rise against the hegemony of the Hellenic clergy. In 1871 the city notables and families signed a petition demanding the nomination by a synod of an Arab bishop for their diocese.[19] It was only in 1899 that the Greek Orthodox Arabs, with the help of Russian diplomats and schools, succeeded in getting an Arab patriarch, Malātiyūs al-Dūmānī, elected to the patriarchate of Antioch.[20]

---

15 Benjamin Braude, "Foundation of Myths of the Millet System," in *Christians and Jews in the Ottoman Empire*, vol. 1, ed. B. Braude and B. Lewis (London: Holmes & Meier, 1982), 69-89.

16 Vincenzo Poggi, "Les chrétiens en Orient durant la seconde période ottomane (l'établissement du régime des millets)," in *Christianity Through its History in the Orient*. Not published yet.

17 Catherine Mayeur Jaouen, "Renaissance."

18 Davie, "Millat grecque," 125.

19 Juliette al-Rāsī, "Min arshīf baṭriyārkiyyat Anṭākiyyah wa sā'ir al-mashriq li-l rūm al-urthūdhuks fī Dimashq," *Dirāsāt al-Jāmiʿah al-Lubnāniyyah*, no. 26 (1997), 435-506.

20 Alexis Bogolioubsky, "Le problème de l'enseignement des langues dans les écoles russes de la société impériale de Palestine," unpublished article.

Here too, Beirut was the first diocese to test and put into practice the demands of communal organizations requested by the Ottoman reforms. Even if this experience was not always successful and even if it covered only a relatively short period, and in spite of the fact that it was inspired by the Ottoman reforms, and that it had, on several occasions, caused a conflict between the clergy and the laity, this tentative practice of involving the latter in the management of church affairs had a very important impact on believers and on the Church's history and future. This period, although sometimes difficult and full of conflict, is constantly rememberd with nostalgia. During the contemporary history of the Antiochian church, all the attempts to reform ecclesiastical organization, all the parish grievances, and all the lay recriminations stemmed from the memory of this period, which is considered as a renaissance, a past golden age which should, at all costs, be updated and revived.

The first attempt to have a secular representation was initiated in 1862 by Hierotheos, Bishop of Beirut. It was referred to as Jamᶜiyyah Qillayat al-Rūm al-Urthūdhuks (association of the Greek Orthodox Bishopric), and was composed of twelve members. Its function was to assist the Bishop in the charitable domain, and with the management of church affairs.[21]

The association ceased activity in 1863 with the departure and later the death of Hierotheos, the Greek Bishop of Beirut. The episcopal seat of the Beirut diocese remained vacant until 1870, when Ghifrāʾīl Shātīlā was elected by the synod as first Arab bishop of Beirut.

During eight years, between 1868 and 1875, the community affairs in Beirut seemed to have been managed by the Beirut Greek Orthodox Welfare Association. This Association became the manager of the Greek Orthodox waqfs for the poor and assumed the management of the five community schools in the city.

The income of this Association came from the management of the waqf estates, the money collected in churches, the subscriptions of members and the numerous donations made by the citizens of Beirut, residing either in this city or in other cities of the empire. Two churches were built during this period thanks to this association's activities, namely Our Lady of the Annunciation inside the old city and St. Nicholas in the new district of Rmayl.

This Association, which helped the community overcome the difficult years and the vacancy of the Episcopal seat, was the basis of a whole network of similar associations in Beirut and in all the cities of the region. Each institution had its own association to ensure administration and fund raising activities.[22]

---

[21] Davie, "Millat Grecque," 170.

[22] Ibid., 264.

The second attempt to elect a community council for the diocese of Beirut and Mount Lebanon was in 1876. Bishop Ghifrāʾīl Shātīlā justified theologically the establishment of this *majlis* on the basis that Christ himself had found it necessary to have disciples to help him in his task. This task proved to be very difficult, especially in Mount Lebanon. Those twelve elected members were similar to the twelve *aʿwān allāh*, disciples of God as stated by Saint Paul. They had to assist the bishop in his mission.[23] The bishop and notables convened the delegates' families, who were to choose by secret ballot the twelve members of the council. As in the case of the Association members, the *majlis* members were community notables and important merchants, landlords and financiers from the city. It was mainly they who paid the largest amounts for military taxes (*badal ʿaskariyyah*) and real estate taxes (*wirko*). They were essentially inhabitants of the new suburban districts located in the eastern side of the city – Qīrāt, Rmayl, and Ṣayfī. The new council's responsibilities were quite heavy. They covered Beirut diocese, including all the villages and monasteries of Mount Lebanon. This council had to satisfy the community's needs, to take care of its development, and to solve its problems within the canonical Ottoman laws. This council was essentially responsible for the city and mountain churches. *Wakīls* (administrators), had to be appointed for a period of two years. The council had to go over the accounts presented by these churches annually. The responsibility of the council also covered the mountain monasteries, which had suffered losses. The by-laws stipulated financial support to these monasteries until their recovery, after which half of their profits would go to the profit of the clerical school. This school, established by bishop Ghifrāʾīl, was also under the jurisdiction of the council.

The council instituted a general fund for the community in order to cover the expenses of the schools, even their deficit. A treasurer, member of the *majlis*, was entrusted with this fund.[24]

An updating of the lay representation in the community council was launched in 1886 by the amendment of the old status and the promulgation of new laws. The new council responsibilities were greater at the level of waqf management. Article 18 of the new statutes specified the new council's obligations as follows:

1. The supervision of all the community activities, charitable activities and the study of its needs both moral and material.
2. The control of affairs relative to personal status, especially the right to rule on inheritance disputes and to execute testaments.

---

23 Ibid., 177.

24 Ibid., 183-184.

3. The nomination and investment of *wakīls* responsible for churches, schools, associations, other commissions and communal institutions, certification of their status and the reason for their appointment.
4. The supervision of the accounts of schools, churches and of the associations and their waqfs.
5. The responsibility for the legal investment of *wakīls* with extraordinary activities.
6. The allotment and collection of the *badal ʿaskariyyah* (tax for the exemption from military service and draft).

The community council was responsible for defending the rights of the community and negotiating the public posts reserved for the Orthodox in the city's administration council and the tribunals. This council had the responsibility over all matters that related to the rights of the community in order to ensure its success and development within the limitations of Ottoman and Canon Laws.[25]

V. 2: Management of the Accounts of St. John the Baptist Dūmā

The study of the accounting records of the administration of the waqf of St. John Dūmā typifies the problems posed in this thesis. The foundation and the development of waqf property and institutions in the modern era occurred later among the Greek Orthodox of Mount Lebanon than it did among the other communities. Here is a classic case of a large 19th-century agricultural estate, where a monastery possessing the means of production (land, mills, tools etc.) divided up labour among the share-cropping families of the surrounding villages. This particular monastery also housed a school, which functioned for only a short time yet was held in great esteem by the inhabitants of the region.

Regarding the administration of its estate, this monastery, like all the others, was little affected by laymen. Throughout its history, its lands were administered by monks in the higher ranks of the church hierarchy, although the numerous peasant sharecroppers who exploited its waqf lands were themselves, of course, laymen. What changed rather was the geographical and administrative structure on which the monastery depended. Until 1901 the monastery was part of the see of Beirut, which included the whole of Mount Lebanon. In 1902, however, following the partition of the see of Beirut, St. John Dūmā was attached to the waqfs of the see of Jbayl and Batrūn (Mount Lebanon). The attitudes of the two hierarchies towards the monasteries were different.

---

[25] Ibid., 217-218.

Before we approach the theme of the book-keeping of St. John of Dūmā monastery, it would be advisable for us to learn about its estate. Unfortunately, we could not find any deeds in the monastery nor in the archives of the bishopric of Mount Lebanon, which were burned in 1978. Instead we have to resort to an assessment of the present situation. The surface area of the property is estimated at approximately two million square meters. In this respect, it is the most important monastery after Balamand and Mār Yaᶜqūb of Diddih. However, we could find in the monastery archives a list of the documents, deeds, and receipts of the *mīrī* tax, concerning the monastery's estate.[26] This document, dated 1880, was written by the *hygoumené* Jirāsīmūs Fawāz himself. It is drawn in columns, four of which specify deed number, plot number, deed date and number of witnesses. In a wider fifth column, the type of the deed is mentioned: acquisition, donation or exchange, the name of the previous owner and sometimes the type of soil and crops (olive trees, *ṣalīkh*, water mills, mulberry trees, press houses, etc.). Often a single parcel is referred to as *qiṭᶜat ᵓarḍ,* and many parcels are referred to as *rizqah.* A sixth column describes the location of the parcel in relation to the surrounding villages of the area. This survey is by region. It is written on a sheet of paper folded in two, thus forming four pages, one page for each of four villages where the monastery owns property. The documents, retranscribed in columns, are acquisition documents, proof of the monastery's expansion. Following the listings for each village, the following documents are enumerated: property deeds, sharecropping contracts, receipts for crops delivered, land partition, cancellation of contracts, power of attorney, and the *mīrī* tax paid. Six villages where the monastery owned lands are mentioned in these papers – Dūmā, Kfar Ḥildā, Kfūr and Bishtūdār, in the district of Batrūn and surrounding the monastery, and two other villages, Kfar Ḥazīr and Amyūn in the district of Kūrah, relatively far from the monastery. The last two are specialized in olive tree exploitation, while the four others had much more diversified crops. Throughout this survey, dates are mentioned according to the Christian era, although a few of the deeds going back to the end of the 18th century and the beginning of the 19th century are dated according to the Hijra era. The purchase and donation of parcels are certified by deeds. Each deed refers to one parcel owned by the monastery waqf. Thus there are 45 parcels in Dūmā, 16 in Bishtūdār, eight in Bayt Shlālah and 29 in Kfūr al-ᶜArbah, six in Kfar Ḥazīr and five in Amyūn. As to certificates and contracts, there are 10 documents for Dūmā, three for Bishtūdār, 26 for Bayt Shlālah, nine for Kfūr and three for Amyūn, a total of 109 parcels and 45 certificates. These parcels are

[26] Archives of St. John the Baptist Dūmā, document nos. 227, 228.

those acquired around the monastery's estate, the central estate having been acquired in 1784, when the monastery was established.[27]

"St. John the Baptist Dūmā"

27 Ibid., Triodi no. 6, colophon.

The book of accounts of St. John of Dūmā monastery were a model which could be used for the management of waqf estates in rural regions. The annual balance sheets for the years 1890 to 1927 are the result of a daily book-keeping, recorded by items in other notebooks of different shapes which served as a draft of the final sheet.[28] The new models of book-keeping are relatively recent, going back to about the middle of the 19th century. The listing by columns of the different chapters defining dates, titles and amounts replaced the traditional book-keeping method, which recorded the accounts horizontally and spelled the amounts above the numbers. The total sum of the different amounts was recorded in the margin, thus allowing a paragraph for revenues and another for expenses. The final operation done to obtain the annual balance sheet was registered and sometimes underlined at the end of the account, followed by the signature of the responsible person. This method was used until the first half of the 19th century. It was probably due to the new reforms and the obligation to keep proper books of accounts that the columnar layout was definitely adopted. At the end of the yearly balance sheet, the bishops wrote a short note attesting the correctness of the accounts, which was signed and sealed. Later on, for certain years we only have the signatures of the superiors and bishop without any explanation.

Beginning in 1891, the different expenses and revenues headings were posted on the balance sheet with the number of the page on which they were registered. Each type of expense was recorded and detailed on other pages of the same book. There were expenses for salaries, food, monks' clothing, maintenance of agricultural lands and flocks and miscellaneous expenses and revenues. Some headings referred to the same pages and recorded both expenses and revenues. This was the case for the different agricultural plots, the cattle, the mills, and the "miscellaneous," which necessitated maintenance expenses and ensured revenues. Another heading, concerning the church, also appears on both pages. The church received donations and vows from pilgrims and from inhabitants of the neighboring villages. It always needed funds for rehabilitation and maintenance. Later on the expenses and revenues of the school and library are recorded under one heading and on the same page.

The figures under these different headings show a tenfold increase over the 35-year period recorded. This increase could well be due, at least in part, to the impact of monetary devaluation which occurred in the region at that time. In 1890, the monastery of St. John the Baptist of Dūmā was in the *mutaṣarrifiyyah* of Mount Lebanon within the frame of Ottoman hege-

---

28 Ibid., Account Books, document nos. 278-339.

mony. In 1927, it became part of the Greater Lebanon state, in the frame of the French mandate. So, these accounts covered the Ottoman period between 1890 and 1918 and the French mandate period between 1919 and 1927. Changes on the levels of commercial circuits, agricultural practices and monetary fluctuations also occurred because of the different political and economic upheavals in the region.

During this period, mulberry growing linked to silk production had already declined. Several spinning mills and trade centers which depended on sericulture went bankrupt.[29] Mountain monasteries and convents, which were the centers of conflection, moved towards new crops less concerned by the market economy and concentrating more on local consumption. Crucial fiscal transformations occurred due to change in the political regime. Within this change, it is natural to point out modifications concerning the usual currencies throughout the different periods. In spite of the different upheavals and throughout the 35 years, the used currencies remained unchanged. During the Ottoman period, the *pāras* and piastres were in circulation. The same symbols were used to designate the piastre fractions: 1/4, 1/2, 3/4. We should ask whether the recorded currency was used only as an account currency or as a real one. We already know that during the Ottoman period, the population of Mount Lebanon had enough available cash coming from abroad thanks to the silk trade revenues. The Ottoman currency, repeatedly devalued and counterfeited, was not trusted by the people.[30] From other sources, we learn that European currencies, such as the gold English pound, the gold Ottoman pound, the gold Napoleon and the Austrian piastre representing Empress Maria Theresia were used. The Ottoman currency was adapted to foreign coins circulating since the 17th century and highly appreciated by the people. Thus, the *ghurūsh* was a transformation of the German big cent (*Groschen*), the *pāra* was an Egyptian currency, introduced into the empire, which kept the label of *miṣriyyah*. The *zulūtah* was an adaptation of the Polish *zloty*, which was widely used at that time in the Empire.[31] We also learned from the archives and heritage items preserved in monasteries, bishoprics and convents, that there were also many paper currencies. They were either the new Ottoman currency or Russian *roubles*. Nevertheless, we could not trace, through these books of accounts, any mention of foreign

---

29 Labaki, 148.

30 Bernard Lewis, *The Emergence of Modern Turkey* (London: Oxford University Press, 1961), 108.

31 GeorgeYoung, *Corps de droit ottoman: recueil des codes, lois, règlements, ordonnances et actes les plus importants du droit intérieur et d'études sur le droit coutumier de l'Empire Ottoman*, vol. 5 (Oxford: Clarendon Press, 1911), 1.

currencies supposedly used in the mountain during that period. Was this fact a token or a proof of Orthodox loyalty to the Ottoman government? Together with the enforcement of the French mandate, the introduction of Mount Lebanon to the markets and the cessation of Ottoman extortion, the foreign currencies should have been more easily accessible to the Lebanese. But in these books of accounts, the constant use of the *ghurūsh* and *pāra* seemed to be due to the easy way of following a familiar system with exchange methods having no secrets for the users. (Thus these *ghurūsh* and *pāra,* which were easily understood, could ensure the follow-up of the book-keeping).

During these troubled years, including the First World War, the books of accounts were properly kept. This regularity and accuracy reflect the importance of the lands of this monastery and the importance of its production to the community. Even during the four years of the war, which were especially murderous for Mount Lebanon, the smallest book-keeping detail was recorded. Expenses seem to have been reduced, especially salaries. For one or two years during the war, expenses were limited to those necessitated by the superior, one monk and one servant. But a specific book-keeping method seems to have distinguished the war years. This method consisted in presenting the accounts of six or 12 months with the six last months of the year and the six first months of the following one. Thus, we have: the first six months of 1914, the six last months of 1914 and the six first months of 1915, the six last months of 1915 and then the whole of 1916 and 1917. Were these changes in the chronology a new reality due to the war events or were they due to the new demands for crops or for the convenience of the ecclesiastical hierarchy? The books do not mention it. Was it an urgent need for money which led the superior, twice during the war, to report a six month balance sheet?

The method to be used for recording this accounting data should exemplify the concept of serial history. It is possible to draw up series of the different headings given in the accounts in order to make a statistical study of the data. For example, the evolution of expenses, revenues and account balances may be reviewed with attention to the various details that have influenced its course. In the case of these accounting records, there is solid numerical data, series of figures to which the method of serial history may be well applied.

In order to assess the value of the modifications of the balance sheet during the period under review, one needs to know its details. Thus, detailed study of the revenues and expenses permits us to better appraise the economic, religious and cultural conditions of the monastery, and to know better its role in the region.

V. 2.1: Expenses

Obligations under this heading are numerous. They are recorded in detail. There are five important groups in which we can classify the expenses: salaries, rural expenses, food, construction and education.

Graph 10 illustrates the monastery of St. John Dūmā's expenditure, which was varied by nature and by amount. Wages seem to have been the least important item, while land acquisitions were the largest expense. Various expenses to cover hospitality and food consumption (marked DIV on the graph) fluctuated from year to year, as they depended mainly on the number of persons who happened to be staying in the monastery. Building expenditure was irregular; it covered repairs or the construction of new wings in the monastery.

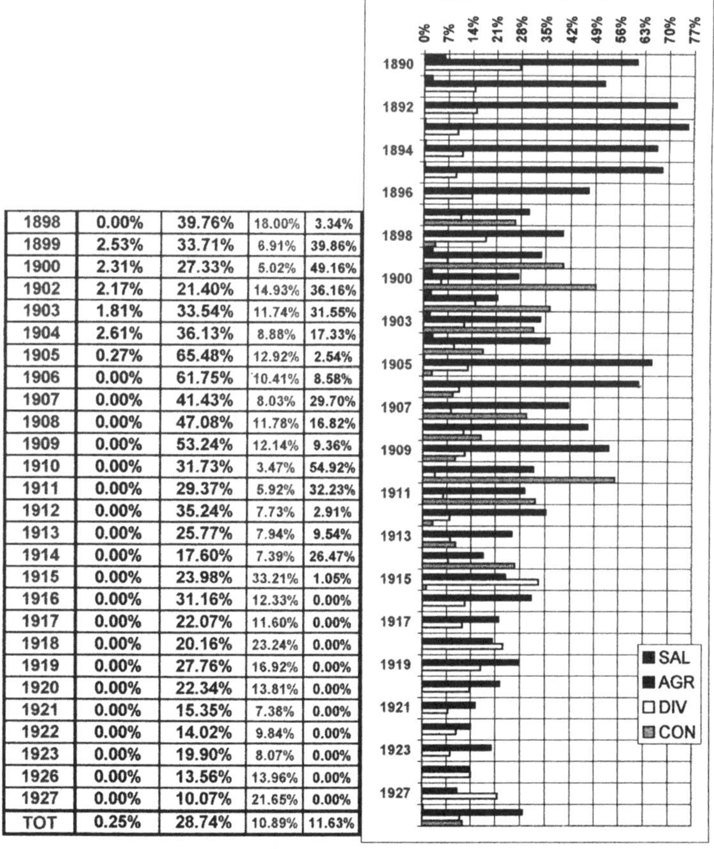

1898	0.00%	39.76%	18.00%	3.34%
1899	2.53%	33.71%	6.91%	39.86%
1900	2.31%	27.33%	5.02%	49.16%
1902	2.17%	21.40%	14.93%	36.16%
1903	1.81%	33.54%	11.74%	31.55%
1904	2.61%	36.13%	8.88%	17.33%
1905	0.27%	65.48%	12.92%	2.54%
1906	0.00%	61.75%	10.41%	8.58%
1907	0.00%	41.43%	8.03%	29.70%
1908	0.00%	47.08%	11.78%	16.82%
1909	0.00%	53.24%	12.14%	9.36%
1910	0.00%	31.73%	3.47%	54.92%
1911	0.00%	29.37%	5.92%	32.23%
1912	0.00%	35.24%	7.73%	2.91%
1913	0.00%	25.77%	7.94%	9.54%
1914	0.00%	17.60%	7.39%	26.47%
1915	0.00%	23.98%	33.21%	1.05%
1916	0.00%	31.16%	12.33%	0.00%
1917	0.00%	22.07%	11.60%	0.00%
1918	0.00%	20.16%	23.24%	0.00%
1919	0.00%	27.76%	16.92%	0.00%
1920	0.00%	22.34%	13.81%	0.00%
1921	0.00%	15.35%	7.38%	0.00%
1922	0.00%	14.02%	9.84%	0.00%
1923	0.00%	19.90%	8.07%	0.00%
1926	0.00%	13.56%	13.96%	0.00%
1927	0.00%	10.07%	21.65%	0.00%
TOT	0.25%	28.74%	10.89%	11.63%

Graph 10 - Expanses of the Monastery of St. John Dūmā

Graph 10 reveals a general decline in expenditure, beginning shortly before the First World War and continuing for the rest of the period under consideration.

A study of these expenses will determine whether or not the monastery strove to maintain a rough balance between its spending and its regular annual income.

We have already stated that some of these obligations also generated revenues.

V. 2.1a: Salaries and Dues

Reported at the beginning of the accounts, these are divided into three groups: expenses for maintenance of the clergy, dues to the bishop, and salaries of the workers and servants of the monastery. Expenses for the maintenance of the clergy, living in the monastery, were allocated to the *hygoumené* and to the monks. The word *kiswah*, meaning clothes, is specially used for these particular expenses. Monks living in the monasteries only needed their cassocks. We do not know whether this modest sum was actually remitted to each one, as clothing or in cash, as stipulated in the accounts. These expenses dedicated to the clergy were quite important for the clothing of the superiors, and minimal for the clothing of the monks and labourers. Over the years covered by these accounts, the monastery had been ruled by two superiors, Jarāsimūs Fawāz and Bāsīliyūs al-ᶜAmm.[32] The first was responsible for the monastery until 1904. In 1890, he was given a cassock worth 480 piastres only. The price increased to 600 piastres in 1902, then it reached 1,200 piastres in 1903 and 1904. The second was a residing monk in Dūmā. His clothing was worth 227 piastres or 418 piastres only. In 1905, he was nominated superior and the price of his clothing reached 1,200 piastres, then 1,418 piastres in 1917 and finally 3,030 piastres in 1919. The monastery superiors had the title of archimandrite.

Under Bāsīliyūs al-ᶜAmm the word *kiswah* was applied to the clothing of all the workers and the servants, although they differed. The worker's *kiswah* was by far more expensive than the monk's, which appears absurdly low and even sometimes just symbolic. Another accounting detail allows us to differentiate between monks and lay workers, although they both received *kiswah*. Monks are recognizable from the fact that they had names of Byzantine saints. Based on the cloth value and the names, we can point out that around twenty monks, including *hygoumenés*, passed through the monastery during this period. Apparently, these monks were

---

[32] al-Bīṭār, 45.

only passing through. They were accomplishing their training and testing their limits before joining bishoprics, parishes or other monasteries. Others even emigrated to foreign countries where the number of Orthodox was increasing. Such was the case of Anṭūniyūs Bashīr, a monk from the village of Dūmā. He became the patriarchal delegate in the diocese of NewYork and North America.[33] He was only mentioned in 1916, when his *kiswah* cost only 30 piastres. Only one resident ensured a permanent presence in the monastery. He was present throughout the 35 years, and his name is Ilyās al-Kfūrī. We cannot ascertain whether he was a manager (*wakīl*) or a keeper (*nāṭūr*) working for the monastery. But the minimal value of his clothes seems to dismiss this hypothesis. We do not know either if he was a monk since no religious title precedes or follows his name. The mention of his *kiswah* appears regularly over the whole period, varying between 90 and 300 piastres, figures which were exceeded in 1920 (404 piastres), and in 1922 (355 piastres). We suppose that he might have been worker and monk at the same time.

Another member of the clergy benefited from the monastery's revenues. Although from 1906 onwards his name was never mentioned, he can be easily recognized from the wording used, beginning in 1906: *li siyādatihi*, which means "to His Eminence." He was Būlus Abū ʿAḍal, bishop of Mount Lebanon. Before 1901, Ghifrāʾīl Shātīlā, bishop of Beirut and Mount Lebanon, was responsible for St. John of Dūmā. The partition of this bishopric into two brought the bishop Būlus Abū ʿAḍal, originally from Damascus, to the see of Batrūn and Jubayl. From the beginning of 1906, he started collecting the royalties of the monastery of Dūmā, amounting to 2,436 piastres, then 2,000 piastres annually until 1921, and reaching 5,000 piastres in 1922.

Among the beneficiaries of these *kiswah*, fourteen women are listed, of whom nine were mentioned for only one year. Five of these nine women received a wage, an *ujrah*, instead of the *kiswah*. They are all listed under their first-born son's name. The traditional Oriental way to designate a woman was by the name of her father, or her husband, or her son.[34] Some of the women whose names were mentioned several times seem to have accomplished an important function in the monastery. The two most common functions were those of servant and cook. It is essentially through the repeated mention of the name that we can make out the difference between salary *kiswah* and welfare *kiswah*. Some of the women worked in the monastery for as long as nine years. There were four whose salaries

[33] Slim, "Balamand," 108.

[34] Jacques Weulersse, *Paysans de Syrie et du Proche Orient* (Paris: Gallimard, 1946), 223.

were regularly repeated. This was the case of Umm Ilyās from 1899 to 1905, Maryam Buṭrus Jirjis, employed at the same time as Jirjis Buṭrus Jirjis, probably her brother, from 1905 to 1913, Ḥannā Ḍāhir and Maryam Simʿān, employed together from 1918 to 1927. Their salaries seem to be as important, if not more, as those of the other workers employed during the same period. Although they had specific functions in the monastery, they were often called upon to do certain agricultural tasks proper to women, like sericulture and the gathering of alimentary stock, etc. These female cooks and workers could have salaries exceeding 600 piastres, as was the case of the cook Umm Ilyās. Other women, whose salaries were sometimes minimal, seem to have been charged with a specific seasonal function. The record specified that the salary covered a specific number of months. It would be interesting to know the degree of kinship, if any, between the servants and the workers employed in the monastery and the other workers or even the sharecroppers living in the neighborhood of the monastery, which was at some distance from the village of Dūmā. Other than the kinship between Maryam and Jirjis, we have no information whatsoever concerning the others.

As far as the men were concerned, most of them were listed as receiving *kiswah*. Here too, we notice the same irregularities and disparities in the importance of salaries. In this case, we have a few regular workers, namely Dāwūd Jibrāyil (17 years), Jirjis al-ʿAfaysh (10 years), Mikhāʾīl Raḥbānī (seven years), and Jirjis Jirjis (seven years). Here too, there is a certain alternation in the employment policy. The mid-period seemed the most regular. Between 1904 and 1914, the monastery hired three workers and a woman servant, while at the beginning and at the end of the period, it employed six to eight workers a year. The same workers were usually rehired for three or four years only (nine cases).

This irregularity of employment is not in accordance with the practice of mountain monasteries, where sharecropping contracts could last up to thirty years.[35] This is due to the fact that agricultural work had its peaks and its slack periods during the year. Was the regularity of employment during the mid-period due to the launching of new constructions? In fact, between 1897 and 1910 the accounts show regular expenses for new buildings and for the church of St. Nicholas.

V: 2.1b: Meals and Food Consumption

We encounter two sources of expenses in the accounts. The heading, "Table expenses" appears in the books from 1890, while the heading

---

[35] Chevallier, "Société du Mont-Liban," 148.

"Kitchen" appears only in 1906. These expenses are essential and are related to the role of the monastery as havens throughout history. In fact, since the Byzantine period, monasteries had an essential role as far as hospitality was concerned. This role was also exploited and misused by some superiors. Some notables, taking advantage of their power and previous donations, abused the lodging and food granted by certain monasteries. The exaggerated generosity and hospitality of these monasteries often trespassed their original functions as places of prayer and monastic contemplation. Transgressions were so exaggerated that Canon Laws contain entire chapters stipulating the interdiction to turn monasteries into hotels. Church laws were not only meant for monastery superiors but were often directed against important notables living near the monastery.[36]

Chroniclers and historians throughout the Arab and Muslim period give us detailed descriptions of the monasteries, where the religious celebration of Christians feasts was followed by popular festivities that were sometimes attended by Muslim officials. During their trips, hunting parties or simply during their visits to their subjects in the different regions, caliphs and sultans and their courts would spend a few days in the monasteries lying on their way. They admired the monastic churches and frescoes and ate with the monks a few of their culinary specialties.[37]

During the Ottoman period, the monasteries maintained the tradition of hospitality.

Monasteries in the Syrian countryside and the Lebanese Mountain became havens and stopovers for travellers. In the cities this role was assigned to the *khānāt*. European travelers in Lebanon, Syria and the Holy Land described their travel experiences, itineraries and stopovers through the mountain. Monasteries were ideal places for stopovers. As havens of peace, free discussion could be held with the monks on different subjects relative to the period and region.[38] Although these travellers regretted the monks' ignorance, and expressed intolerant opinions about others, those who had an official status would often do the monks special favors such as giving them travel passes for their goods, advancing cash, and bringing precious liturgical objects as guarantees. Whether officially or informally,

---

36 Ḥanāniyyā Ilyās Kassāb, ed., *Majmūʿat al-sharʿ al-kanasī aw qawānīn al-kanīsa al-masīḥiyya al-jāmiʿa* (Beirut: Manshūrat al-Nūr, 1985), 820. (The Seventh Council, Law 13).

37 Joseph Nasrallah, "La peinture monumentale des patriarcats melkites," in *Exposition icônes melkites organisée par le Musée Nicolas Sursock du 16 mai au 15 juin*, ed. S. Agemian (Beirut, 1969), 67-84.

38 Henry Maundrell, *A Journey from Aleppo to Jerusalem in 1697* (Beirut: Khayats, 1963), 46-47.

these monasteries benefited from the protection of the foreign consuls who visited or sojourned in their premises.[39]

The accounts of St. John of Dūmā monastery did not include the details of food expenses. But from the preceding heading, we can estimate that ten to twelve individuals, monks and workers, were fed at the monastery table. Important guests are not mentioned in the books, although the journal of Dāwūd Bashīr, one of the village notables, points out that in 1902 alone, four important personalities visited the village and were invited to St. John monastery. Notables of the village, guards and companions were included in these invitations.[40]

Food and kitchen expenses are an important part of the monastery budget. At the beginning of this period and until 1900, this hospitality cost only one-sixth to one-eighth of the monastery's expenses and obligations. During the four years preceding the war food expenses increased. Was this increase due to the higher cost of foodstuffs or to the decline of the silk sector, both of which occurred before the First World War? During those years, the cost of food reached almost a quarter of the total expenses, but during the war food expenses diminished on average. Nevertheless, food expenses in 1915, 1916, and 1917 reached one-third and sometimes even one-half of the total expenses. After the war, these expenses increased spectacularly: from 15,154 piastres in 1919, table and kitchen expenditures reached 60,830 piastres in 1920. 1920 is in fact the date of the reopening of the school. Here we notice that the students had their meals at the monastery table despite the fact that meals were not included in the school budget but recorded in the monastery accounts. Knowing that most of these pupils were boarders, the increasing cost of food in the total budget of the monastery can be easily justified.

V. 2.1c: Miscellaneous Expenses

These expenses were those incurred during a year but not recorded under a specific heading. At the beginning of the period under review miscellaneous expenses constituted a large proportion of the total expenses. Later on, this proportion decreased to no more than 10 to 15% of the total expenses. This reduction could have resulted from better experience in book-keeping. As time went by, superiors learned to register their expenses under the proper heading. This method of double entry was relatively new, and we can assume that experts in this matter were not numerous, especially as monks and monastery superiors were not specialised in this new field.

---

39 Guys, "Beyrouth et le Liban," vol. 1, 52.

40 Private archives, personal diary of Dāwūd Bashīr.

The importance of these unlisted expenses has raised doubts among researchers concerning the accuracy of the monks' book-keeping. According to these researchers, the doubts regarding the importance of these expenses and the accuracy of these accounts caused a reaction of mistrust among parishioners, believers and pilgrims who, because of their mistrust, significantly reduced their donations to these monasteries.[41]

However, concerning this period, there are several Arabic books, which are simplified manuals of the new book-keeping method. One of these books was written by Master Ḍāhir Khayrallāh, from the village of Shwayr, who taught this discipline in Balamand school.[42] So, monks and superiors educated in this seminary were in principle able to control and record the monastery's expenses and revenues for economical spiritual, liturgical, and later educational purposes.

V. 2.1d: The Case of Mār Yaᶜqūb Monastery

This trial appears between 1902 and 1909 in the expenses of St. John monastery. Mār Yaᶜqūb is a Maronite monastery dependent on the Lebanese Maronite Order. It is located on top of the mountain overhanging the village of Dūmā. The lands that are the subject of the conflict are given in sharecropping to inhabitants of Bishtūdār. They comprised a forest, goat pastures and a tobacco plantation. It was stated that during the first year mentioned in the accounts, namely 1902, 1,277 piastres were spent as a result of trespassing and provocations by monks of Mār Yaᶜqūb monastery on the lands of St. John monastery. In 1903 expenses amounting to 1,254 piastres were referred to as trial expenses. This trial cost St. John monastery 3,355 piastres, unevenly spread over a period of seven years.

The correspondence found in the monastery's archives reveals that 27 letters mentioning this trial were received.[43] They referred to trespassing and sometimes crop damage by cattle. Already in 1892, Ghifrāʾīl Shātīlā, bishop of Beirut, addressed a letter to the superior of Dūmā, Jirāsīmūs Fawāz, alerting him that the superior of Mār Yaᶜqūb Maronite monastery had complained to the Bashīr notables of Dūmā, claiming that six *qīrāṭs* of *al-Shikkā* and *al-Dhuhayrah* forests been given in sharecropping contracts to the inhabitants of Bishtūdār were Mār Yaᶜqub properties. In fact, these lands, which included a church, a shed for goats and an area for drying tobacco leaves were the property of St. John monastery. Ten years later the

---

41 Fayyad, Michel, *The Greek Orthodox Monasteries of Syria and Lebanon* (M.A. thesis, American University of Beirut, Beirut, 1931), 53.

42 Ḍāhir Khayrallah, *Lamḥat al-nāẓir fī mask al-dafātir*, 4th ed. (Beirut: al-Ittiḥād, 1911).

43 Archives of St. John Dūmā, nos. Dou 191, 193, 197, 198, 203, 207.

conflict between the two monasteries was brought to court. These letters also mentioned damages caused by the cattle. Indeed, the letter of patriarch Malāṭiyūs addressed in 1902 to the monastery superior states that he has informed the governor (*mutaṣarrif*) of Mount Lebanon about the goats trespassing while on their way to graze on St. John monastery lands, and the cows ploughing the lands of the said monastery. This last accusation leads us to think that the lands of the monastery were exploited without the patriarch's approval. In spite of the modest productivity of the lands in litigation (only six *qīrāṭs*) this trial necessitated the intervention of important personalities. On the clerical side, there were the bishops, the two patriarchs of the two communities and, of course, the superiors of the two monasteries; on the official side, the *qāʾimaqām*, the *mutaṣarrif*, the judges, the *wakīls* and the village notables. In this double ecclesiastic and civil hierarchy, it seems that the contacts were made between personalities of comparable rank. The patriarch wrote to the *mutaṣarrif*, the bishop to the *qāʾimaqām*, and the monastery superior to the village notables. Book-keeping, reports and orders generated a great deal of correspondence, which sheds light on the different responsibilities in the monasteries and on the management of their estates.

In addition to judicial contacts and formalities, this conflict stimulated a great deal of necessary cadastral measures. Following several infringements of the monastery's properties, the authorities decided to set the exact limits of the plots that were the reason of the conflict. In 1898, a first ruling, issued by the court of Batrūn and ratified by the *mutaṣarrif* Naʾūm Pāshā himself, empowered the monastery to use these lands. Then in 1902, the *mutaṣarrif* ordered the prevention of trespassing against the monastery lands. Legal action continued in order to solve the conflict, which was finally settled in favor of St. John of Dūmā monastery.

V. 2.2: Common Expenses and Revenues

In this section, there are three headings, under which both expanses and revenues are shown. There are agricultural expenses and revenues, educational expenses and revenues, and church expenses and revenues.

V. 2.2a: Agricultural Expenses and Revenues

There are three expense sources, which are at the same time sources of income. They are the six main estates of the monastery, cattle, and mills. These expenditures were incurred for fertilizers, terrace construction, daily wages, etc. These lands were entrusted to sharecroppers from the nearby villages of Dūmā, Kfar Ḥildā, Bayt Shlāla, and Kfūr. More detailed accounts, classified according to region, inform us about the production of each plot, its price, the expenses incurred and the distribution between the sharecroppers and the monastery. These expenses also included the taxes due to the Ottoman State and then to Greater Lebanon under the French mandate.[44]

The monastery's lands are formed of donations and purchases made during the two preceding centuries. Several terms were used to designate the six parcels. In Shammāyā, they were referred to *kurūms*, in al-Tallah, al-Bahassīs and al-Nubūh, they were called vineyards and orchards. Other regions are simply designated as *arḍ*, meaning land (soil). That was the case at al-Qabbūt, al-Shammīs and al-Kfūr. In the accounts of some years, the revenue of market garden produce was not reported separately. For example, we have the word *dindānī* used for two years regarding al-Shammis lands and then for two years for al-Bahassīs orchards. The most important agricultural lands were those directly surrounding the monastery and designated in the accounts as *kindar al-dayr*, the domain. Because of their large area the monastery was at some distance from the nearby villages. The houses and plots entrusted to the sharecroppers were located inside this *kindar*.

Regarding revenues, there was an alternation of good and bad years. Olive orchards were known to have rotating productions, one good year and then a bad one. Even lease-farming or sharecropping contracts were concluded for an even number of years. Taxes were also evaluated on the basis of two consecutive years, taking into account the revenue difference between the two years.

Bad years varied due to differences in location, altitude, soil, irrigation, and climatic conditions. Some crops were more resistant than others to certain diseases or insect attack. This is clearly shown in the detailed accounts during 35 years.

Thus we can see that regarding the same year, namely 1897, the domain (*kindar*) revenues went down from 7,802 piastres to 4,425 piastres, while al-Shammāyā vineyard revenues climbed from 676 to 2,390 piastres. Between 1905 and 1906, as well, while al-Tallah orchards revenues decreased greatly (from 4,448 to 631 piastres), those of Shammāyā, Shammīs and Qabbūt vineyards went up appreciably.

In addition to the lands, there are two other headings that were essential for the role of the monastery in rural life: cattle and mills.

Cattle: Cattle seemed to have been used essentially for the monastery and its inhabitants' domestic needs. A minimal part of cattle production was sold and gave infinitesimal revenues. Nevertheless, expenditures undertaken for the upkeep of the cattle often exceeded the income. Those animals were not always bred for meat or milk products. There were also

---

44 Archives of St. John Dūmā, nos. Dou 251, 254, 257, 260, 261, 262, 264, 266, 304, 327.

draught, transport and plough animals: donkeys, horses and mules were essential in rural life. They were the only means of transport in this steep and remote region. They carried men and pulled the swing-plough. The area of an orchard of mulberry trees was estimated from the number of donkey- or mule-loads of leaf it produced. The measure used was the *ḥiml*, which was equal to 75kg for a donkey and 100kg for a mule. Although they were costly to keep, these animals were necessary for the proper functioning of the rural economy.

The cattle, which were a source of income, could also be a source of conflicts. Pastures where flocks spent spring and summer were disputed between villages. Due to clan or family rivalry, one party would send its flocks to graze on the ploughed fields of its adversary. The area of cereal plots was estimated from the number of days it took a pair of cattle to plough it. The unit used was the *fiddān*, i.e. the area ploughed in one day by one pair of cattle. An important consequence of the movement of flocks between winter and summer pastures was the accompanying movement of herdsmen and their families, a practice reminiscent of nomadic life. Gradually families started to settle down in the new location, resulting in the creation of satellite villages inhabited by members of the same original village. Such population movement or migration was not unique to Lebanon but was seen throughout the Mediterranean countries. Probably the best examples of this phenomenon in Lebanon are the villages of Zghartā and Iḥdin, and Bsharrī and Dayr al-Aḥmar.

Mills: Water mills were vital in the production of flour and *burghul*, two basic components in the diet of the people. Practically every monastery owned one or more mills, which it used for its own crop and also made available to the inhabitants of the neighboring villages for a fee. The establishment document of the monastery mentioned the acquisition of two mills in Kfūr village. One century later, in 1869, with the arrival of bishop Ghifrāʾīl Shātīlā, a new mill was acquired. It was built by the bishop's brother, the *mutawahhid* Aftīmūs, who was superior of the monastery, at a cost of 32,000 piastres. The colophon relating this fact also reported that this same monk Aftīmūs planted Shammāyā vineyards in the region of Kfūr and also renovated the tobacco plantation.[45] According to the books, during the 35 years under review, losses were recorded only in three years, 1871, 1907 and 1916.

The reasons for losses in those years are not known. Perhaps they were due to repair works or new construction. Although profits were relatively limited, grain ensured a regular income. The mill fees were based on the total weight of the grain. These mills produced not only the different kinds

---

[45] Archives of St. John Dūmā, Triodi no. 6.

of flour and *burghul*, but also leguminous plants and grain mixtures and fodder for the cattle.

Despite climatic changes and the vicissitudes of the rural economy, graph 11 shows that agrarian revenues were for the most part in surplus, i.e. that revenues exceeded expenses. Therefore agriculture remained the monastery's principal source of income, both to supply the needs of its inhabitants and to finance various activities, including the construction and maintenance of buildings and infrastructure in the monastery's domain.

Agric

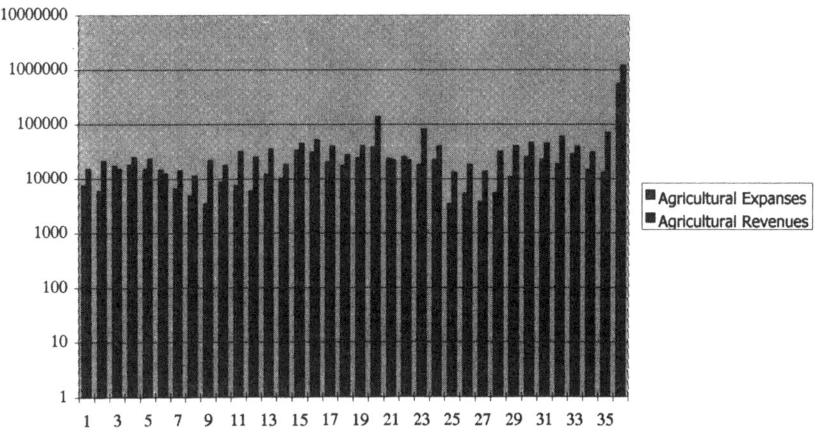

Graph 11 - Agricultural Balance Sheet of St. John Dūmā

Graph 11 reveals certain periods in which spending exceeded income, such as the years 1892-1895 and 1911-1912. However, in each case, the deficit was tiny and could easily be met. The revenues of the different plots of land scattered throughout the region, along with the revenues of mills and flocks, all together complemented one another: diversity of production was profitable and tended to maintain financial stability in the monastery's rural economy.

V. 2.2b: The Church Income & Expenses

Revenues from donations to the church funds are to be studied in the light of the expenditures needed for repairs of the monastery church and for building a new church, St. Nicolas church. Building started in 1897 in the monastery. St. Nicolas church, a very modest structure, cost only 4,791 piastres over four years (149 + 289 + 3,897 + 456), slightly more than the expenses resulting from the maintenance of the church. Altar candles, oil, icons, liturgical objects, repairs etc. were regularly recorded every year. Donations deposited in the box near the candles tray were affected by church embellishment and decoration and by the amount of attention given to this church. The colophon reporting the establishment of the monastery mentioned brass items and a silver crucifix, which the superior had acquired at the same time he purchased the agricultural fields and mills. This chapel appears to be older than the cloister. At its base, the facade is made up of very large stones. The chapel consists of two rooms that communicate through two archways. Each of these rooms contains an altar, one in the name of St. John the Baptist and the other in the name of the Virgin Mary. This type of church reminds us of the church in St. Dimitri, built during the Middle Ages in Kusbā. If we take into consideration the church only, we find that its balance sheet was in deficit in four years only: 1894, 1895, 1904 and 1913. For the remaining years, donations in cash (vows, contributions, altar candles) covered the church's maintenance costs. Construction was the cause of the church deficit. In addition to St. Nicholas church, there was new construction in the monastery which lasted 18 years and which cost a total of 212,344 piastres.

Graph 12 shows the expenditure and income of the monastic church, extending over nearly the whole period under study. Works undertaken from 1897 to 1914 incurred an expenditure that reached a maximum in 1910. The revenues coming to the church were small but regular.

The graph shows that these revenues were not sufficient to cover the expenses occasioned by the new construction. Yet even though building works were not justified on a strictly economic basis, they were made necessary by the religious character of the place.

The church building's very existence demanded that the value of its architecture and building be increased. These new buildings were connected to the monastery and were in the style common to houses and monasteries of that period, i.e. constructions around an inside open-air court. The end of the 19th and beginning of the 20th centuries saw the liberalisation of the Ottoman attitude towards the construction of new churches and rehabilitation of old ones. All over the empire new *faramāns* were granted to the different non-Muslim communities permitting the establishment of new places of worship.[46]

These new churches, built outside old districts, attracted new inhabitants who settled in those new areas. In the countryside and under the

---

[46] ʿAbd al-Raḥīm Abū Ḥusayn and Ṣāliḥ al-Saʿdāwī, *al-Kanāʾis al-ʿarabiyyah fī al-sijill al-kanasī al-ʿuthmānī: 1869-1922* (Amman: al-Maʿhad al-malakī li-l-dirāsāt al-dīniyyah, 1998), 119-187.

influence of foreign missionary schools, churches sprang up and benefited from educational services. Monasteries expanded and were turned into seminaries or schools. Because of the lack of transport, the scarcity of roads suitable for vehicles, and the distance between villages, the majority of schools were boarding, with children going home only during holidays.

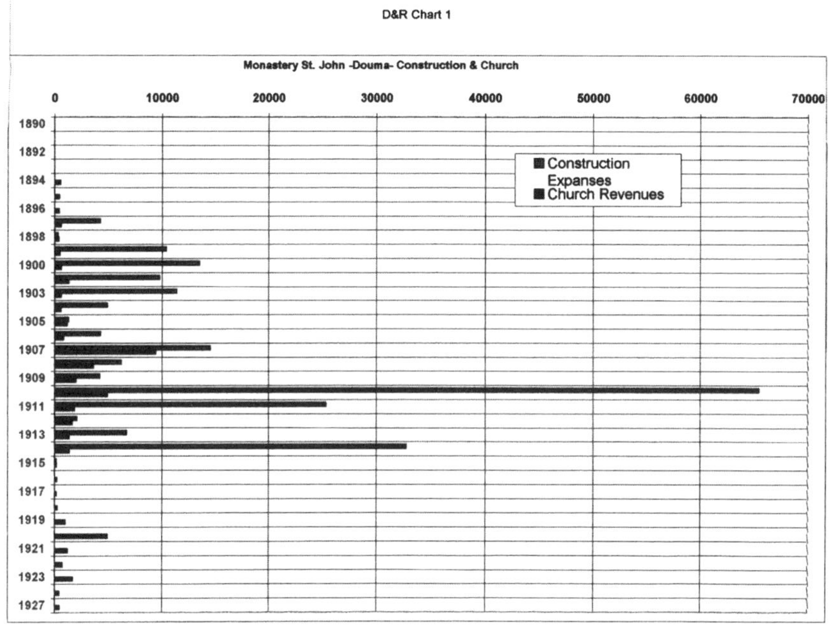

Graph 12 - Construction Expenses and Church Revenues of St. John Dūmā

V. 2.2c: The Bookstore and the School

It was in this framework that the Dūmā monastery expanded its buildings and opened a boarding school, which proved to be very important for the region. From the start, the school provided library/bookstore facilities.[47]

The operation seems to have been profitable. Thus the monastery launched a new activity, which was as successful as its agricultural vocation. This teaching activity was also introduced into several Mount Lebanon monasteries, such as Mār Ilyās Shwayyah, St. Georges in Dayr al-Ḥarf, Sayyidat al-Nūriyyah near Ḥāmāt, Our Lady of Bkaftain and others. Economic activities and the presence of students and teachers had to be reconciled with traditional activities. School quarters, dormitory space, canteen,

[47] Archives of St. John Dūmā, Register recording names of borrowers and buyers.

study rooms and library had to be distinct from monks' cells, cellars, kitchen and church. According to oral testimony, seminary students also helped in the fields at harvest time.[48]

The opening of the Levantine markets and the arrival of foreign religious missions pushed local institutions to follow the missions' path, in order to benefit from the new economic and cultural opportunities available in the region. Regarding the Orthodox, the stakes were not only cultural and economic but also religious. The establishment of Protestant and Catholic mission schools was coupled with a proselytism practiced on a very large scale. Most of the converts to these new communities were recruited from among the Orthodox. The race to establish schools in the mountain villages was a source of competition, not only between the concerned communities but also between the interests of the powers backing them. At the beginning of the twentieth century, the small village of Shwayr saw the establishment on its territory of four schools: Russian, Protestant, Catholic and local. These schools were meant to gain the sympathy of the inhabitants towards the foreign powers and to advance their interests through linguistic teaching, cultural indoctrination, and religious conversions.[49] For the Greek Orthodox of the mountain, the establishment of a new bishopric in their region led to the concentration of efforts on education and religious teaching. This effort also aimed to improve the parish services to resist proselytism.

Dūmā, Kfar Ḥildā and Kfūr villages, surrounding St. John monastery, were in the same situation as Shwayr village, which benefited from its central location in Mount Lebanon. The opening of the school in the monastery was supposed to serve primarily the three villages, where the majority of the inhabitants belonged to the Greek Orthodox community.

The opening of the school proved to be positive for the monastery's revenues, although it only functioned for eleven years. In fact this school, which opened in 1911, had to stop its activities in 1914 due to the First World War. It reopened in 1920, and remained functioning until 1929. The accounts mention 212,344 piastres as the cost of buildings within the enclosure of the monastery. These works lasted from 1897 to 1915. Also during the same period, the school necessitated expenditures amounting to 18,603 piastres. But during the same period, the school provided the monastery with an income of 520,213 piastres, thus making a profit of 121,837 piastres. The school revenues could sometime exceed the revenues derived from agriculture. Along with the school's profitable activities came the sale of books, also profitable although more limited. Here too, the total of the

48 Interviews with Bishops Elias Ṣalībā (Ḥamā), Elias Qurbān (Tripoli), Elias Najm (Superior of Mār Elias).

49 ʿAun, 100-102.

sums earned over eleven years shows some net profit. During a few years the sale of books and stationery were clearly more than the mill revenues. But here, we notice an important investment regarding the library at the school opening. The first time was in 1911 and 1912 when the monastery spent 3,442 piastres and 5,401 piastres. The second time was in 1920 and 1921, when the monastery spent 2,917 and 9,560 piastres. These sums were recuperated over a few years. The balance sheet of these operations was far from being in deficit.

V. 2.3: General Balance Sheet

Study of the balance sheet (graph 13) over the 35 years of book-keeping gives a different picture of the monastery's supposed prosperity. Indeed the budget statement shows a deficit for 20 of the 35 years. However the gaps between revenues and expenses were not important. One year's losses were covered in the following year. Sometimes these losses resulted from supplementary expenses following a year of excess revenues. Although educational activities were very limited, agriculture remained the most important source of income. Except for the years 1895, 1911 and 1912, for which the total deficit was about 4,000 piastres only, agriculture revenues always exceeded expenses.

BIL Chart 12

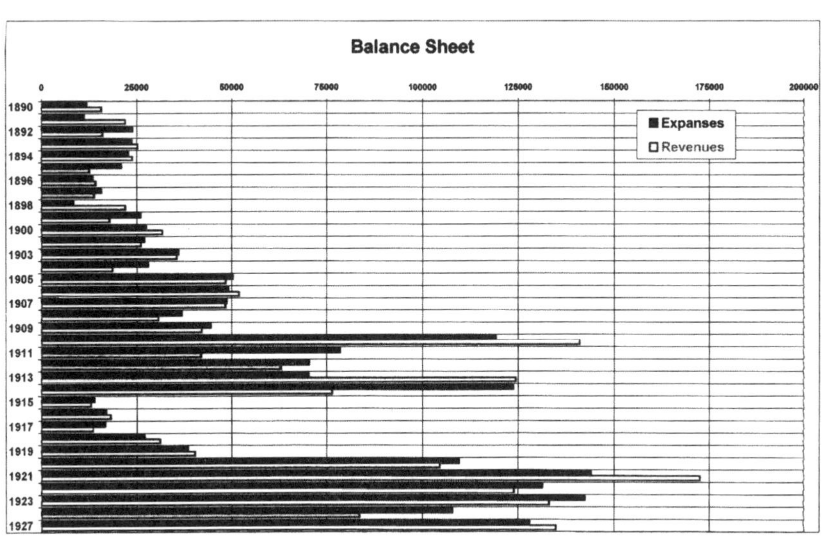

Graph 13 - General Balance Sheet of St. John Dūmā

Over this 35-year period the graph 13 shows that 1910 was the year with the highest agricultural revenues. They reached 136,194 piastres. During this year too, expenditures for the construction of the new wings reached their highest level. In fact, 65,453 piastres were paid in 1910 for the construction of school buildings. Effectively, the school opened its doors in 1911. The expenses necessitated at the eve of the opening could only be covered thanks to the excess in agricultural revenues.

The graph 13 also shows that during the 35 years under review, agricultural land revenues, although still important, decreased enormously. In the beginning, they amounted to 80 to 95% of the revenues, while after 1920 they were only 40 to 50%. As for the expenses, during the earlier years the monastery spent 60 to 75% of its revenues on the maintenance of agricultural lands. Following the First World War, land maintenance claimed only 10 to 20% of the total expenses. Was this evidence of the increasing lack of interest in agriculture, which started with the First World War? Or was it due to the fact that infrastructure works had been completed once and for all during the earlier years? Terrace construction, installation of irrigation canals, and quarrying stone were done only once, while ploughing, manuring, and maintenance had to be carried out at least annually.

Depending on the parcel, these expenses could be distributed over several years. The less important they were, the more crop revenues could be reinvested in other activities.

There were three years for which the agricultural balance sheet showed an excess of revenues over expenses: 1913, 1921 and 1927. As we can note in graph 13 profits obtained during these years were used to cover the losses in other years. These losses were not the results of bad crops, but were mainly due to the accumulation of deficits from the preceding years.

The graph of expenses and revenues shows a sharp rise during the time when the school is functioning. The curve for agricultural revenues rises gently. The increase in the volume of currency used, resulting from devaluation, is not too important. The opening of the boarding school had the greatest impact, not only on the economic level (increase of expenses and revenues), but also on the cultural and the social level.

The school was not only an asset for the village as far as culture was concerned, but it was also positive regarding the monastery's economy. It offerred the choice of a new way of life, different from the rural life. Amid this rural context, in this high mountain village, the choices of a profession had already started to diversify since the end of the 19th century. Emigration, public function, trade, services and finance already had their specialists. These tendencies increased with the establishment of the boarding school in the monastery.

Trade was already practiced in rural life. The village of Dūmā, was well known for its very important *sūq*.[50] But starting from the end of the 19th century and the beginning of the 20th, a change of exchanged products and destinations occurred.

Despite the rise of commerce, the different authorities that managed the agricultural estates always acted on the basis of a subsistence economy. The territory of the waqfs, and that of Mount Lebanon generally, was integrated into the market economy through mulberry monoculture and silk production; yet self-sufficiency in food persisted. Table menus, for example, included the agricultural produce of the monastic estate. At the start of the 20th century, the school pupils at St. John Dūmā, whether boarders or day-pupils, ate meals comprising the main products of the monastery's waqf lands.

The school's accounts were attached to those of the monastery, unlike Balamand, where the school's autonomy was clearly stated and maintained in the monastery's directives. At St. John Dūmā too, we can observe a difference in the style of administration. During the 19th century, Dūmā depended on the bishopric of Beirut. To this see Ghifrā'īl Shātīlā, the first Arab bishop since the schism of 1724, was elevated in 1870. He made it his task to recover the losses caused by the departure of his predecessor, the Greek bishop Irotheus, who had carried off all the revenues of the diocese before retiring to his native village in Greece. Shātīlā's policy partly explains the importance of investments and agricultural expenses at the end of the century. The monastery came under a new administration in 1902; once its functioning and sufficient income were assured, the new hierarchy progressively increased its share from 2,000 to 5,000 piastres. Previously, the monastery's accounts mention no special sums to be remitted to the bishopric of Beirut.

Emigration, which had already started during the 19th century, increased with the First World War and the economic crisis following it.[51] The educational vocation of this monastery, as of others, was short lived. In spite of the interest that the school had given the area and the church, it had to close its doors.

The world economic crisis of 1929 broke St. John of Dūmā monastery's expansion and was the main cause of the decline of Mount Lebanon's agricultural economy, after it had survived centuries of persecutions, Mamlūk military campaigns, and the different economic crises and demographic upheavals of the Ottoman period. Contrary to what we suppose, and in spite of the catastrophes caused by the First World War, it was in 1929 that the Lebanese economy started turning away from agriculture.[52]

---

50 al-Bāshā, 167, 231.

51 Youssef Courbage and Philippe Fargues, *Christians and Jews under Islam* (London: Tauris, 1997), 192.

52 Ibid., 192.

The waqfs, which were production centers and places of cultural and religious influence, entered a period of hibernation and decline. The exploitation of monastic lands had continued until recently by yearly sharecropping contracts through long-term tenant farming. But under the cover of land development contracts, sharecropping agreements were cancelled and turned into tenant-farming contracts for the benefit of certain notables.[53]

Monasteries that had at times around fifty sharecroppers working on their lands with their families, now entrusted their waqfs to notables or developers, who, in return for their investments, required their tenant-farming contracts to be drawn up for a period of 99 years.

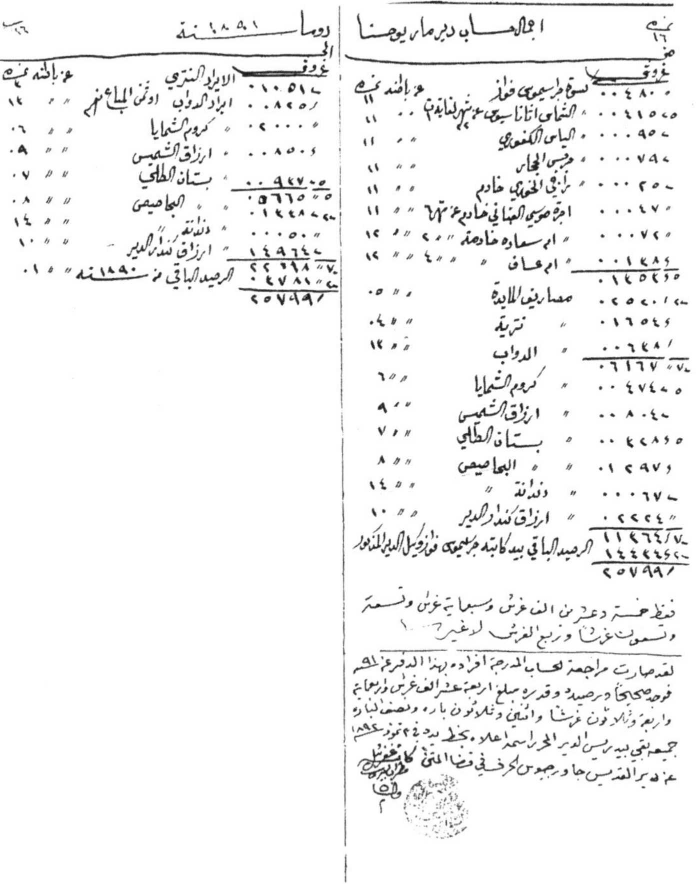

Doc 7 - Expanses and Revenues of the monastery of St. John Dūmā

[53] Masʿūd Ḍāhir, *al-Judhūr al-tārīkhiyyah li-l-masʾalah al-zirāʿiyyah al-lubnāniyyah 1900-1950* (Beirut: Lebanese University, 1983), 116.

V. 3: Exploitation of Urban Waqfs

The exploitation and management of urban waqfs was undertaken mainly by renting shops and houses belonging to the waqf. Rural properties attached to urban waqfs have been mentioned. In these properties, rents were not the main form of exploitation, but rather sharecropping in the form of the *musāqāt* contract. The scattering and fragmentation of waqfs in urban areas has also been mentioned. Study of the exploitation of urban waqf revenues reveals some important variations. Two regions provide sources for such study: Aleppo at the end of the 18th century and Beirut during the 19th century. This study does not include Syria; however, since the archives of the justice courts in Tripoli and Beirut have not yet provided waqf accounting documents, we must suppose that the two cities had the same judicial structures as did Aleppo.

The documents from Aleppo concern annual accounting reports made in the name of the community's bishop and submitted to the Muslim religious authorities. The documents from Beirut are more varied, but they were also drawn up at the episcopal see and approved by the courts. Some contracts were printed in Turkish and French. From rental contracts it is possible to make lists of prices, names, and places for some waqfs over a period of one or two years. These 19th-century waqfs, which were mainly managed by lay notables, are more difficult to examine than the waqfs of the previous era, which were administered by the bishop alone. In the period of emancipation of Christian communities, laymen took charge of all aspects of waqf business, such as leasing property, collecting rents, making accounts, preparing reports, registering with the authorities, paying taxes, and so on. This change at the level of waqf management is revealed in the archives and in accounting documents by a corresponding change in methods of presentation.

The absence of archives before the 19th century may be due to the fact that accounting reports by Christian waqfs were sent to Muslim courts in the main cities. Numerical data is arranged differently, either horizontally or vertically, for different centuries. Study of the ways in which waqfs were exploited reveals much about such diverse topics as the occupation of urban space, waqf revenues, co-existence of different communities, methods of payment, different currencies in use, conditions of exploitation, etc. Exploitation took place at different levels and in different forms. *Ījār* rents in the cities, for example, could be accompanied at a higher level by revenue-farming contracts.

Rental revenues were collected by notables or "banks" that guaranteed the Church a return by themselves paying in advance. *Ḍamān* and *Ījār* in the cities were comparable to *muzāraʿah* and *musāqāt* contracts in the countryside. The presence of Christian waqf documents in Muslim courts reveals the importance of local municipal authorities in the administration of the waqfs. Moreover, the extent and variety of 19th century archive material in the episcopal sees should not lead us to suppose that the Christian urban populations had become in any way independent of the courts. The accession of the Christians to full citizenship as a result of the Tanzimats did not of course release them from most of their legal obligations. Therefore waqf donations, *juʿliyyah* trials (in which family waqf was recuperated by religious waqf), and purchases, sales, and exchanges of lands by Christian religious institutions were all still supervised by those same courts. The judges remained the *qāḍīs* and *muftīs* of the city, and the witnesses were the same officials, whose names are written in the documents.

The data provided by the documents on the renting of shops and houses belonging to the waqfs of Aleppo and Beirut are partly numerical. Dates, rental amounts and duration are all given. Data describing real estate, legal regulations, details on the identity of tenants, and the different clauses of contracts constitute a body of information that is very useful in analysing the general urban situation. It is perhaps less useful for the quantitative and economic history of urban waqf administration. Nevertheless, here too the mass of qualitative information on tenants, quarters, and rents can be handled in a serial manner; this should reveal the functioning of a traditional institution which, by force of urban life and the particular historical moment, attempted to modernise and adapt to a new environment.

V. 3.1: Rented Premises in Aleppo in the 18th and 19th Centuries

Waqf accounts from Aleppo give information on the four Christian communities, one of which was called the Rūm.[54] At this period, the term probably meant the Greek Catholic community, which had become more numerous than the Greek Orthodox in Aleppo in the late 18th and early 19th centuries. The other three Christian communities mentioned in the documents are the Maronites, the Syrians, and the Armenians. In the case of the last two, it is not quite clear whether Uniate Catholic or Orthodox communities are referred to. This period was one of bitter and often violent conflict between the two communities.[55] Nevertheless, both Catholic and Orthodox at that time may still be regarded as parts of a single community in human, sociological, and economic terms.

---

54 The accounts are available in the National Archives at Damascus.

55 Hidemitsu Kuroki, "The Orthodox-Catholic Clash in Aleppo in 1818," *Orient* 23 (1993), 1-20.

These documents include accounts of the waqfs' income and expenditure. Income was provided mainly by rent from shops and houses belonging to the waqf. By examining the accounts of each community, it is possible to understand the inner workings of this kind of exploitation, which was very common in the cities. The chief official involved was the bishop, always named at the beginning of the document.

Accounts for the year 1229 (1813) state that the Rūm owned 17 houses, called *dār*, and eight shops, called *dukkān*. Different parcels of real estate are recorded under the names of individuals, each identified by his surname, first name, and profession, by the name of his father, or by the name of the district where the waqf was situated. Three persons were mentioned twice as tenants of houses or shops. The total rental income amounted to 717.5 piastres.

The Armenian waqf consisted of ten *dārs* and three *dukkāns*, with an income of 357 piastres and expenses of 396.75 piastres, resulting in a deficit of 39.75 piastres. The Maronite waqf owned four *dārs* and four *dukkāns*, with an income of 424 piastres. Expenses were 474 piastres, leaving a deficit of 50 piastres. The Syrian waqf owned 11 *dārs* and four *dukkāns* with an income of 464 piastres. Expenses necessary for maintenance and taxes amounted to 536 piastres, leaving a deficit of 72 piastres.

Communities	Revenues	Expenses	Deficit	Avanias (extrataxes)
Rūm	715.5	744.75	29.25	25
Armenians	357	396.75	39.75	27
Maronites	424	474	50	32.75
Syrians	464	536	72	40.5

Although the deficits were not very high, they were slightly higher for each community than the amounts paid for *avanias*, which came to 25, 27, 32.75, and 40.5 piastres for each community respectively.

In the listed revenues of houses and shops, an association of the property with other beneficiaries is mentioned several times. This may suggest that waqf in the urban environment was becoming more fragmented. A number of shops and houses belonged to several Christian communities in different quarters of the city. Probably these waqfs were concentrated in the so-called Christian quarters of Ḥārāt al-Naṣārā, Maḥallat Ṣalībiyyah, Maḥallat al-Akrād (the Kurds), Zuqāq al-Arbaʿīn (referring to the Forty Martyrs, a common place-name in the cities of Syria), Maḥallat al-Māwardī (rose-water), and al-Rawwās.[56]

---

56 André Raymond, "Alep à l'époque ottomane," *Revue du monde musulman et de la mediterranée*, no. 62 (1992).

As for the waqfs known by the names of tenants, it is not possible to say whether these are surnames or first names. After settling in a district or quarter, families were usually known either by their place of origin or by their profession. After a period of integration which could last for up to three generations or one century, families tended to divide into lineages, each of which took the first name of its founder. Thus, the surnames (which are also common first names) Qusṭanṭīn, Jirjis, Yaᶜqūb, Anṭūn, Yuwāṣaf, and Ghaḍbān are those of tenants among the Rūm. There is also the name of a woman, Hīlānah (Helen), among the tenants. First names are likewise found among tenants of other communities, such as Karkūr (Krikor or Gregory) and Wannis (John) among the Armenians; Jibrāyil and Ḍāhir among the Syrians; and Jirjis, which is certainly the most popular among all communities.

Very often in the towns, the inhabitants are known by their professions and trades, which are specified, for example: al-Jawharī (jeweller), al-ᶜAttār (perfume-seller), al-Khayyāṭ (tailor), al-Khūrī (priest), al-Qass (parson), al-Shammās (deacon). These names are common among both Greek Catholics and Greek Orthodox.[57]

Expenses are everywhere greater than revenues. They consist mainly of construction costs or roof repairs. The Rūm waqf was building new houses in three districts of Aleppo: Maḥallat al-Akrād, Zuqāq al-Arbaᶜīn, and al-Ṣalībiyyah. A relatively large sum of 261 piastres was allocated for the construction or repair of waqf *musaqqafāt.*

The word *taᶜmīr*, "construction," appears in another document under the word *tarmīm*, "repair," although the latter word is usually more applicable. The construction and repair of buildings belonging to Christian waqfs required, in addition to their cost, special authorisation that could hardly be obtained without paying more taxes or bribes.

Other expenses were necessary for liturgical celebrations; they concerned mainly the purchase of oil and candles. These were necessary for lighting and ceremonies and required an annual outlay of up to 170 piastres, a relatively large sum.

Other expenses imposed by the authorities were important. These included the *mīrī* and *avanias*. The value of the official *mīrī* tax was the same for all the city's Christian communities. The word *mīrī* was mentioned beside the word *shamaᶜa*, "candle," but this probably meant taxes on candles, whose price was stated with that of oil. This tax did not exceed five piastres.

The *avanias* amounted to large sums that seem disproportional to the income or wealth of the communities' waqfs. These *avanias*, listed un-

57 Salibi, xxii.

der the heading *ʿawāriḍ sulṭāniyyah*, were not regarded officially as unjust exactions. They are regularly collected by the city's religious authorities and recorded in the tax-registers as impositions of the sulṭān, the empire's supreme authority. They were imposed on each of the city's quarters and divided among the inhabitants.[58]

Archive documents reveal that the *avanias* were similar to the traditional poll-tax on the Christians known as the *jizyah*, and that they took into consideration the social and economic situation of the tax-payers. These *avanias* were invariably imposed from one year to another, since the official *mīrī* tax, imposed as a fixed tribute after the occupation of Syria by Sulṭān Salīm, was not sufficient to fill the coffers of the Ottoman treasury.[59]

Under the heading of "expenses" there were a number of items that may be grouped as administrative costs. The relatively high cost of registering documents and other formalities is marked down as payable to the scribe (*khidmat al-katabah*); it amounts to 25 piastres for the Greek Orthodox but is not mentioned in the accounts of the other communities.

With this sum goes a special stipend, also quite high, which is to be paid to the tax-collector, *al-jābī*. The Rūm and the Syrians pay large amounts to the tax-collectors – 40 piastres and 30 piastres respectively. The Armenians and the Maronites do not pay this stipend. We may ask whether the sums were so high in order to avoid bribing the tax-collectors, or rather an indirect, yet virtually official way of paying those very bribes and "gifts."

Other, much lower, registration and accounting charges were included in the documents. They seem to be taxes that had been fixed long before. The accounting tax varied from five to seven piastres according to the community. The registration tax, *qalamiyyah wa qaydiyyah*, did not exceed one piastre for each community.

One expense that was common to all the Christian communities was included in the accounts. This was the financial aid paid by each community to the poor. The mention of the phrase "service to the poor," *khidmat al-fuqarāʾ*, varies from one community to the other.[60] The Rūm do not mention it for the year 1229 A.H. The Armenians and the Maronites pay 176 and 131.75 piastres respectively. The Syrians do not mention the poor, but rather the parsons and their servants, *al-qusus wa-l-farrāshūn*. Very often the latter are recognised by the authorities as "poor and modest."

Various other expenses are mentioned. Important sums may be listed under a heading in the accounts of one community that is not found in the

---

58 Polk, 40-41.

59 Volney, vol. 2, 271.

60 Harīz, 102.

accounts of the others. Thus we may find the expenditure of 130 piastres for "community losses" in the Armenian accounts, 240 piastres for "community affairs" in the Syrian accounts, or 264.5 piastres for "necessary expenses" in the Maronite accounts.

Under the heading of expenses there is also a payment, common to all waqf accounts, known as *ḥikr*, meaning the subletting of waqf property. They are either grouped under the heading "various *aḥkār*" or distributed among several separate headings. The sums described as *ḥikr*, or *aḥkār* in the plural, differ widely for each community. They amount to 33.5 piastres for the Rūm, only seven piastres for the Armenians, and seven, eight, and sixteen piastres for the Syrians. The last community is the only one to include its cemeteries in its accounts, so that 16 piastres are registered as *aḥkār al-maqbarah*. It is not clear whether the revenue of these *ḥikrs* derived from the tax-farming of rural properties, or whether it was a fixed proportion of waqf revenues, owed to the administrator whom the bishop appointed to collect the rents of the waqf.[61]

V. 3.2: Rented Premises in Beirut in the late 19th and early 20th Centuries

The relevant sources date from the end of the 19th and beginning of the 20th centuries. They consist mainly of contracts between the tenants and the bishopric. These contracts are printed in booklets, in which each page contains two copies of the contract, one for the tenant and one to be kept by the bishopric. Two kinds of contract were drawn up by the bishopric, one dating from 1883 and the other from 1911. The first is written in Arabic; in addition to information about the property, it includes ten conditions written on each contract. The second specimen is written in French and Ottoman Turkish, a fact that reveals the simultaneous measures in favour of Turkish nationalism and modernisation taken by the Young Turk government, which came to power after 1907. The 1911 contract also states the rights and duties of both parties, although it is somewhat strict with regard to the tenant.[62] The 20th century contracts use a more precise juridical language than those of the preceding period. In particular, they give more details on certain conditions of payment or cancellation. According to the laws of the religious and political authorities, waqfs enjoyed privileges regarding rents and exchanges, because their revenues were destined for the poor and needy. Indeed, these contracts seem to have been specially drawn up for waqfs.

This kind of exploitation tended to create many kinds of problems that were often only resolved in the courts. Problems often arose between the

---

[61] Encyclopédie de l'islam, Nov. ed., s.v. "Waqf."

[62] Archives of the Greek Orthodox Bishopric of Beirut, nos. Bey 961, 963, 1141.

owner, in this case the waqf, and the tenant. Conflicts could also break out between the administrators, who were members of the community council, and the clergy, particularly the bishop. Extant documents reveal court trials that involved the administrators themselves, in cases where one or more of them were opposed by one of their colleagues. In short, several kinds of documents can give information about the ways in which urban waqfs were rented. Contracts, trials, correspondence, and accounts all shed light on some of the practices that coloured and influenced the lives of our ancestors.

The series of contracts consulted in the archives reveal a body of data that can be grouped over three years, 1883, 1887, and 1888. Most of these contracts were drawn up for the Waqf of the Poor of St. Georges's Church, one of the main Greek Orthodox waqfs in the city. Separately, there are contracts covering a single year for the Waqf of the Rūm Poor. Altogether, there is a total of 136 contracts; 23 for the Waqf of the Rūm Poor in 1883, 35 for the Waqf of St. Georges in 1883, 41 for the Waqf of St. Georges in 1887, and 37 for the same waqf in 1888. This series of documents gives data on the identity of tenants, the price of rents, the nature and location of properties, and the methods of payment. The contracts for the year 1887 are the most complete; they seem to provide the most accurate information on how urban waqf was utilised.[63]

The first item in the contract is always the identity of the tenant. His name appears at the top of the page, preceded by a title that helps to identify him. For example, the names of Christian tenants are preceded by the title *khawājah*, while the names of Muslim tenants are preceded by the titles *al-sayyid*, or sometimes *al-ḥājj*. Of 41 tenants listed for 1887, 16 were Muslim and 25 Christian. All these were in quarters regarded as mainly Christian, since they had churches, for example St. Georges, Nūriyyah, the bishopric, Birkat al-Muṭrān, and St. Nicolas in the quarter of Rmayl. These quarters also contained the main Greek Orthodox waqfs in Beirut. The tenant families were of very different backgrounds. They included bourgeois families native to the city, Sunnīs and Greek Orthodox who had long lived in co-existence. In contrast, the properties of the Waqf of the Rūm Poor had no Muslim tenants: all 23 of them bore the title *khawājah*. Since this waqf was the oldest, it was perhaps more resistant to communal intermixing at the levels of habitation and professional activity. Other tenants included Maronite and Greek Catholic families, one Jew, and several families newly arrived from the Mountain, Damascus, or Wādī al-Taym after the events of 1860.

---

63 Archive of the Greek Orthodox Bishopric of Beirut, nos. Bey 928, 929, 934.

One might suppose that after two decades these new families, having settled down and established themselves in business, might become fully integrated in the circuit of social-confessional relations. Such was not the case, however. In 1901 the leaders of the Damascene families settled in Beirut decided, on the model of the native Beirutis, to found an association that would help their co-religionaries in need and overcome the segregation, albeit minor, that was imposed by the native bourgeois of the city. One of the periodical reports of this association clearly states the wish of these families to retain their native customs and habits, which are a great deal more conservative and traditional than those of Beirut.[64] This attitude pleased the Church, which tended to distrust the modernisation of social and cultural life, and the attraction of many of its flock towards the Western Christian communities, both Latin and Protestant. The religious authorities naturally favoured this association. Moreover, new communities in the city were helped to survive and prosper by the mediation of the waqf. On their arrival, they were housed in waqf schools. Later, they often chose to rent shops belonging to the waqf, which were available either in the city-centre or in the new quarters.

Similarly, the sites and buildings rented by the waqf are very diverse. The different nature and function of rented buildings are described by the same terms in both the contracts and the inventories: shop (*dukkān*), house (*ḥārah*), bakery (*furn*), warehouse (*makhzan*), cellar (*qabw*), and room (*ʿudd*). Sometimes the same tenant rents two, three, or even four shops, but this is exceptional. The 41 rental contracts made by the Waqf of St. Georges in 1887 cover 30 shops, three *ḥārāt*, four warehouses, one cellar, two bakeries, and six rooms. The 23 contracts made by the Rūm Poor Waqf cover six shops, four *ḥārāt*, two cellars, one bakery, and 17 rooms. The Rūm Poor Waqf had more residential space available than the other waqfs. The rooms mentioned in the contracts are rented with kitchens. For example, two rooms with kitchen were rented in Rmayl and two rooms with kitchen in Sābā Alley for 800 and 400 piastres per annum respectively. Sometimes buildings rented to individuals are mentioned in the contract under the name of the original donator of the waqf. Thus, for the Rūm Poor Waqf there are four contracts referring to the *waqfiyyah* of Ḥannā al-Jammāl in the Rmayl district on River Street. This *waqfiyyah* comprised: a large *ḥārah* rented to *khawājah* ʿAṭallāh al-Ḥamawī for 3,550 piastres; a shop rented to Shwayrī al-Shaghūrī for 300 piastres; two rooms and kitchen rented to the same tenants for 800 piastres; and a *ḥārah* of three rooms, a kitchen, and a covered *dār* rented

64 Annual Report of the Association of Damascus Families, 1902.

to Andrāwūs and Salīm Faraḥ for 1,500 piastres. This waqf comprised a number of buildings for residence and commerce and yielded a fairly large annual income of 6,150 piastres.

Most of the rented commercial premises were held by the Waqf of St. Georges. This waqf owned many shops in the city-centre, in addition to cellars and warehouses that were useful for business.

Districts or quarters in the city are mentioned in the contracts, along with alleys and *sūqs*. The quarters are the same as those stated in the inventories, except that the rental contracts very often name the quarter after a particular family with which it is associated. The word *ḥārah* is also used to mean "quarter." For example, the contracts of the Waqf of St. Georges mention ḥārah bayt Ṭrād and ḥārat bayt Būstrus, while those of the Rūm Poor Waqf mention ḥārat bayt al-Jubaylī and ḥārat bayt Sursuq eight and three times respectively.

The new layout of the city transformed even the old buildings of the city wall. Thus Burj al-Kashshāf (the guard tower) became Ḥārāt al-Arnaʾūṭiyyah, named after the Ottoman janissaries who garrisoned the city. In this old military building, the waqf owned a *ḥārāt* of six rooms rented to Asʿad Ṣahyūn for 900 piastres. In 1887, one of the city gates is mentioned in four contracts that cover altogether one house and four shops. Bakeries, it seems, were essential elements in city waqfs. The two waqfs considered here owned three bakeries, one of which delivered bread to the bishopric by contractual requirement. The tenant of this bakery was Muslim and paid an average rent of 1,800 piastres. The other two bakeries, one in ḥārat bayt Būstrus and one in Rmayl, were rented for 2,140 piastres and 1,400 piastres respectively.

The locations of the waqf rented premises show that urban space was utilised to the utmost. Several contracts mention churches as landmarks. These are, principally: the Maronite Church of St. Georges (mentioned three times), the Greek Orthodox Church of St. Georges (mentioned eight times), the Chapel of al-Nūriyyah (mentioned three times), and the Church of St. Nicholas (mentioned four times). It is clear from this data that the facades of these churches were surrounded by shops. For example, locations are described by phrases such as "near the door of the Church of St. Georges," "above the door of the church," "below the bishopric," "to the south" or "to the west of the church." Six contracts mention shops or rooms near church doors, which suggests a state of overcrowding. The waqf sought to remedy this problem by demolishing several houses and shops in order to build the Sūq of St. Georges and open up access to the church.

Rents are paid for three months, six months, or one year in advance. It is not possible to give the sum total of revenues derived from waqf rentals.

But a comparison of the names of districts with the nature of rented premises reveals some shops and warehouses whose rents rose slightly over a period of five years (1883 to 1888). We do not know if the tenant gained a rent rebate by paying in advance. These rents clearly reveal the priority accorded to commercial rentals. Shop rentals are higher than those of houses and *ḥārāt*. There were also large price differences among shop rentals. The level of rent depended on size, position, goods sold, but also the number of doors (not mentioned in these contracts). Commercial rentals include warehouses, which were most profitable to the waqf. Warehouses were used for storing goods and permitted merchants to import in bulk, thereby paying lower purchase prices per item. The warehouses of Sūq al-Ḥaddādīn were rented for 1,900 piastres per annum in 1883. Those of Sūq al-ᶜAttārīn were rented for 2,750 piastres in 1888, and those of Sūq al-Quṭun for 3,600 piastres in the same year. Some shops were rented with working equipment. One contract of 1883, for example, specified that the shop contained six dyeing-vessels.

Houses, although larger, were not as profitable for the waqf. A *ḥārah* above the door of the church was rented in 1883 for 430 piastres, rising to 600 piastres in 1888. Housing rents in the new quarters were higher. A ground-floor house in the district of Rmayl was rented for 1,700 piastres in 1888.

Ḥārah-houses belonging to the Rūm Poor Waqf were expensive: one at Sūq al-Khamāmīr in ḥārat bayt al-Jubaylī was rented for 1,600 piastres and another at Rmayl for 3,550 piastres in 1883. Most rents due to this waqf were paid monthly.

It is interesting to note that one tenant might make two contracts for two different places in the same waqf. For example, in 1883 Ṣāliḥ Kanᶜān rented a room for 180 piastres per month and two cellars for 120 piastres per month in Sursuq Alley. We do not know whether both rentals were in the same building. The total rent paid was 3,600 piastres per annum.

Contrary to the widespread notion that waqf rentals were stable and long-term, the turnover of tenants appears to have been high. In the three years – 1883, 1887, 1888 – for which contracts are available, less than half of the tenants are mentioned for every single year. Was this turnover due to economic difficulties, to emigration, or to the transfer of residence and business outside the city walls? The stable tenants are mainly Muslim merchants who occupied the *sūqs* specialising in crafts and traditional commerce near the Orthodox and Maronite Churches of St. Georges.

The problems of administering urban waqfs were not limited to individual court cases. Delays in payment, petitions made by tenants, farming contracts offered by banks to the bishopric, the judgements of civil and religious tribunals – all these show that conflicts were common and involved many people. In particular, the administration of Greek Orthodox waqf rentals in Beirut posed problems for both tenants and waqf officials.

As an example of the former case, in 1912 the tenants of the Waqf of St. Georges addressed a petition to Bishop Jirāsīmūs Masarrah, complaining of the difficult economic situation. These tenants asked the bishop to intervene on their side in the conflict between them and the waqf administrators. They asked the bishop to reduce by 25 to 30 % those rents that they had not been able to pay for two or three years.[65] However, after several delays most of the tenants were evicted, and in 1914 only five recalcitrants were still refusing to quit. One of these was a merchant renting two warehouses and another lawyer renting an office in St. Georges Street. These five tenants had not only stopped paying rents due by contract to the waqf administrators, but they had also ceased paying official taxes due to the Ottoman authorities, particularly the *wirko* fixed tax on real estate. For this reason, measures were taken by the representative of the town-clerk of Beirut to cancel the rental contracts.[66] The tenants, who seem to have been well-informed, invoked a novel interpretation of new laws decreed by the government. These forbade eviction in cases such as this and allowed tenants to make a rental contract with the official *ijrāʿiyyah* rent authorities. Such a contract was initially made for three years and allowed delays of payment for fixed periods, thereby giving the tenants ample opportunity to pay according to their means. In the view of the tenants, this contract could not be cancelled and did not permit their eviction, for eviction would have to be preceded by a court case against each of the tenants and each case would certainly result in a demand for payment, not eviction. In this juridical interpretation, the tenants were invoking the special waqf status of the rented premises, which exempted them from many of the laws and formalities enforced in public life. Moreover, the new laws exempted the waqfs from paying many taxes, according to the moratorium rule that had recently been published in the newspapers.[67]

From other court cases and letters concerning other tenants, all dating from 1915, we learn that unpaid rents were subject to interest of 15%. The tenants had only paid 5%, and the waqf administrators demanded that the bishop pay the remaining 10% in their place, "so that things should be done

[65] Archives of the Greek Orthodox Bishopric of Beirut, no. Bey 1573.

[66] Ibid.

[67] Ibid.

according to the rules *al-uṣūl*," i.e. in order to avoid a court case and the evictions that would follow.[68]

Other conflicts may also have been provoked by economic crisis. These conflicts involve the waqf administrators responsible for making contracts and collecting rents. In 1914, a large number of them advised the bishop to summon two administrators to pay sums that they owed the waqf. Otherwise the community council would be forced to mortgage their belongings and place seals on their property until the waqf could recover its revenues. The amounts in question were rents on urban properties; they were normally collected by *wakīl*-administrators and sent to the waqf, which was now administered by the community council. The two administrators were accused by their colleagues of making contracts for their own profit. The members of the council summoned them to pay at least one-third of the waqf's revenues within 15 days, or they would be taken to court. For more than a year the council had received no waqf revenues. The losses, both from tenants who refused to pay and to quit the premises, and from administrators who did not remit revenues to the waqf treasury, seem to have been very considerable.[69]

Such conflicts must have been serious, for very large sums were at stake. These sums paid for the operation of all the waqfs' institutions and associations. Yet it seems too that they were a source of private profit for a group of notables and financiers. Thanks to the documents that concern these conflicts, we have a better understanding of how waqf rents were collected. The financial responsibilities of the community council covered all the waqfs belonging to the community in the city. The economic crisis that occurred a few years before the First World War reveals the personal interest of important financiers and bankers in this matter. The vacation of waqf commercial premises could permit a further increase in waqf rentals. In this same year (1912), the bishopric received an offer from three bankers to farm the rents of the Greek Orthodox community in Beirut. They simply offered an increase of ten and a half pounds (one pound equalled 100 piastres) over and beyond the amount reached at the auction. Another more complex proposal offered 10,000 piastres extra each year, if the proponents could have the farm of waqf rentals for four years, along with the right to manage the shops that were already rented. This proposal specified that payment would be made in two instalments, one immediately after the agreement was made and the other after six months. A note also specified that the bank making the proposal would guarantee the operation.

---

[68] Ibid.

[69] Ibid., no. Bey 1520.

A third offer proposed simply to farm the rents of Sūq St. Georges according to the prices and conditions fixed by the bishop.[70]

These proposals all came from well-known banks in the city. These were family-owned banks established on the basis of commercial and industrial businesses whose capital had been formed over one or more generations. These new financial institutions were a recent development in the cities and ports of the Levant. What is surprising is that modern businesses like these banks should have resorted to obsolete traditional practices that even the Ottoman Empire was trying to abandon. The farming of revenues was essentially a method of fiscal collection. It was tied to the military and administrative organisation of the whole empire and was associated with many financial and fiscal measures. With the coming of the empire's reform policy, revenue-farming was regarded as the source of all evils. Although suppressed several times, it was always soon re-established because it brought the treasury more revenues, more quickly, than any other method of collection.[71]

Obsolete though it was, the form of revenue-farming adopted by the waqf and the banks at the beginning of the 20th century was, for the waqf, a quick way of recovering the losses incurred because of economic crisis and conflicts with tenants. For their part, the bankers were sure of taking a percentage of the rents collected and so profiting from their guaranteed services to the waqf.

The urban waqf was being renewed and modernised by measures such as decentralisation, the creation of institutions, and the appointment of laymen to the management of the Church's affairs. Nevertheless, it did not shrink from resorting to traditional methods in order to expand its revenues and re-establish its economic viability.

New methods of exploitation, capital accumulation, interest-bearing loans, and the existence of banks, albeit family-owned: all are to be found in the framework of urban waqf administration. Yet they did not prevent the waqf from remaining above all a traditional institution.

---

[70] Ibid.

[71] Young, vol. 5, 305-307.

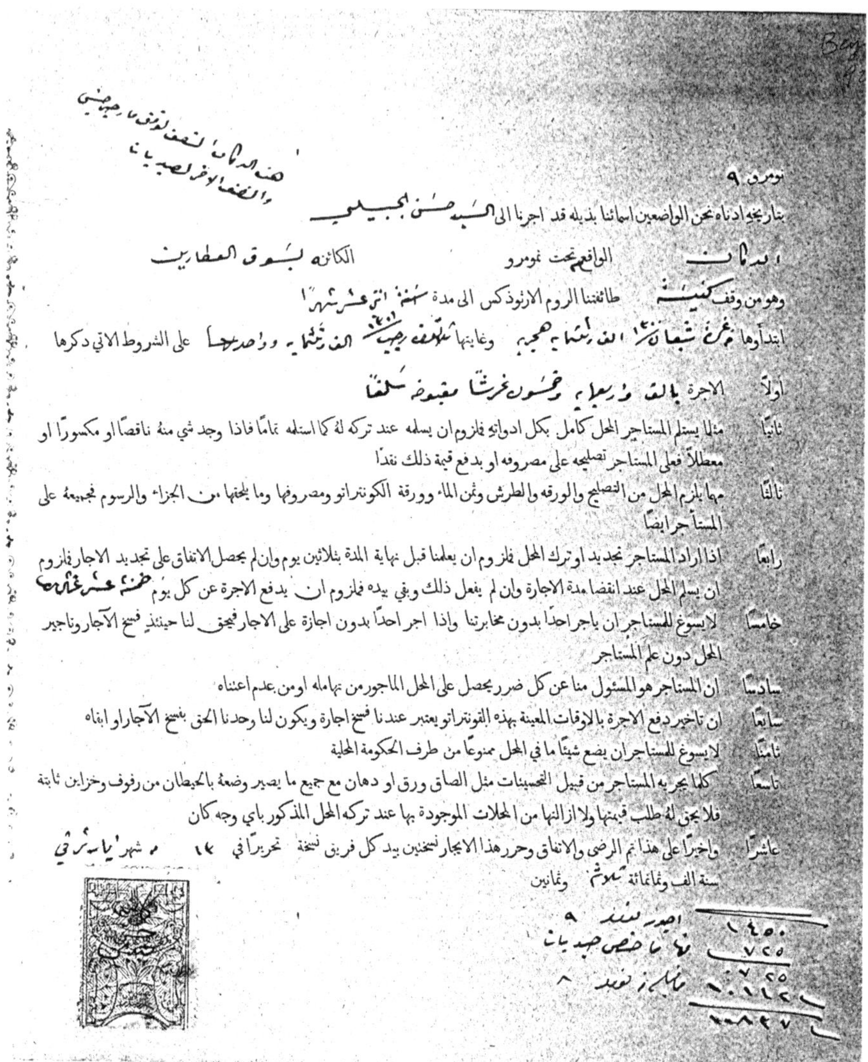

نومرو ٩

بتاريخه ادناه نحن الواضعين اسمائنا بذيله قد اجرنا الى

الواقعه تحت نومرو الكائنه بسوق العطارين

وهو من وقف طائفتنا الروم الارثوذكس الى مدة سنة اثني عشر شهرًا

ابتدأوها وغايتها على الشروط الاتي ذكرها

اولاً الاجرة بالف واربعماية وخمسون غرشا مقبوض سلفا

ثانيًا مثلما يستلم المستاجر المحل كامل بكل ادواته فملزوم ان يسلمه عند تركه له كما استلمه تمامًا فاذا وجد شي منهُ ناقصًا او مكسورًا او معطلاً فعلى المستاجر تصليحه على مصروفه او بدفع قيمة ذلك نقدًا

ثالثًا مهما يلزم المحل من التصليح والورقه والطرش وثمن الماء وورقة الكونترانو ومصروفها وما يلحقها من الجزاء والرسوم فجميعهُ على المستأجر ايضًا

رابعًا اذا اراد المستاجر تجديد او ترك المحل فملزوم ان يعلمنا قبل نهاية المدة بثلاثين يوم وان لم يحصل الاتفاق على تجديد الاجار فملزوم ان يسلم المحل عند انقضا مدة الاجارة وان لم يفعل ذلك وبقي بيده فملزوم ان يدفع الاجرة عن كل يوم

خامسًا لايسوغ للمستاجر ان ياجر احدًا بدون مخابرتنا واذا اجر احدًا بدون اجازة على الاجار فيحق لنا حينئذٍ فسخ الآجار وتاجير المحل دون علم المستاجر

سادسًا ان المستاجر هو المسئول منا عن كل ضرر يحصل على المحل الماجور من تهامله او من عدم اعتنائه

سابعًا ان تاخير دفع الاجرة بالاوقات المعينة بهذه القونترانو يعتبر عندنا فسخ اجارة ويكون لنا وحدنا الحق بفسخ الآجار او ابقاه

ثامنًا لايسوغ للمستاجر ان يضع شيئًا ما في المحل ممنوعًا من طرف الحكومة المحلية

تاسعًا كلما يجريه المستاجر من قبيل التحسينات مثل الصاق ورق او دهان مع جميع ما يصير وضعهُ بالحيطان من رفوف وخزاين ثابتة فلا يحق لهُ طلب قيمتها ولا ازالتها من المحلات الموجودة بها عند تركه المحل المذكور باي وجه كان

عاشرًا واخيرًا على هذا تم الرضى والاتفاق وحرر هذا الايجار نسختين بيد كل فريق نسخة تحريرًا في ١٢ شهر سنة الف وثمانماية وثمانين

١٤٥٠
٧٢٥

Doc 8 - Deed of Location of the Waqf of Beirut 1883

CONCLUSION

We have noticed in this research a series of elements that were essential to the evolution of waqfs among the Greek Orthodox of Lebanon during the Ottoman period. Certain of these aspects were common to the other communities and depended on measures taken by the Ottoman authorities; others were specific to certain regions and villages of Mount Lebanon.

Regarding the foundation of Greek Orthodox monasteries in the mountain, we may say that this was a movement of renewal, which took place quite late by comparison with other communities. *Mīrī* lands belonging to the *tīmār* were ceded, rented or sold to the monasteries. The Greek Orthodox had no political leaders among the tax-farming class of Mount Lebanon and so they were unable during this period to acquire lands, which was not the case for the other communities. Also, their numbers were fewer in the mountain than the Maronites or the Druze and their notables were mainly urban merchants. The foundation of waqfs, favoured by the change of the administrative system from *tīmār* to *iltizām*, did not benefit the Greek Orthodox, except where they were numerically significant and possessed an important community. This was the case at Balamand in Kūrah, for example, where they also had a political agent in the entourage of the wālī of Tripoli. In the mountain, however, the secretaries and treasurers of the emirs who acted as governors and tax-farmers were Maronites and Greek Catholics. In this situation, the foundation of waqfs was a way of regrouping the followers of a confession around religious institutions.

Founded with the aid of the notables, the waqfs soon rivalled and surpassed both them and the *muqāṭaʿjīs* in the extent of their lands and wealth. The period during which waqfs were founded, like the period before, was restrictive in that the measures taken by the Ottoman Porte with regard to waqfs were generally contrary to the precepts of Islamic *sharīʿah*. Confiscations and alienations were made to restrain the extent of waqfs, just as waqfs were being constituted from *mīrī* lands, all in response to the particular socio-economic situation in each period. All these actions were in contradiction with the state's duty of protecting religious property and institutions, and with the condition that a waqf could only be sound (*ṣaḥīḥ*) if it were constituted from *mulk* property.

These measures, whether restrictive or favourable to waqf, were applied to both Christian and Muslim communities. The Christian communities had moved their religious centres to monasteries in the mountains; popular piety became fixed on these institutions as centres of pilgrimage, prayer, refuge and great liturgical feasts. All these were occasions for believers to manifest their religious identity and reinforce their community spirit. Whereas the Maronites usually made donations in land, the Greek Orthodox did so in money. Land was at this time the main source of production and wealth, so that even money donations were soon reinvested in land. Nevertheless, not only money and land were donated: manuscripts, icons, liturgical objects and other more utilitarian objects were also constituted in waqf.

With the expansion of waqfs through the purchase of *mulk* lands or the renting of *mīrī* lands, the monasteries were transformed into centres of production and distribution. A study of the acts of acquisition of the monastery of St. Elie Shwayyah shows that this monastery's land expansion began in the second half of the 18th century. The expansion took place along with a diversification of production and regional specialisation. This monastery was a stronghold of the Greek Orthodox in a region where the Uniates were established in force, and where the struggle among different religious factions was very important. Naturally the monastery became a centre of influence for several pressure groups. After the monastery was refounded and the Shihāb and Abīllamaᶜ emirs had granted tax-farming rights to Niqūlā Jubaylī notable, who were very influential in Beirut, the monastic superiors were mainly members of the local clergy, attached to the bishops and notables of Mount Lebanon. After the first half of the 19th century, the Uniate party was strengthened and the superiors of the monastery came to be Greek nationals. The whole ecclesiastical hierarchy of the Greek Orthodox community was Hellenised. The Greek patriarchs were closer to the Ecumenical patriarchate, and therefore to the Ottoman authority; they were better able to defend the interests of the Greek Orthodox of the patriarchate of Antioch.

This period is essential in that it demonstrates the access that the monasteries had to the local courts of justice. The Greek monastic superior was allied to the *muqāṭaʿjīs*, formerly Druze and now Maronite, and also on good terms with the Egyptian governors; the local inhabitants resorted to him for justice and he handed down judgements. Towards the end of the 19th century, the patriarchal see of Antioch was taken back by Arab nationals; at this time Russian monks came to live in the monastery and constructed new buildings and installations. The Imperial Russian Association for Palestine built a school there.

From the 18th century, this monastery acted as a deposit bank for wealthy Greek Orthodox of the Matn and the town of Zaḥlah in the Biqāᶜ. Through its sharecropping contracts, it also acted as a lending bank to the peasants who worked the monastic lands, repaying their debts after the delivery of the harvest. These loans were offered at interest rates of 10-12%; they are clearly recorded in the monastery's accounts.

The financial role of the monasteries of Mount Lebanon resembled in a way the practice of waqf *al-nuqūd*, which permitted loans on interest, forbidden in principle by Islam. This kind of waqf was very common among Muslim waqfs during the Ottoman period; it was an adoption of traditional local customs that went back to the Byzantine era. This financial activity undertaken by Christian and Muslim waqfs was essential for providing the cash deposits needed by the population in various circumstances.

The administration of the waqfs also contradicted Islamic *sharīʿah* law. The Ottoman reforms of the 19th century handed over the administration of waqfs to laymen. These measures weakened the *ʿulamāʾ* class who had lived from these waqfs since time immemorial. The measures weakened the Greek Orthodox clergy too, but the impact of the reforms was different for each of the two communities. Among the Muslims, the new and inexperienced administrators employed by the State impoverished the waqfs to such an extent that their revenues could no longer support them. Their buildings deteriorated and their institutions fell into decay. In contrast, among the Greek Orthodox, the laymen charged with adminstering the waqfs were drawn from among the urban notables of Beirut. They were experienced in managing business affairs, were open to modern innovations and possessed much wealth in the form of commercial and financial businesses and property. These new, and sometimes old, aristocrats became the leaders of their community.

The organisation of the waqf, which had long been in the hands of a bishop or patriarch, became decentralised. The four monasteries of the mountain which depended on Beirut now each had its own *hygoumené* responsible for all the monastery's affairs: administration, spiritual and liturgical life, agriculture, hospitality etc. To these duties were added, at the end of the 19th and the beginning of the 20th century, reponsibilities for the new schools, such as teaching and housing of pupils. In the city also, there was a decentralisation, seen in the breaking-up of the great traditional waqf centres and the establishment of new churches and especially new institutions run by charitable associations. The new lay administrators were mostly sympathetic to the national/liberal ideology of the era and were not necessarily confessional in their thinking and behaviour; nevertheless, it had become clear to them that their prosperity and the progress of their business affairs were tied to the prosperity of their community.

This growing difference at the level of community development and prosperity had a harmful effect on inter-confessional understanding and coexistence. Although there were no serious incidents or problems, the Christian bourgeoisie, which was already under Western influence, now came to identify itself with the European way of life. The waqfs extended this influence, generalising it to the rest of the population through the schools, which were conceived along European lines. Just at the moment when the Ottoman Porte had established legal equality among the communities and had suppressed distinctions in clothing, other elements of community differentiation arose in the society of the time.

Education was a great value, which from the start of the 20th century became a means of social emancipation. It now came to be regarded more highly than agriculture. Waqfs which derived their income and profits from food production now seemed unsuited to the aims and ambitions of the new society. A negative and deprecatory attitude towards waqfs entered the minds of people along with the new ideas and modern ways of life. The reform of waqf administration, which was intended to make it more efficient, seems ironically to have been responsible for the beginning of the waqf's decline.

Regarding the mobility of waqf lands, it may be said that although they were permanent and their sale was forbidden, these lands were nevertheless rented, exchanged, given in sharecropping contracts, leased etc. According to the clauses of Islamic *sharīᶜah* law, all these procedures could take place in the interest of the waqfs, whether they were Christian or Muslim. Muslim courts of justice nearly always gave favourable judgements to religious institutions. The immobility of waqf domains was the basic reason for the accumulation of land by these foundations.

Even apart from the fact that private properties inevitably disintegrated due to successive partitions, waqf domains were in any case more productive, contrary to the opinion that waqfs were reluctant to adopt new techniques and were a source of economic stagnation. Indeed, new cultures were first adopted in the monastic estates. The monks were innovators in the field of agrarian development. In Kūrah in North Lebanon, for example, the first banana plantation and the first cypress windbrakes were planted by the convent of Our Lady of Kaftūn. Likewise, the monastery of Balamand was the first to obtain authorisation from Sulṭān ᶜAbd al-Ḥamīd to cultivate top-quality tobacco. In the 19th century, when most of the country depended on mulberry cultivation, the monasteries had a much more diversified economy. When the Lebanese silk industry collapsed and the producers were ruined, there was no longer a need for mulberries. The monasteries, which already had experience in a diversified agrarian economy, helped the population to overcome the crisis.

The change from one form of cultivation to another was not merely a matter of a different technique. It was also a social and political problem, since agriculture was not only a source of income but a way of life. Over the centuries, the monasteries have played the role of a ministry of agriculture, introducing new forms and methods of cultivation. Experimentation leading to productivity growth took place on monastic lands first. Once the success of a new crop had been established there, the general population could adopt them. In the event of failure, only the monastery would suffer losses. This experience of changing agriculture and crop diversity was not restricted to the production of waqf lands alone, but was an important factor in the general influence of waqf institutions.

The mobility of waqfs is not only a matter of their landholdings but also applies to their liquid assets and vocation. During the Ottoman period, waqf foundations responded to the demands and needs of the population. Originating as ascetic institutions devoted to prayer and the spiritual life, the waqfs expanded their landholdings and became centres of production and distribution of labour. From the middle of the 19th century, these monasteries began to devote their agricultural revenues to schools, which were established in the ancient cells and great halls of the old monasteries. Such was the case at St. Elie Shwayyah, St. John Dūmā and Our Lady of Balamand. Other initiatives, specifically aimed at the needs of the city, were offered by the Poor waqfs of the churches of Beirut. Their schools, hospitals, orphanages, asylums and other institutions all formed what may be regarded as a nascent civil society amid the galloping pace of modernity at the end of the 19th century.

The evolution of waqf among the Greek Orthodox of Mount Lebanon was clearly tied to their history in the Ottoman world. The waqf was indeed an organ of social solidarity, but it was also a tool of political and economic power; its study may help us to follow the emergence of a new social category.

The relation between the waqfs and the notables has often been stressed in historical research, yet it should not be forgottent that the governing elite underwent some thoroughgoing upheavals over the centuries.

The founders and donators of waqfs in the 16th and 17th centuries were governors and tax-farmers of the different districts: Sīfā and Ayyūbī for Balamand, Abīllamaᶜ for St. Elie and Shihāb for St. John Dūmā. These families were Druze or Sunnī. The monasteries and the Christian communities were protected by the *muqāṭaᶜjī* leaders of the different regions and formed part of their clientele. In the 18th century there arose Christian families who, because of their political and cultural emancipation and economic prosperity, became more and more influential in public life and with the monasteries and clergy. This new social class was formed of tax-farming businessmen, installed in the towns but retaining interests in the mountain. Such whose the family of Niqūlā Jubaylī at Beirut and St. Elie Shwayyah and the Maᶜlūf family at Dūmā. These handled formalities with the local authorities and established the religious orders in their properties and, in so doing, reinforced their own local authority.

Responsibility for the administration of the institutions of the church moved on several occasions from laymen to clerics, and vice-versa. But with the period of the *tanzimat*, the modernisation of the Ottoman Empire's structure and the development of a civil society, laymen established their domination over the affairs and property of the church. This category of notables was formed from the new bourgeoisie of city merchants and financiers, who frequently reinvested their profits in purchasing land or in leasing the great waqf estates. The change in the personnel of waqf founders and administrators was accompanied by a change in the means of exploitation of the great estates. The contracts made between peasant cultivators and big landowners at first presupposed that part of the land would pass into the peasant's hands. But the transfer of the status of *mulk* and *mīrī* lands into waqf lands resulted in a change from *muzāraᶜah* contracts into *musāqāt* contracts in which the peasant cultivator could only claim a part of the crop, since waqf lands remained indivisible.

With the decline of agriculture and the growing rural exodus, most of the monasteries began to cancel the sharecropping contracts and lease their lands to big urban and rural merchants and financiers. These monasteries at first profited from quick cash returns, which were used to establish seminaries and schools. But these profits were soon devalued because of inflation and the abandonment of agriculture.

The waqf institution also sheds light on relations between city and countryside. These relations, often described as hostile, were economic, human and cultural in nature. Through their fiscal demands, the cities had long been stripping the countryside of its wealth. Very often the waqfs were located in the mountains and other rural areas, while their beneficiaries were institutions and *mutawallīs* based in the cities. The establishment of monasteries in the mountain was made possible by the initiative of city notables of Beirut and Tripoli. But this period, the 18th and 19th centuries, seems to have witnessed an attempt to restore relations that were more to the advantage of the mountain. Everywhere else in Syria, the countryside had been devastated by the rise of bedouin tribes. The cities were places of refuge protected by the central government. But Mount Lebanon during this period was itself a place of refuge, assuring security to its inhabitants. The mountain, which in this period was experiencing rapid demographic growth, represented a place of refuge for the notables, who were welcomed by the monasteries in time of war or epidemic. Here exchanges of services were rendered, but also exchanges of products and merchandise.

This alliance between clergy and notables cannot mask the various conflicts that broke out in the religious orders of all the communities at the start of the 19th century. For example, the monks of Aleppo separated from the local monks, called Baladites by the Maronites and Shwayrites by the Greek Catholics. These different schisms caused the division of waqfs and the transfer of monks from one monastery to another. Not until the end of the 19th century did the Greek Orthodox experience such a conflict and in the event they resolved it. In 1901, the diocese of Beirut, which included Mount Lebanon, was divided into two bishoprics: the bishopric of Beirut, reduced to the city and its close suburbs, and the bishopric of Jbayl and Batrūn, which included all the monasteries of Mount Lebanon.

This schism, which was in principle made for the benefit of the mountain, did not in fact do so, for the general situation of the period was tending to bring about a decline of agriculture. In the years before this conflict, the monasteries attached to the patriarchate or to the bishops had to provide regular cash returns but also had to supply their institutions with food, firewood etc. The agricultural lands, which were a main source of wealth during this period, and especially the great extent of waqf land, were the main stake in this conflict. The conflict reveals a Greek Orthodox attitude quite different to that of the other communities of the mountain. The monasteries under the direct rule of the towns were quite impoverished on the eve of this schism. Their surpluses and profits, instead of being invested locally, were sent to the towns. Even the inhabitants of the villages, the peasants and the secular clergy, complained about the attitude taken towards them by the urban clergy and lay notables. This attitude tended to deepen the cultural divide and to envenom already poor relations, but above all to devalue an ancestral way of life organised around agriculture.

There are several indications that the waqf acted as a centre of production and a supplier to the international market. Among a range of agricultural products, the one that was specially grown for export was silk. The production and marketing of silk gave rise to a very detailed and complicated accounting system. The profits from silk were gained by European, particularly French, companies that drew their supplies from Mount Lebanon. Silk was exported in the form of cocoons, skeins and cloth. Silk was not the only product exported to Europe or sold in the cities: oil, soap and even wine were also sold by the monasteries' commercial agents. Despite the tendency to a mulberry monoculture, wheat was still widely grown in the mountain, and *ṣalīkh* lands were still acquired by the monasteries. We may ask whether the superiors of the Greek Orthodox monasteries were neglected by European businessmen or were themselves reluctant to work with the Latins. Did they have fewer contacts with French merchants, or did they prefer to export their silk to Syrian towns where it was woven in Arab style?

We know that in the 19th century most of the business intermediaries working in the silk export trade were Greek Orthodox of Beirut and Tripoli, but also of Hims, Alexandria, Izmir and other places. These merchant notables formed part of the community councils of the different dioceses.

Market economy and subsistence economy coexisted; trade with the Syrian cities and trade with Europe complemented each other. The context of the Ottoman Empire encouraged many kinds of solidarity, both Christian-Muslim and intraconfessional. The great waqf domains supplied the market for silk and, in part, the demand for food also. They also facilitated the collection of taxes and provided disposable cash for village communities or urban confessional groups.

The study of urban and rural Greek Orthodox waqfs during the Ottoman era, with attention to their foundation, expansion and administration offers a variety of contradictory and complex situations. The waqf served both the wealthy and the poorest class. Whether immobilised or active, open or closed upon themselves, archaic or progressive, these institutions reproduced the problems of Ottoman society yet profited from its structures. The study of their history will help us better to understand the present situation of the waqfs and to increase their potential value.

APPENDIX

Actual Situation of Waqf

This study of the waqf in the Christian communities during the Ottoman era has been prompted by the present condition of these great domains, which are now in a regrettable state of dilapidation and neglect. Having once played an essential social and political role, they are now reduced, for the most part, to a pitiful level in several aspects:

Economic. Most farmland has been left fallow or is being cultivated in a very superficial and unprofitable manner. Urban waqf properties have long been rented out to private citizens for ridiculous amounts that do not even cover their upkeep.

Social. Since the second quarter of the past century, waqf tenants have sought to reinvest in industry, housing and construction. Since agriculture is no longer a profitable activity, the great estates have been broken up and sharecropping contracts cancelled. Although the sharecropping tenants were fairly indemnified at the time, our mountain towns and villages today present a dismal spectacle of desolation, with abandoned houses everywhere except the Biqāᶜ, ᶜAkkār and southern Lebanon.

Human. The problem of the administration of waqfs remains a serious bone of contention among cultivators, administrators and beneficiaries of charity institutions, family waqfs and properties belonging to pious foundations. Each party tries to reap the greatest profit possible without going to the source of the problem and without seeking to reinvest income for the benefit of the community. If that were to happen, the restoration of these properties might become the core of a development project for the whole of Lebanon.

Patrimonial. Most waqf buildings possess the very elegant architectural style, aesthetic yet functional, which prevailed at the time of their construction. These buildings need to be restored in a manner fitting the use that will be made of them, yet respecting the original style. Most of these convents, monasteries and episcopal sees harbour archives and manuscripts that are essential for understanding the history of the country, religious life and the evolution of ways of thinking in different periods.

Environmental. With the exception of olive production, agriculture has clearly failed as a remunerative occupation, some waqf lands have been converted to other, more lucrative activities. This has resulted in the cutting of trees to clear land for residential areas, and the digging of quarries that eat away the mountainsides. Areas still preserved are becoming intensively exploited. The legal status of waqf lands, long term leases, and promises to develop land and increase revenues – all have contributed to a deterioration of the environment. During the seventies of the past century sand quarries caused landslides in the land property of Mār Ilyās Shwayyah convent in Qinnābah Brummānā where a sizable area of the 200,000 sq.meters property slided down the slope thus causing confusion and error to the cadastral services of the Lebanese government.

This negative picture is not true everywhere. Fortunately, many waqf foundations are flourishing. Some agricultural estates, especially those closest to the monasteries, are still verdant and fruitful. Waqf domains formed a solid foundation for charitable and educational institutions. The vast monastic buildings served as a refuge for thousands of people displaced during the war. The aid dispensed by the monasteries was not confined to shelter only, but extended to the channelling of all aid coming from individuals and charitable institutions.

It is essential to understand the main reasons for the decline of the waqfs. A study about administration of waqf was done at the beginning of the French mandate period.[1] A number of projects have been undertaken in the context of the Green Plan (a Lebanese Ministry of agriculture autonomous adminsitration that renders services material to farmers) and by some sees and convents with the aim of evaluating and upgrading the revenues of the waqfs which are at their disposal. During the preparation of the Catholic Church's Pastoral Synod for Lebanon, several studies were made proposing, as part of a solution to social and economic problems, to revalue the goods and property of the Church.

The *Lineamenta,*[2] drawn up as a preparatory to the Synod, and which bore the title "Witness of Love," insist on the role of the Church as servant, affirming:

The Church's traditional social doctrines rest on a double principle: human solidarity and the universal destination of goods. God intended the earth and all that it contains to be for the use of all men and peoples, in such a way that the goods of creation should pass equitably among the hands of

---

1 Michel Fayyad, *The Greek Orthodox Monasteries of Syria and Lebanon* (M.A. thesis, American University of Beirut, 1931).

2 Document edited for the preparation of the Catholic Pastoral Synod for Lebanon, 1993.

all, according to the law of justice, which is inseparable from that of charity. Whatever form the ownership of property may take, we must always keep in mind the universal destination of goods.

Further on, the same text, under the title "Social action of the ecclesiastical body," raises the subject of waqfs and, after defining them according to their different kinds, specifies:

The Church has an innate right to acquire, possess, administer and alienate temporal goods with the aim of realising its ends, namely: organising public worship, procuring an honest livelihood for the clergy and other ministers, and accomplishing apostolic works of charity.

Study groups were formed, each with the aim of preparing a theme. A commission to study Church property, formed of economists, lawyers and engineers, presented a report advocating the reform and revaluation of church waqf lands.

This report analysed the demographic and economic situation of Lebanon's Christians, which since 1975 has suffered because of emigration. The report warns that "the Church in Lebanon risks becoming a group of pastors endowed with land property but without flocks." Faced with this slow haemorrhage, the Church must deal with its problems. Each of the estates spread across the territory of Lebanon may become a centre of development, a sort of pilot project suited to the needs of the region. These centres, which would be the base of the socio-economic infrastructure of the Lebanese countryside, might lead to a real development of rural areas, by creating hospitals, rest houses, asylums, vocational, technical and agricultural schools, artisanal and cottage industries of high quality, value added niche products, village and hotel complexes for touristic purposes, and other requirements dictated by the local environment and economy. These different projects would necessitate coordination between the different religious communities and institutions, in order that the Church's social and economic activity might be put at the service of the community.[3]

In the same setting, Reverend Father Sharbil Kassīs[4] proposed the revaluation of monastic and ecclesiastical lands in Lebanon, while categorically opposing their sale or break-up. Far from limiting the role of the waqfs to the socio-economic field, Father Kassīs linked them to the dignity and liberty of man, and to the idea of the motherland and the solidarity of the national community. He advocated the revaluation of monastic farmlands, but also advanced suggestions relating to housing, ecology, leisure and

---

[3] Boutrus Labaki, ed. *Rapport de la Comission des Biens de l'Eglise*, Beyrouth, 25.4.1992.

[4] Superior of the Lebanese Maronite order during the first years of the civil war. Doc. Revalorisation des domaines monastiques et ecclosiastiques, 11.1.1993.

pilgrimages. Likewise, the report insisted on the role of waqfs in training farmers as part of a practical "schooling of life," which would seek to reintroduce young country dwellers to agricultural work. Concerted action by the monasteries, those "schools of life," the sharecroppers attached to the monastic lands, and the owner-cultivators of the surrounding areas, should lead to the creation of agrarian cooperatives, food processing industries and the marketing of agricultural produce.

These studies do not take into account the underlying causes of the present bad condition of the waqfs. The basic cause of the problem seems to lie in their juridical nature. The archaic origins and structures of these institutions renders them unfitted to the evolution of the modern economy.

The new sees founded by Antiochian Greek Orthodox emigrants to Europe and America are not at all based on waqf property. This has not in any way impeded their growth and development. The new churches established in the Western world have contented themselves with the gifts and contributions of their parishioners and with a simple administrative organisation adequate to their situation.[5]

The economy of Lebanon, which was previously centred on agriculture, has, in the space of a century, completely turned towards trade and services. The small size of the fragmented and dispersed land parcels (less than one Ha), the break-up of landholdings and the lack of investment in the agricultural sector have all led to an enormous shrinking of income from agrarian activities. Even the food processing industry seems to have been affected.

There is another reason, apparently dependent on the first, but really stemming from a fundamental change in mentality. The great majority of Lebanese, especially among the younger generation, prefers to avoid any kind of agricultural work. But fields of Poultry, field crops, plastic tunnels still attracts the young generation. Even those relatively well-paid as sharecroppers in cash-crop farming would prefer to take positions in public administration or teaching, where salaries are clearly inferior. The example of some flourishing waqfs, especially in Egypt, where monks are farming land in an oasis, seems not at all to have professionally attracted the younger generation in Lebanon.[6]

The clergy is not alone to blame for the causes of the decline of waqf lands. For very long periods, and in our own times, the clergy has been to a large extent excluded from the administration of the waqfs, especially those dependent on rural and urban parishes. Even in the waqfs attached to

---

5 Athanasios Ṣalībā, *al-Nūr*, 198.

6 Adiḇ Bathich, Official of the Waqf Administration of Mount-Lebanon, interview.

monasteries, long term contracts have entrusted very large lots to the care of laymen whose only aim has been to make the most profit in record time with the least effort. Investments that would have improved yields at the cost of a partial or temporary halt in revenues were totally refused. In addition, the continual monetary devaluations which occurred during the 1980s have reduced all the various waqf rents and revenues to a very modest and often insignificant level.[7]

The Orthodox Church of Antioch in Lebanon; an Assessment of its Belongings and Future Projects

In 1970, the Synodical Committee for Awqaf and finance was established by the holy Synod. Its chairman was Bishop Spiridon Khūrī of the Diocese of Zaḥlah with other laymen. This committee noting the state of neglect and misallocation of waqf resources, requested Mr. Georges Ḥannā Jiḥā, Agricultural Engineer, to assess the situation and submit a report that would help in planning any future development project aiming at improving the situation. The study was to begin with the rural sector, and then it would put emphasis on the waqf in Beirut and the Biqāʿ.

This chapter begins with an overall assessment of the land the Greek Orthodox Church owns in the rural regions of Lebanon. We will review the estates of the dioceses of Mount Lebanon, of Tripoli and Kūrah and of the monastery of Our Lady of al-Balamand. The study will be divided into two parts:

1. An assessment of the situation in the last quarter of the twentieth century.
2. A brief mention of recommendations and proposals submitted to improve the yield of the lands in some of the dioceses.

1: Assessment of the Situation

The total area of the lands owned by the two dioceses and the monastery is as follows:

The diocese of Jbayl and Batrūn	6,651,954 m^2	6,652 *dunum*
The diocese of Tripoli	3,548,813 m^2	3,549 *dunum*
Monastery of Balamand	2,823,700 m^2	2,824 *dunum*
Total	**13,024,467 m^2**	**13,024 *dunum***

[7] Ibid.

The total land area is huge in comparison with individual land ownership in Lebanon. The waqf estates include arable land, woods, orchards, buildings, and wasteland. The latter constitutes the major proportion of the total area.

Later in this chapter we will show that most of the wasteland could be reclaimed to become productive if properly planned for.

We will begin by studying the estate of the diocese of Jbayl and al-Batrūn. The land is spread over seven regions and is dedicated in its greatest part to the convents of Kaftūn, al-Nūriyyah, Ḥamāṭūrā, and to the monasteries of Saint John of Dūmā, al-Ḥarf, Baqᶜātā, and to the former see at al-Ḥadath. Only 2.4% of the land is arable and 32% is built-up or suitable for building. The remaining 94.4% is composed of pastures and non-agricultural land or wasteland.

Thus the yearly total yield per *dunum* of land is about 400 times less than the general average yield of a *dunum* in Lebanon; it would be ten times less if we only consider the 2.4% arable land. It is actually irrelevant to give exact amounts of revenues because of the depreciation of the Lebanese pound; the figures have lost their comparative meaning. These figures are true for most of the church properties whose production is very poor. But why is the production so low?
Many reasons can be found:

1. No agricultural roads that facilitate access of machinery or the transportation of crops.
2. Long-term lease of these agricultural lands tends to aggravate carelessness of the peasants.
3. Choosing traditional partners who do not have the proper tools or knowledge to invest in the land commensurate with its value.
4. No repair or maintenance of water canalization.
5. Introduction of non-agricultural enterprises such as tourism and industry within agricultural areas.

It is obvious that most problems are due to the leasing process arising from the inadequacy of human resources available in most monasteries, added to the fact that leasing requires no investment or budgeting.

Statistically, approximately half of the land is leased to partners for a long period of time. The other half is mainly leased for one year (woods). Therefore the land that is directly managed by the convent or monastery is very little.

The property of the diocese of Tripoli and al-Kūrah, as previously mentioned, is 3,548,813m^2 or 3,549 *dunum* or 355 hectares. It includes woods, grazing land, agricultural land, reclaimable non-agricultural land, reclaimable land, and wasteland. It is distributed among six convents and monasteries: our lady of Bkiftīn, Mar yaᶜ*qub* Diddih, our lady Al Naṭūr, Mār Mitr Kusbā, St. Elie al-Nahr and al-Kafr and the see of Tripoli.

The land of the diocese is under-exploited for the reasons already mentioned and due to the fact that the nature of the soil, in many areas, is difficult and expensive to exploit.

Finally the property of the convent of our Lady of Balamand is spread over eleven regions: Balamand, Barghūn, al Ḥurayshah, Dārayyā, Fīʿ, Qilḥāt, Batrūmīn, Bdubbah, Kusbā, Bhinnīn and al-Tall. Here the total percentage of agricultural land is 54.7% and of wasteland is 38.5%, which is reclaimable and should be taken care of and invested in.

Generally the area is divided into real estate and agricultural land, which includes woods, grazing land and arable areas. The remainder, which is not used for agricultural purposes, could be reclaimed for agricultural use if the necessary funds became available. Still, there remains a part, which is wasteland that cannot be used for anything. The land suitable for building is classified into three different categories A, B and C based on price; i.e., category A is the most expensive and C is the least expensive. This classification is dictated by a variety of conditions such as its closeness to main roads, or to industrial projects, or to beaches suitable for tourist projects. Added to that is the fact that it is not suitable for agriculture or similar endeavours.

We shall examine the agricultural sector. To begin we note that only a small area of the land is irrigated while the rest depends on rainfall (2.4% of the land of the diocese of Jbayl, and 1.4% of the land of Balamand monastery are irrigated, while 5% of the land of Tripoli is irrigated due mainly to the good investment of the land in Bkaftīn). Thus we see that an acceptable level of agricultural production under such conditions is almost impossible. What should be done is reclaiming the areas, but study of the nature of the soil, the needs of region, as well as significant investment are all required. This has been demonstrated in other parts of the country

For the two dioceses and the Patriarchate there is an area of approximately 11,721,607m^2 which is not suitable for either tourist or industrial projects but is suitable for agriculture. This area is subdivided into arable lands, natural pastures, scrub forest and garigue, forestry, and wasteland. The problem here is that the first three subdivisions are under-productive because they are insufficiently invested in, and the last, labeled "waste land," is to a great extent transformable into an arable area if there is adequate investment of labor and funds. In the irrigated part, one finds trees, vegetables as well as a fallow land. In the remainder of the land, or the unirrigated part, one finds olive groves, pasturage, forestry and a huge waste area.

As was said before, the land is mostly reclaimable but at varying cost. The land labeled A is very easy to reclaim with a very low budget. Land B needs more money since it is not level and contains some surface rocks. Finally the land C is expensive to transform since its slope dictates the use of terracing and levelling, and the clearing away of the deep rocks that are often encountered.

A look at the figures gives a better view of the situation.

	Arable Land	**Land A**	**Land B**	**Land C**	**Wasteland**	**Wasteland/ Total area**
Diocese of Jbayl	476,217	349,000	915,000	4,882,000	690,271	10.7%
Diocese of Tripoli	797,264	172,000	215,666	474,622	804,293	32.7%
Monastery of Our Lady of Balamand	504,734	149,342	202,845	91,600	1,862,128	65.9%
	1,778,215	670,342	1,333,511	5,458,222	2,367,692	

One can conclude from the above table that even though the arable area is small compared to the total area of the land (around 15%), the reclaimable area is 63.7% of the total, which means that the 15% can be greatly increased with proper projects. Finally the wasteland is only 21.3% and not 85%.

But of course, all this needs proper planning, which means an investment project. The agricultural investment requires seven steps:

1. Construction of agricultural roads. Agricultural roads would facilitate mechanisation, modernization of agricultural techniques and transportation of produce, and increase the value of agricultural lands.
2. Investment in the land considered "wasteland." We have shown before that 63.7% of the land can be reclaimed to become arable but of course that needs a proper budget, especially for the land labeled C. In addition, one must not forget the fact that the services of an engineer and the transportation of materials must be provided for.
3. Increase of the production of the olive groves by planting olive saplings. Increasing the production of the olive groves may happen if all the leased groves are returned to the direct management of the monastery, which will allow scientific supervision and good agricultural practices conductive to a high increase in yields of different crops: like fertilizing, spraying against pests and disease, and so on.

4. Improvement of the natural pasturage. The natural pasturage needs deferred grazing for some time to help the forage crops grow and also to plant some forage species that are palatable to small rumiants (sheeps and goats) and to improve the outcome of these meadows. But this needs supervision and special care by specialists, plus a budget.
5. Starting a program of reforestation. Investment in reforestation will pay off in timber production, and will contribute to the protection of the environment and beautifying the scenery.
6. Provision of the human resources needed. Human resources are needed to manage and execute this agricultural project and it will involve human skills from planning by engineers to planting, cultivating and harvesting by workers.
7. Soil fertility and pest control. The materials might be expensive but they last for approximately ten years. Therefore their price can be spread over that period and become affordable. Some of the other items needed are fertilizers, insecticides, and fungicides, and a canning factory for olives and other produce.

Of course, all these steps are important but priorities are to be set, e.g. the human resources are the most urgent at the beginning. The project should be designed to accommodate variations which may be necessitated by budgetary or technical constraints.

It is essential here to give some information about the distribution of waqfs. Each waqf is related to a church or other ecclesiastical institution, i.e. they are independent from one another. For each waqf a council is chosen to take care of its endowment.

The study of the waqf is relevant to the nature of the relationship between the people and the church. In Beirut, one notices that for a long period the church neglected many of its waqfs because it considered them unproductive, not worth the trouble, or simply out of carelessness. This led to people taking advantage of the situation and settling and building on that land, which they did not own. There are documents for many waqf churches, schools, and charitable organizations, and so on. We propose to begin by listing these and examine some relevant figures to illustrate the above statement:

The church of our Lady of al-Niyyah, the church of Dayr al-Nabī Ilyās Btīnah, the church of the Archangels Michael and Gabriel, the church of Dayr Our Lady of Dukhūl, Ashrafiyyah, the church of St. Ilyās Muṣaytbah, the Orthodox Charitable Organization, the Hospital organization of St. Georges, the organization of Ittiḥād al-Birr, the Orphanage of St. Michael, and the al-Salām School.

In all the documents we find that first there is an assessment of what was on the land in the past; and below it a list of what actually exists after a check by the real estate department in the government real estate department, mostly done in 1962-1963. In the past these lands were woods or little convents of one room. After the check was made, the trees were cut down and instead there are buildings, gas stations, cemeteries, factories, shops, orphanages, Palestinian refugee camps, and so on. The church did not make any of these. The people did. These lands are situated mostly in the regions of Rās Bayrūt, Mazraʿah, Ashrafiyyah, Ṣayfī, Muṣaytbah, Bashūrah, and Rmayl. According to the documents, these lands are about 370,000 m^2. It is interesting to point out that a very small proportion of these belongings are labeled waqf for the poor, which was the principal waqf foundation in the nineteenth century. However, approximately all are owned by Greek Orthodox institutions.

2: The Projects

From the agricultural viewpoint, the majority of the land is fertile, even through part of it is steep and rocky. However with the help of a government agency (the Green Plan) all these problems can be overcome. Around 10% of the total area is of a nonagricultural nature and more suitable for construction of factories, schools, hotels, and hospitals, or for tourism.

Most of the land is neglected at present. Sharecroppers or tenants, under the supervision of the monasteries and convents, exploit only a small productive part. Most of the land has good productive potential and needs reclamation, i.e., deep plowing, removal of stones and rocks, terracing, construction of support walls, cleaning, clearing, etc., to become suitable for economic production.

As a result of this, the heads of the Greek Orthodox Church approved a plan proposed by agricultural experts to try to transform all the church holdings into resources dedicated to raise the standard of living of the people by helping them financially, educationally and socially. The plan includes many parts or stages all directed at helping the community. These are:

2.1: The Diocese of Mount Lebanon

Kaftūn, a Typical Convent

A major project is the one related to the convent of Kaftūn. The diocese of Mount Lebanon owns tremendous areas of land of different fertility levels, yet there is a large productive area as well as other areas that can be rendered more productive by applying land reclamation techniques, as was done at the convents of Kaftūn's lands during 1972-1974.

Of the arable land of the convent of Kaftūn about 50,000m^2 are irrigated by the al-Jawz River, and 30,000 m^2 of dry land. The project aims at making the land a prototype of an economically productive area. This is achieved by taking the following steps:

a. Land reclamation of both the irrigated and the dry land
b. Repairing and rebuilding the support walls
c. Repairing the main public irrigation canal
d. Planting citrus seedlings
e. Planting banana seedlings
f. Rejuvenating the existing olive orchards and planting new ones
g. Reforestation
h. Leasing the natural pasture land
i. Constructing agricultural roads

This plan involves the improvement of existing resources and cultivation of arable land, especially the irrigated part.

Housing Projects in Kaftūn and Beirut's Suburbs

The housing projects of the diocese of Mount Lebanon consist of 110 land parcels were offered for sale for the purpose of house construction to help the people of Kaftoun settle in their village. Only one land lot was sold for one individual family at cost price. Construction of the houses or apartments took place in the villages of Kaftūn (90), Ḥāmāt (2), and Mkallis (24), and they were mostly sold to families displaced by the Lebanese war. A project has been executed during the five past years, it aims at constructing 250 apartments on the land of the diocese of Mount Lebanon at Ḥadath, a suburb of Beirut.

Tourist Project

A tourist project was proposed to build a cable car between the shores of the regions of al-Ḥīrī near Shikkā to the convent of Our Lady al-Nūriyyah, but it failed to be approved by the leaders of the Church because, they said, the public might disturb the nuns in the convent who need solitude, calm and decorum. In the end the project was not executed and the lands were sold to finance other social and charitable projects in Mount Lebanon.

2.2: The Monastery of Balamand

The Institute of Theology

The project of Balamand is mainly educational since it comprises the construction of a theology institute and a university. St. John of Damascus Institute of Theology was finished on 26 October 1970. Teaching began that year. A board of trustees was formed on 6 April 1965, to follow the procedures and supervise the creation of the institute of theology. The project cost $294,000, donated by the Archbishop Anthony Bashīr ($250,000) and by metropolitan Philip and the Council of Trustees of the diocese of New York and North America ($44,000).

The University

His Beatitude Patriarch Ighnātiyūs IV established the university in 1988. It goes beyond the church's traditional function of preparing priests and monks. It is an institution of higher education for all citizens in Lebanon and the Arab Countries. The university is licensed by the government and authorized to grant degrees in all the existing seven faculties. It is a private non-profit independent Lebanese institution, which is deep rooted in its long Eastern Orthodox tradition. Its stated aims are teaching and service to the community, with a high priority on science and the moral value of knowledge. Although it teaches in Arabic, English and French, it is mainly English-oriented.

Agricultural Projects

In addition to the university and the institute of theology, an agricultural project was started in 1985. It aimed to increase the value of the land and make it more suitable for agriculture. Many deep wells were drilled, agricultural plastic tunnels were built for off-season vegetable crops, irrigation canals restored, and about 4,000m^2 of land were reclaimed and made ready for agriculture.

2.3: The Patriarchate

The Convent of St. Ilyās of Shwayyah and Abū Mīzān

Finally the lands of the Patriarchate were intended to be invested with a project on the land of the convent of St. Ilyās of Shwayyah at Abū Mīzān. This project has two sub-projects related to olive plantation and promotion of a silk industry. The establishment of an olive plantation is a project under the supervision of the consultant Mr. Georges Ḥannā Jiḥā, an agricultural engineer. It is important here to point out that the same Mr. Jiḥā made all the agricultural projects, some of which were executed and the others not. The olive plantation project aimed at planting a new variety of olive (also called table olives), which is better suited for presentation than the local varieties, which are more suitable for oil extraction. The land can contain more than 1,000 trees but since the irrigated area is small, the project aims at planting 300 only. According to a feasibility study done by Mr. Jiḥā, the revenues from planting a Greek, Spanish or Italian variety will pay back the cost of the project during the first three years of production, i.e., after nine years of the implementation of the project although the trees will only begin to produce after six years. The total cost is estimated at about $12,000 at the 1971 exchange rate. The effects of the project on the community should be:

1. More employment opportunities.
2. Becoming a model for the peasants who will introduce the new varieties and use scientific methods.
3. Establishing a small canning factory on a cooperative basis.

The other project, to promote the silk industry, was also studied in 1971 by Mr. Jiḥā and is the result of both the setting-up in 1956 of the Silk Office as part of the Lebanese Ministry of Agriculture, and the past history of Lebanese silk production. The project involves the establishment of a cooperative by farmers and their families. The materials and items needed include mulberry trees to feed the silk worms and silk houses. The probable client for the silk cocoons would be the Silk Office. The cost at a minimum is estimated at $4,500.

Unfortunately, these two projects were not executed and those responsible for the land found that it would be financially better to cancel sharecropping contracts, to parcel the land and enter into new agreements for land improvement and exploitation of the land. During the civil war, these contracts were misused and taken as a justification for extensive quarrying of huge quantities of rocks, which were used to produce building-stone and gravel without any respect for the environment.

3: Some Actual Problems in the Concept and Administration of Waqfs

At present, the waqf estates of all the communities cover almost 27 % of the surface of Lebanon. This proportion reaches 40% in the region of Kisrawān.[8] Nevertheless, as far as the properties of the Orthodox Church are concerned, there is no central authority that can provide information about these waqfs.[9] Throughout the Middle East the waqfs were a source of problems; there was and still is a debate whether to eliminate or to maintain them. Under the French mandate, the mandating countries often took up restrictive measures towards religious or domestic estates turned into waqfs. Measures undertaken by these mandating powers spared the Christian waqfs.[10] When socialist regimes came to power, they put an end to several of these estates through nationalisation, which mainly affected the large rural domains. Sometimes, the state assigned these waqfs to the public estate, serving the interests of rural communities. Despite economic liberalisation in Egypt, there remains the problem of the restitution to the Coptic Church

8 Nadīm Ḥaydar, 6.

9 Georges Khuḍr, *Raʿiyyatī*, January 22, 1995.

10 Encyclopédie de l'islam, Nov. ed., s.v. "Waqf."

of waqf estates, which had been dispossessed by nationalization under Nasserism. Negotiations and talks are still continuing between the Egyptian government and the religious authorities in order to recuperate the estates given by donators to the benefit of humanitarian services. Religious laws consider these estates as inalienable.[11]

This problem is not specific to the Middle East; for example, in Greece the Church's real estate and land ownership causes tension between the Church and the State. Archbishop Christodoulos of the Greek Autocephalous Church declared: "The Church doesn't plan a split from the state, but, nevertheless, it has to be prepared for such an eventuality."[12]

Real estate consisting of agricultural lands, exploited or not, and in the cities, of immovable properties and buildings, is a source of income to waqf beneficiaries. Nevertheless, the fact is that the church estate is mainly constituted of wide lands, exploited badly or not at all.

At present in Lebanon, all the communities have problems with their waqfs; trials, mismanagement, takeover of premises, trespassing, shortage of income, and problems with the state are frequent.

In the Druze community, the rivalry between political parties has extended to the waqfs especially since the promulgation in 1999 of the new law organizing the waqfs. This rivalry has resulted in a number of law suits.

According to Salīm ʿAbd al-Khāliq, responsible for the waqfs service, these properties do not exceed 250 (excluding the properties in Ḥāṣbayyā region which do not depend on the general administration of waqfs).[13] According to Mr. Ḥasan Ḥamādah, member of the National Council of Information, there should be more than 750 properties,[14] and even 1,000 parcels, as stated by the lawyer Farīd Abū Shaqrāʾ.[15]

Regarding the waqfs of the Catholic churches, 250 religious establishments are accounted for. Their agricultural domains and fixed properties are spread all over the Lebanese territory at different altitudes. These agricultural domains are either directly exploited by establishments depending on the church or leased to farmers. Direct exploitation is becoming increasingly scarce, due to the fact that even the clergymen are departing from manual tasks generally depreciated in modern Lebanese society.

On the other hand, sharecropping is presently only a remnant of the past and is disappearing, but the means of settlement are often a cause of

---

11 *Ecumenical Courier (correspondence) of the Middle East*, no. 39 (1999) chronicle, 24.

12 *Orthodox Press Service*, no. 242 (Nov 1999), 2.

13 *al-Nahār*, October 8, 1999.

14 *Nidāʾ al-Waṭan*, October 20, 1999.

15 *al-Safīr*, October 12, 1999.

conflicts opposing sharecroppers to monasteries, bishoprics or patriarchates. The most common exploitation system of agricultural properties belonging to the churches is farm-leasing, covering renewable periods of 30 to 99 years.

Being simple peasants with limited means, the farmers often lack technical possibilities and know-how. This fact is the cause for the non-application of new methods of exploitation and management.[16]

Nevertheless, it is impossible, nowadays, in the context of the outburst of international commercial exchanges, to separate a modern concept of profitable agricultural exploitation and trading practices. But the principle ruling waqf possessions, which states that these possessions are inalienable, forbids any commercial activity in their exploitation, due to the inherent risks in trading. But the different Lebanese laws applied by communities or waqfs, and forbidding their sale, nevertheless authorize their exchange with other estates which become waqf. This possibility of replacing one waqf estate by another has been recognized by the law, in order to enable the tenants to better realize the initial aims of the waqf, namely piety and charity. Nevertheless, they do not involve the authorization of activities implying risks, such as industrial or commercial activities.[17] However, we notice nowadays that some churches, such as the church of Cyprus, have accepted to exchange waqfs against industrial exploitation in order to benefit from greater income.[18] Archbishop Christodoulos of Athens has declared that the Greek Church estates should be managed in complete harmony with the market rules.[19]

Attempts to exploit waqf estates in the domain of tourism have been established. Hotels have been built in the cities by religious institutions. The Orthodox have built the Lattakieh Hotel; the Greek Catholic the Qādrī Hotel in Zaḥlah (built by the monks of the Basilian order).

But is it possible to apply the rules of a modern economic management in traditional institutions and ignore the accumulation of wealth in order to renew them? And is it acceptable that the church accumulates wealth, even if it is done in view of redistributing its income in the future? Some persons thought that, even if the Oriental churches could acquire waqf estates due to historic circumstances favorable to Christians, they did not have to act as agricultural managers dedicating themselves to the fructification of these lands. Today these questions and opinions get different answers depending

---

16 Report of the Church Properties Commission.

17 Nadīm Ḥaydar, 7.

18 Khuḍr, "al-Awqāf."

19 Orthodox Press Service, 2.

on whether or not one accepts the idea of church institutionalization.[20] In this specific respect, Ighnātiyūs IV, Greek Orthodox patriarch of Antioch, denies that the church is wealthy: "It has the possibilities of being wealthy but does not take advantage of its potential. We wish to become wealthy, if God allows, when we will be able to fructify our potential wealth. It is a must for us to create and develop our institutions in the aim of helping our people. We have to become rich in order to allow the people to learn and to work in our institutions. People are surprised by the fact that our institutions could develop and flourish during the war. We have to make up for lost time."[21]

Also regarding institutionalization, a clear opinion is given by the Lebanese Maronite Order "the foolish rich man" (Luke 12-16-21) is definitely not the example to follow. The monastery in Lebanon is not poor, but it is the monastery of the poor. And it is for them that it intends to remain so. Inciting the monastery to get rid of its possessions or to hoard them is equally absurd, as unjustifiable as it is senseless.[22] For centuries, the existence of waqf real estates was justified by the aim to use the income of the church possession for piety and charitable services. This income consisted of an agricultural crop or its counter-value, or of rents collected according to leasing contracts. This type of traditional economic activity is seen today as limited and does not suffice to generate wealth, compared, for example, to that generated by commercial, industrial, banking and other activities. Churches in Lebanon are important real estate owners, and find themselves in the awkward situation where needy people see them as wealthy and avaricious institutions. They were accused several times of betraying their vocation of love and charity. In fact, churches are facing opposition in some circles. Traditional economic activity is no longer enough to ensure sufficient income for charitable services. Furthermore, the inalienabilitity of their real estate prevents the sale of a part of them to raise funds to finance the functioning institutions. The reason that prevents the selling off of a waqf estate is not only a legal interdict, which could be bypassed by waqf exchange, as authorized by the legislator or by a special patriarchal authorization. But the idea that church estates are "sacred property" is still prevalent due to the fact that popular tradition considers as waqf land an application of the will of the presumed late donators, although most of the waqf lands were acquired

---

20 Georges Naḥḥās, "al-Ma'sasah fī'l-kanīsah," *al-Nūr*, series of nine articles, 1998-2000.

21 Ighnātiyūs IV (Hazim) Patriarch of Antioch, interview in *al-Āfāq*, June 8, 1988.

22 Report on Revalorization of Monastic and Ecclesiastical Property in Lebanon, January 11, 1993.

thanks to the amassing of riches and the initiative of members of the clergy and occasionally some notables. The idea of sacred property is found again in the waqf concept as understood by conservative personalities and religious institutions.

Mgr. Georges Khuḍr, Orthodox bishop of Mount Lebanon, states in this respect: "The inalienable character of waqf estates, as stipulated in the ancient texts, has created in people's mind, the idea of a sacred waqf, which is intangible because it is an ancient heritage which is, for many, part of the communal identity. Also we know that collective mentalities change with difficulty."[23]

Quite often, the most determined opposition to the sale of a monastery or church *waqf* estates comes from the inhabitants of the nearest village. They are the ones who, throughout history, benefited the most from these waqfs, on the economic level as well as on the educational and religious levels. The waqf is a part of their heritage and a part of their village life. Some of them think that the total or a part of the income generated by the sale of the church waqf should be reinvested in the village. Municipalities, associations, and clubs often consider themselves accredited to use waqf land to enlarge roads, open sports field, etc. Thus, the church waqfs are also in danger of becoming village waqfs similar to *mashāᶜ* lands (collective properties of a village located outside residential areas).

In Islam church waqfs are considered as waqfs of the poor. They have become village waqfs in the collective consciousness of the villagers.

The same idea of the waqf being sacred is upheld in a report on the "revalorization of monastic and clerical properties in Lebanon" presented by the Order of the Lebanese Maronite Monks. It rejects all theories on liquidation of monastic properties. Written under the title "A tomb for each acre: the land taken back against the payment of its value and taxes," this report asserts that getting rid of monastic properties would be a triple blunder, consisting of a denial of the past, an easy misjudgment of the present, and an alienation of the future. The land to preserve is the land of Lebanon, which, in the past, "was made of sweat, tears and blood for the dignity of free man." This land was humanized and protected from the greed of conquerors who occupied the Near East, reducing it to a *ḥamāyūn* or imperial land. This allowed "the idea of homeland to spread and defeat the totalitarian empire" and also to defend the value of the national community solidarity in opposition to the *umma* conception of a monoreligious sacred community.[24]

---

23 Khuḍr, "al-Awqāf."

24 Report on Revalorisation of Monastic and Ecclesiastical Property in Lebanon, January 11, 1993.

The waqf is seen here as a materialisation of collective identity, both national and confessional. During the Lebanese civil war, 1975-1990, this amalgam between confessional Maronite and national Lebanese identity was common to the conservative Christian parties.

According to popular belief and conservative circles, the waqf represents a sacred land that is bound to the place it is located in. Only the institutions (church, parish, and convent) given to the waqf by the initial donator could profit from its revenues. In case there was no indication, the revenues should go to the benefit of the donator's village. That is why conflicts occur sometimes between parishioners or their representatives and the ecclesiastical superiors (bishops, monastery superiors) when the latter try to liquidate or replace waqf estates in their villages.

Nevertheless, Mgr. Khuḍr asserts a clear theoretical position and points out: "From the point of view of ecclesiastical law, the waqf is one entity, divided waqfs do not exist. When people speak about this or that parish waqf, it is only to give a geographical indication. This does not mean that the parish priest or his lay assistants are the managers of the waqf. However, it is only natural that the bishop entrusts the local inhabitants with the mission of watching over the properties of the locality. From the theological and legal points of view, nothing prevents a central and modern administration with employees subordinate to the center, from watching over the exploitation of the waqf estate since the local inhabitants are not entitled to use these properties."[25]

The interpretation of the initial donator's will can also be the cause of conflicts. By suing the Beirut bishopric, Lady Cochrane challenged its right to build a church and lodging premises for the clergy inside its gardens, since the land where the bishopric was built was originally given by the Sursuqs (Lady Cochrane's ancestors) "in order to serve as a site for a building representing the Greek Orthodox community of Beirut." The bishop answered, stating that there is no law forbidding the use of a waqf.

The establishment of the inalienability of waqfs was inspired by the love the believers had for their Church and their fear of the people's greed. They wanted to ensure their Church's needs and, as they saw it, to strengthen it as an earthly entity. But as time went by, these properties became an excuse for people to be avaricious, claiming that possessions given to the Church in the past were sufficient.[26] In fact, needs increase along with charity, which doesn't acknowledge limits to donation.

---

[25] Khuḍr, "al-Awqāf."

[26] *L'Orient le Jour*, January 14, 1995.

According to the bishop of Mount Lebanon, in order to remain loyal to those who established the waqfs, two points are necessary: develop the possessions we have in the best possible way and move towards the realization of a social aim expressing our charity and love.[27] In this context, where theological, social, economical, psychological and political considerations intersect, churches face increasingly urgent social requests, and more important expense needs.

Forced to handle these considerations carefully and being unable to believe in a management based on a purely economic rationality, the churches are trying to obtain a better exploitation of their possessions, keeping in mind the demands arising from their status of inalienable properties.

27 Khuḍr, *Raʿiyyatī*.

BIBLIOGRAPHY

ᶜAbbūd, Sanāʾ. *Dayr al-Balamand wa madrasatuhū al-iklīrīkiyyah.* B.A. thesis, Institute of St. John of Damascus, Balamand, 1978.

Abdel Nour, Antoine. *Etude sur deux actes de waqf du XVI et du XVII siècles des wilayaets de Damas et de Sayda.* Thèse de doctorat, 3ème cycle, Paris, 1977.

Idem. *Introduction à l'histoire urbaine de la Syrie ottomane (XVI-XVII siècle).* Beirut: Librairie Orientale, 1982.

Abou Nohra, Joseph. *Contribution à l'étude du rôle des monastères dans l'histoire rurale du Liban: recherche sur les archives du couvent St. Jean de Khenchara et de cinq autres couvents maronites et melkites (1710-1963).* Ph.D. thesis, Strasbourg, 1983.

Idem. *Etude d'histoire rurale libanaise, édition, traduction et commentaire de quelques actes du couvent St. Jean de Choueir, 1815-1836.* M.A. thesis, Beirut, 1975.

Abū Ḥussayn, ᶜAbd al-Raḥīm and al-Saᶜdāwī, Ṣāliḥ. *al-Kanāʾis al-ᶜarabiyyah fī al-sijill al-kanasī al-ᶜuthmānī: 1869-1922.* Amman: al-Maᶜhad al-malakī li-l-dirāsāt al-dīniyyah, 1998.

al-Aḥmar, Nafīẓ. "Dayr al-Balamand: taʾsīsuhū wa dawruhū ʾabr al-tārīkh," in *Jawānib min tārīkh al-kūrah fī-l-ᶜahd al-ᶜuthmānī,* edited by Rifᶜat Sābā. Beirut: n.p., 1999.

Aouad, Ibrahim. *Le droit privé des Maronites aux temps des émirs Chéhab (1697-1841) d'après des documents inédits.* Paris: Geuthner, 1933.

Argyriou, Asterios. *Les exegèses grecques de l'Apocalypse: l'époque turque (1459-1927).* Tessaloniky: Etaireia Makedonikon Spoudon, 1982.

ᶜAun, Sāmī. *Abᶜād al-waᶜy al-ᶜilmī: dirāsah fī al-fikr al-ᶜarabī al-ḥadīth.* Beirut: al-Maktabah al-Būlisiyyah, 1986.

Bacel, Paul. "La congrégation des basiliens choueirites," *Echos d'Orient,* 4 (1903).

Baiḍūn, Aḥmad. "Bayn arkhabīl al-aḥyāʾ wa-l-majāl al-ʿumūmī," *al-Marqab*, 1 (1997), 179-214.

Idem (Ahmad Beydoun). *L'identité confessionnelle et temps social chez les historiens libanais contemporains*. Beirut: Librairie Orientale, 1984.

Barnes, John Robert. *An Introduction to Religious Foundations in the Ottoman Empire*. Leiden: E.J. Brill, 1986.

al-Bāshā, Qusṭanṭīn. *Tārīkh Dūmā*. 2nd ed. Jūniyyah: al-Maktabah al-Būlisiyyah, 1991.

Belin, Alphonse. *Essai sur l'histoire économique de la Turquie d'après les écrivains originaux*. Paris: n.p., 1865.

Idem. "Sur la propriété foncière en Turquie," *Journal Asiatique* (1861).

Birbarī, Georges. *Nashʾat abrashiyyat Jubayl wa-l-Batrūn wa mā yalīhā*. M.A. thesis, Institute of St. John of Damascus, Balamand, 1993.

al-Bishʿalānī, Isṭfān. *Tārīkh Bishāʿlī wa Ṣalīmā*. Beirut: n.p., 1948.

al-Bīṭār, Tūmā. *Tārīkh dayr al-qiddīs Yūḥannā al-Maʿmadān Dūmā wa urthūdhuks al-minṭaqah*. Dūmā: Dayr al-Qiddīs Yūḥannā al-Maʿmadān, 1991.

Bogolioubski, Alexis. "Le problème de l'enseignement des langues dans les écoles russes de la société impériale de Palestine." Unpublished article.

Braude, Benjamin. "Foundation of Myths of the Millet System," in *Christians and Jews in the Ottoman Empire*, edited by Benjamin Braude and Bernhard Lewis. New York, N.Y.: Holmes & Meier, 1982.

Braudel, Fernand. *The Mediterranean and the Mediterranean World in the Age of Philip II*. Berkeley, CA: University of California Press, 1995.

Buheiry, Marwan. *Beirut's Role in the Political Economy of the French Mandate*. Oxford: Center for Lebanese Studies, 1986.

Burckhardt, John Lewis. *Travels in Syria and the Holy Land*. London: Kessinger Publishing, 1822.

Busson de Janssens, Gérard. "Les waqfs dans l'Islam contemporain," *Revue des Etudes Islamiques* (1951), 5-72.

Cahen, Claude. *L'Islam: des origines au début de l'Empire Ottoman*. Paris: Hachette Littératures, 1997.

Chaunu, Pierre. *De l'histoire à la prospective*. Paris: Robert Laffont, 1975.

Idem. *Histoire quantitative, histoire sérielle*. Paris: SEDES, 1978.

Chevallier, Dominique. "Christianisation et nouvelles règles de la vie sociale," vol. 2, *Histoire du Christianisme*, Harissa, Jérusalem, 1949.

Idem, ed. *L'espace social de la ville arabe*. Paris: Maisonneuve et Larose, 1979.

Idem. *La société du Mont-Liban à l'époque de la révolution industrielle en Europe*. Paris: Geuthner, 1973.

Chikhani, Rafic. *Etude d'histoire rurale libanaise, édition, traduction et commentaire de quelques actes du couvent St. Jean de Choueir, 1684-1738*. M.A. thesis, Beirut, 1974.

Chrysostom, St. John. "In Epistulam I ad Timotheum 12:4, PG 62, cols. 562-4," in *Les pères de l'église*, edited by Jaques Liébaert. Paris: Desclée de Brouwer, 1986.

Courbage, Youssef and Philippe Fargues. *Christians and Jews under Islam*. London: Tauris, 1997.

Crecelius, Daniel. "The Organization of Waqf Documents in Cairo," *International Journal of Middle Eastern Studies*, 2 (July, 1971), 266-277.

Creswell, Robert. "Parenté et propriété foncière dans la montagne libanaise," *Etudes Rurales*, 40 (1970), 7-79.

Crone, Patricia. *Roman, Provincial and Islamic Law: the Origins of the Islamic Patronate*. Cambridge: Cambridge University Press, 1987.

Dāghir, Asᶜad Yūsuf. *al-Madrasah al-Muskūbiyyah al-Manshūrāt al-Urthūdhuksiyyah.* Tripoli: Dār al-Kalimah, 1979.

Ḍāhir, Masᶜūd. *al-Judhūr al-tārīkhiyyah li-l-masʾalah al-zirāᶜiyyah al-lubnāniyyah, 1900-1950*. Beirut: Lebanese University, 1983.

Davie, May. *La millat grecque orthodoxe de Beyrouth, 1800-1940.* Ph.D. thesis, Paris IV, Paris, 1993.

Idem. "Le couvent St. Georges de Bayroûth al Qadîmat," *Chronos*, 1 (1998), 7-32.

"Deeds of Mār Elias," *Dictionnaire encyclopédique du christianisme ancien.*

Deguilhem, Randy, *ed. Le waqf dans l'espace islamique: outil de pouvoir socio-politique*. Damascus: IFEAD, 1995.

Idem. "Waqf Documents: a Multi-Purpose Historical Source; the Case of 19th Century Damascus," in *Les Villes Ottomanes*, edited by Daniel Panzac. Paris: CNRS editions, 1994.

Delaroière, M. *Voyage en orient.* Paris: Debécourt, 1836.

Delin, Alphonse. *"Sur la propriété foncière en Turquie," Journal Asiatique* (1861).

al-Dimashqī, Mīkhāʾil. *Tārīkh ḥawādith al-Shām wa Lubnān, aw, tārīkh Mīkhāʾil al-Dimashqī*. Damascus: Dār Qutaybah, 1982

Ducousso, Henri. *L'industrie de la soie au Liban*. Paris: n.p., 1913.

Al-durr al-manẓūm fī tārīkh mulūk al-rūm. Balamand manuscript no. 187.

Engelhardt, Edward. *La Turquie et les tanzimat*. 2 vol., Paris: A. Cotillon et Cie, 1882-1884.

Fattal, Antoine. *Le statut légal des non-musulmans en terre d'Islam*. Beirut: Imp. Catholique, 1958.

Fayyad, Michel. *The Greek Orthodox Monasteries of Syria and Lebanon*. M.A. thesis: American University of Beirut, Beirut, 1931.

Furzlī, Faraḥ. *Ṣūrat ghayr al-muslimīn fī kitāb Ṣubḥ al-Aᶜshā fī ṣināᶜat al-inshāʾ*. Ph.D. thesis: Usek, Kaslik, Lebanon, 1983.

Furet, François and Nora, Pierre. "Le quantitatif en histoire," in *Faire de l'histoire: nouvelles approches, nouveaux problèmes*, 1. Paris: Gallimard, 1974.

Gardet, Louis. *La cité musulmane: vie sociale et politique*. 2nd ed. Paris: J. Vrin, 1961.

al-Gemayel, Nasser. *Les échanges culturels entre les Maronites et l'Europe: du collège maronite de Rome (1584) au collège de ᶜAyn-Warqa (1789)*. 2 vol., Beirut, 1984.

Gibb, H.A.R. and Bowen, Harold. *Islamic Society and the West: A Study of the Impact of Western Civilization on Moslem Culture in the Near East*. 2 vol., London: Oxford University Press, 1950-1957.

Le Goff, Jacques, ed. *La nouvelle histoire*. Paris: Retz, 1978

Guys, Henri. *Beyrouth et le Liban: Relation d'un séjour de plusieurs années dans ce pays*. 2 vol., Paris: Challamel Ainé, 1850.

Idem. *Esquisse de l'état politique et commercial de la Syrie*. Marseille: s.p., 1863.

Ḥaddād, Rashīd and Fāyiz Furayjāt. *Fihris makhṭūṭāt dayr al-Balamand*. Beirut: Dār al-Kalimah, 1970.

Ḥaqqī, Ismāᶜīl Bayk. *Lubnān: mabāḥith ᶜilmiyyah wa ijtimāᶜiyyah*. Beirut: Lebanese University Publications, 1970.

al-Ḥalabī, Ilyās. "Nubdhah tārīkhiyyah ᶜan dayr al-Balamand," *al-Kalimah* (1907).

Hamman, A.-G. and France Quéré-Jaulmes, eds. *Riches et pauvres dans l'église ancienne*. Paris: Grasset, 1962.

Haneda, Masashi and Miura, Toru, eds. *Islamic Urban Studies*. London, 1995.

Ḥarfūsh, Ibrāhīm. "Tārīkh dayr Mār Shallīṭā," *al-Mashriq* (April 1902).

Harīz, Salīm, *al-Waqf: dirāsāt wa abḥāth*. Beirut: Lebanese University Publications, 1997.

al-Ḥattūnī, al-Khūrī Manṣūr. *Min tārīkh Lubnān: nubdhah tārīkhiyyah fī al-muqāṭaʿah al-kisrawāniyyah*. Beirut: Awrāq lubnāniyyah fī khidmat al-tārīkh, 1956.

Ḥaydar, Marlène. *Mustashfā al-Qiddīs Jirjis 1877-1934*. M.A. thesis: Lebanese University, Beirut, 1992.

Ḥaydar, Nadīm. "al-Awqāf," *al-Nūr*, no. 7 (1984), 6-13.

Heyberger, Bernard. "Les chrétiennetés d'orient au XVIIIème siècle," vol. 10, in *Histoire du christianisme*, Paris: Desclée, 1995.

Hourani, Albert. *Political Society in Lebanon: A Historical Introduction*. Oxford: Centre for Lebanese Studies, 1982.

Huot, Jean-Louis, Thalmann, Jean-Paul et, Dominique Valbelle. *Naissance des cités*. Paris: Nathan, 1990.

Ibn Jawziyah, Muḥammad Ibn Aḥmad. *Qawānīn al-aḥkām al-sharʿīyah wa masāʾil al-furūʿ al-fiqhiyyah*, edited by ʿAbd al-Raḥmān Ḥasan Maḥmūd. Kairo: ʿĀlam al-Fikr, 1985.

Ignace IV. *Le martyr du silence*. Sermon of 17th Nov. 1990 at St. Louis des Invalides, Paris: Service orthodoxe de presse, no. 153.

Issawi, Charles. "British Trade and the Rise of Beirut, 1830-1860," *International Journal of Middle East Studies* 8, no. 1 (1977), 91-101.

Idem, ed. *The Economic History of the Middle East 1800-1914: A Book of Readings*. Chicago, Ill.: University of Chicago Press, 1966.

Johansen, Baber. *The Islamic Law on Land Tax and Rent: The Peasants' Loss of Property Rights as Interpreted in the Hanafite Legal Literature of the Mamluk and Ottoman Periods*. New York, N.Y.: Croom Helm, 1988.

Juraydīnī, Rāʾid and al-Asmar ʿAllām, Dunyā. *Awḍāʿ al-Rūm al-Urthūdhuks al-wāfidīn ilā Bayrūt fī maṭlaʿ al-qarn al-ʿishrīn: dirāsah maydāniyyah fī ʿilm al-ijtimāʿ al-madīnī*. Balamand: University of Balamand, 2000.

Jurdāq, Mitri. *Awdāʿ al-rūm al-urthūdhuks fī madīnat Bayrūt wa ʿalā qātuhum bi-l-dawlah al ʿUthmāniyyah (1876-1906)*. M.A. thesis: Lebanese University, 1999.

Kaplan, Michel. "Les moines et le clergé séculaire à Byzance," *Moines et monastères dans les sociétés de rite grec et latin*, edited by Jean Loup Lemaitre. Geneva: Droz, 1996.

Karam, Mārūn. *Qiṣṣat al-milkiyyah fī al-rahbāniyyah al-lubnāniyyah al-mārūniyyah*, Beirut: Dār al-Ṭibāʿah al-Lubnāniyyah, 1972.

Kassāb, Ḥanāniyyā Ilyās. *Majmūʿat al-sharʿ al-kanasī aw qawānīn al-kanīsa al-masīḥiyya al-jāmiʿa*. Beirut: Manshūrāt al-Nūr, 1985.

Kahdr, Mohamed. "Deux actes de waqf d'un qarahanide d'Asie centrale," *Journal Asiatique*, Tome CCLV (1967), F. 3-4.

Kassatly, *Houda. La communauté monastique de Deir el Ḥarf*. Balamand: University of Balamand, 1996.

Khalifeh, Issam. *Des étapes décisives dans l'histoire du Liban*. Beirut: Librairie Avicenne, 1997.

Khayrallah, Ḍāhir Amīn. *Lamḥat al-nāẓir fī mask al-dafātir*. 4th ed. Beirut: al-Ittiḥād, 1931.

Khuḍr, Georges. "L'activité et la reflexion sociale chez les orthodoxes arabes de 1800 à 1920," in *L'église et les pauvres*, edited by Julio Santa Anna. Suisse: Lausanne, 1982.

Idem. "al-Awqāf," *al-Nahār*, June 14, 1994.

Idem. *Raʿiyyatī*, January 22, 1995.

Krymskyj, Ahatanhel. *Bayrūt wa Jabal Lubnān ʿalā mashārif al-qarn al-ʿishrīn: dirāsah fī taʾrīkh al-ijtimāʿī min khilāl mudhakkirāt al-ʿālim al-Rūsī al-kabīr A. Krīmskī: rasāʾil min Lubnān, 1896-1898*. Trans. Yūsuf ʿAṭʾallāh. Beirut: Dār al-Madā, 1985.

Kuroki, Hidemitsu. "The Orthodox-Catholic Clash in Aleppo in 1818," *Orient* 23 (1993), 1-20.

Kustī, Jamīlah. *Madrasat Zahrat al-iḥsān: khaṣāʾiṣ al-nashʾah wa-l-taṭawwur min khilāl "ʿIqd al-jumān" (1881-1928)*. D.E.A. thesis: Lebanese University, Beirut, 1993.

Labaki, Boutros. *Document sur la valorisation des waqfs*. Beirut, 1982.

Idem. *Introduction à l'histoire économique du Liban*. Beirut: Lebanese University, 1984.

Idem, ed. *Rapport de la Comission des Biens de l'Eglise*. Beirut, 25.4.1992.

Lammens, Henri. *Tasrīḥ al-abṣār fī mā yaḥtawī Lubnān min āthār*. Hazmieh, Beirut: al-Maṭbaʿa al-Kāthūlīkiyyah, 1913.

Latron, André. *La vie rurale en Syrie et au Liban: étude d'économie sociale*. Beirut: Mémoires de l'Institut Français de Damas, 1936.

Van Leeuwen, Richard. "Monastic Estates and Agricultural Transformation in Mount Lebanon in the 18th Century," *International Journal of Middle Eastern Studies*, no.23 (1991), 601-617.

Lemerle, Paul and Paul Witteck. "Recherches sur l'histoire et le statut des monastères athonites sous la domination turque," *Archives d'histoire du droit oriental*, 3 (1947).

Lewis, Bernard. *The Emergence of Modern Turkey*. London: Oxford University Press, 1961.

Leroy, Jules. *Moines et monastères du Proche Orient*. Paris, 1979.

MacFarlane, Charles. *Turkey and Its Destiny: The Result of Journeys Made in 1847 and 1848 to Examine into the State of that Country*. Philadelphia, 1850.

Idem. *Al-Maḥabba*, 1 (1899).

Maḥfūẓāt abrashiyyat Bayrūt li-l-rūm al-urthūdhuks. 2 vol., Beirut: University of Balamand, 1998-1999.

al-Maḥfūẓāt al-ʿarabiyyah fī al-adyira al-urthūdhuksiyyah al-anṭākiyyah fī Lubnān, 2 vol., Beirut: University of Balamand, 1991-1994.

Maḥfūẓāt Dayr Sayyidat al-Balamand al-baṭriyarkī wa Dayr al-Nabī Ilyās al-baṭriyarkī, Shwayyah wa Dayr al-Qiddīs Yūḥannā al-Maʿmadān Dūmā. Beirut: University of Balamand, 1995.

al-Makhṭūṭāt al-ʿarabiyyah fī-l-adyira al-urthūdhuksiyyah al-anṭākiyyah fī Lubnān. 2 vol., Beirut: Institute for Antiochian Orthodox Studies, n.d.

al-Maʿlūf, ʿĪsā Iskandar. *Dawānī al-quṭūf fī tārīkh banī al-Maʿlūf*. Baʿabdā: ʿUthmāniyya, 1907-1908.

Idem. "al-Shaikh Abū ʿAskaryūnis Niqūlā al-Lubnānī," *al-Niʾma*, (February 1911), 533-542

Idem. *Tārīkh madīnat Zaḥlah*. Beirut, 1911.

Idem. "Zajaliyyāt fī waṣf al-ghalāʾ wa-l-jūʿ wa-l-ḍīq," *al-Mashriq* (May 1920), 338-348.

Mandaville, Jon E. "Usurious Policy: the Cash Waqf Controversy in the Ottoman Empire," *International Journal of Middle Eastern Studies* (1979), 289-308.

Mantran, Robert. *Histoire de l'Empire Ottoman*. Paris: Fayar, 1994.

Idem. *Istanbul de la seconde moitié du XVIIème siècle à 1914: essai d'histoire institutionelle, économique et sociale*. Paris: Maisonneuve, 1962.

al-Maqdisī, ʿAbd al-Raḥmān Ibn-Ibrāhīm. *Al-ʿudda, sharḥ al-ʿumdah fī fiqh imām al-sunnah Aḥmad Ibn-Ḥanbal al-Shaybānī*. Cairo: al-Maktabah al-Salafiyyah.

Maundrell, Henry. *A Journey from Aleppo to Jerusalem in 1697*. Reprint, Beirut: Khayats, 1963.

Mayeur Jaouen, Catherine. "Les chrétiens d'Orient au XIXième siècle: un renouveau lourd des menaces." in *Histoire du christianisme*, 11. Paris: Desclée, 1995.

Idem. "La Renaissance dans les églises d'Orient à la fin de l'époque ottomane," in *Christianity through its History in the Orient*. Not published yet.

Messara, Antoine, ed. *L'église de la réconstruction*. Beirut: CEDROC, 1995.

Mohasseb, Sabine. *L'extension de la propriété foncière du couvent de Mār Challita 1615-1878*. M.A. thesis, Beirut, 1988.

Moubarac, Youakim, ed. *Pentalogie antiochienne domaine maronite*. 7 vol., Beirut: Cénacle Libanais, 1984.

Musset, Henri, ed. *Histoire du christianisme: spécialement en Orient*. 3 vol., Harissa etc.: Imp. Saint Paul etc., 1948-1949.

al-Nabhān, Muḥammad Fārūq. *Al-ittijāh al-jamāʿī fī-l-tashrīʿ al-iqtiṣādī al-islāmī*. Beirut: al-Risālah, 1988.

Naḥḥās, Georges. "al-Maʾsasah fī'l-kanīsah," *al-Nūr*, series of nine articles, 1998-2000.

Nasrallah, Joseph. *Histoire du mouvement littéraire dans l'église melkite du Vème au XXème siècle: contribution à l'étude de la littérature arabe chrétienne (1250-1516)*. Paris: Peeters 1992.

Idem. "La peinture monumentale des patriarcats melkites," in *Exposition icônes melkites organisée par le Musée Nicolas Sursock du 16 Mai au 15 Juin*, edited by Sylvia Agemian. Beyrouth, 1969.

Niebuhr, Carsten. *Voyage en Arabie et en d'autres pays circonvoisins*. Amsterdam: Baalde, 1780.

Padel, Wilhelm and L(ouis) Steeg. *La legislation foncière ottomane*. Paris: A. Padone, 1904.

Perrier, Ferdinand. *La Syrie sous le gouvernement de Méhémet-Ali jusqu'en 1840*. Paris, 1842.

Pietri, Charles. "Constantin et l'inflexion chrétienne de l'Empire," in *Histoire du christianisme : spécialement en Orient*, edited by Henri Musset, vol. 2. Harissa: Imp. Saint Paul, 1949.

Poggi, Vincenzo. "Les chrétiens en Orient durant la seconde période ottomane (l'établissement du régime des millets)," in *Christianity Through its History in the Orient*. Not published yet.

Polk, William. *The Opening of South Lebanon 1788-1840*. Cambridge: Harvard University Press, 1963.

al-Qattar, Ilias. *Les conditions sociales au Liban au début du XIXème siècle*. M.A. thesis: St. Joseph University, Beirut, 1974.

al-Rāsī, Juliette. "Min arshīf baṭriyārkiyyat Anṭākiyyah wa sāʾir al-mashriq li-l rūm al-urthūdhuks fi Dimashq," *Dirasāt al-Jāmaʿah al-Lubnāniyyah*, no. 26 (1997), 435-506.

Raymond, André. "Alep à l'époque ottomane," *Revue du monde musulman et de la Méditerranée*, no. 62 (1992).

Rustum, Asad. *Bashīr II: bayn al-sulṭān wa-l-ʿAzīz: 1804-1841*. Beirut, 1988.

Idem. "Dayr Mār Ilyās wa-l-kathlakah," *al-Nūr*, no. 6 (1962).

Idem. *Kanīsat madīnat Allāh Anṭākiyyah al-ʿuẓmā*. 3 vol., Beirut: al-Maktabah al-Būlisiyyah, 1988.

Ṣalībā, Athanasios. Interview in *al-Nūr*. 1986.

Saliba, Nagib. "The Achievements of Midhat Basha as Governor of the Province of Syria 1878-1889," *International Journal of Middle Eastern Studies*, no. 9 (1978), 307-323.

Salibi, Kamal. *The Modern History of Lebanon*. Delmar, N.Y.: Caravan Books, 1965.

Sauma, Victor. *Sur les pas des saints au Liban*. [Beirut]: FMA, c1994.

Shaw, Stanford. "The Land Law of Ottoman Egypt. A Contribution to the Study of Landholding in the Early Years of Ottoman Rule in Egypt," *Der Islam* 38 (1963), 106-137.

Idem. *Ottoman Egypt in the Eighteenth Century*. Cambridge: N.p., 1962.

Slim, Souad. *Balamand: Histoire et patrimoine*. Beirut: Dār an-Nahar, 1995.

Idem. *Etude d'histoire rurale libanaise, édition, traduction et commentaire de quelques actes du couvent St. Jean de Choueir, 1780-1815*. M.A. thesis, Beirut 1978.

Idem. "Khané et Hara dans le patrimoine architectural de la ville de Beyrouth," in *Patrimoine urbain au Liban*, edited by Michael Davie. Balamand: Alba, 2000.

Idem. *Le métayage et l'impot au Mont-Liban aux XVIII et XIX siècles*. Beirut: Dār al-Mashriq, 1993.

Smith, R. Payne, *Catalogus codicum manuscriptorum bibliothecae bodleianae pars sexta, codices Syriacos, Carshunicos Mendaeos*. Oxford: Clarendon Press, 1864.

Tarazi Fawaz, Leyla. *Merchants and Migrants in the Nineteenth-Century Beirut*. Cambridge Mass, London: Harvard University Press, 1983.

Touma, Toufic. *Paysans et institutions féodales chez les Druzes et les Maronites du Liban du XVIIème siècle à 1914*, 2 vol., Beirut: Lebanese University, 1996.

Idem. *Un village de montagne au Liban: Hadeth el-Jobbé*. Paris: Mouton, 1958.

Idem. *Les pères de l'église*. Translated by M. Spannent. Paris: Desclée de Brouwer, 1986, 1990.

Urquhart, David. *The Lebanon (Mount Souria): a History and a Diary*. London, 1860.

Verney, N. and Dambman, G. *Les puissances étrangères dans le Levant, en Syrie, et en Palestine*. Paris: N.p., 1900.

Vezely, Rudolph. "Procès de la production et rôle du waqf dans les relations ville-campagne," in *Le waqf dans l'espace islamique; outil de pouvoir socio-politique*, edited by Randy Deguilhem. Damascus: IFEAD, 1995.

Volney, C.F. *Voyage en Syrie et en Egypte pendant les années 1783-1785*. 2 vol., Paris, 1804.

Weulersse, Jacques. *Paysans de Syrie et du Proche Orient*. Paris: Gallimard, 1946.

Young, Georges. *Corps de droit ottoman: recueil des codes, lois, règlements, ordonnances et actes les plus importants du droit intérieur et d'études sur le droit coutumier de l'empire ottoman*. Oxford: Clarendon Press, 1911.

Zaydān, ʿAbd al-Karīm. *Aḥkām al-dhimmīyīn wa-l-mustaʾminīn fī Dār al-Islām*. Baghdad: University of Baghdad, 1976.

al-Zayn, Ḥasan. *al-Awḍāʿ al-qānūniyyah li-l-naṣārā wa-l-yahūd fī al-diyār al-islāmiyyah ḥattā al-fatḥ al-ʿUthmānī*. Beirut: Dār al-Fikr al-Ḥadīth, 1988.

Ziyādah, Khālid. *Tārīkh al-muqāṭaʿāt al-lubnāniyyah fī al-qarn al-thāmin ʿashar*. Beirut: N.p., 1995.

Zurayq, ʿĪsā. "Maṭbaʿat al-Balamand," *al-Manār* (1901).

INDEX

المعهد الألماني للأبحاث الشرقية

ORIENT-INSTITUT BEIRUT

BEIRUTER TEXTE UND STUDIEN

1. MICHEL JIHA: Der arabische Dialekt von Bišmizzīn. Volkstümliche Texte aus einem libanesischen Dorf mit Grundzügen der Laut- und Formenlehre, Beirut 1964, XVII, 185 S.
2. BERNHARD LEWIN: Arabische Texte im Dialekt von Hama. Mit Einleitung und Glossar, Beirut 1966, *48*, 230 S.
3. THOMAS PHILIPP: Ǧurǧī Zaidān. His Life and Thought, Beirut 1979, 249 S.
4. ʿABD AL-ĠANĪ AN-NĀBULUSĪ: At-tuḥfa an-nābulusīya fī r-riḥla aṭ-ṭarābulusīya. Hrsg. u. eingel. von Heribert Busse, Beirut 1971, unveränd. Nachdr. Beirut 2003, XXIV, 10 S. dt., 133 S. arab. Text.
5. BABER JOHANSEN: Muḥammad Ḥusain Haikal. Europa und der Orient im Weltbild eines ägyptischen Liberalen, Beirut 1967, XIX, 259 S.
6. HERIBERT BUSSE: Chalif und Großkönig. Die Buyiden im Iraq (945–1055), Beirut 1969, unveränd. Nachdr. 2004, XIV, 610 S., 6 Taf., 2 Karten.
7. JOSEF VAN ESS: Traditionistische Polemik gegen ʿAmr b. ʿUbaid. Zu einem Text des ʿAlī b. ʿUmar ad-Dāraquṭnī, Beirut 1967, mit Korrekturen versehener Nachdruck 2004, 74 S. dt., 16 S. arab. Text, 2 Taf.
8. WOLFHART HEINRICHS: Arabische Dichtung und griechische Poetik. Ḥāzim al-Qarṭāǧannīs Grundlegung der Poetik mit Hilfe aristotelischer Begriffe, Beirut 1969, 289 S.

9.* STEFAN WILD: Libanesische Ortsnamen. Typologie und Deutung, Beirut 1973, XII, 391 S.

10. GERHARD ENDRESS: Proclus Arabus. Zwanzig Abschnitte aus der Institutio Theologica in arabischer Übersetzung, Beirut 1973, XVIII, 348 S. dt., 90 S. arab. Text.
11. JOSEF VAN ESS: Frühe muʿtazilitische Häresiographie. Zwei Werke des Nāšiʾ al-Akbar (gest. 293 H.), Beirut 1971, unveränd. Nachdr. Beirut 2003, XII, 185 S. dt., 134 S. arab. Text.

12.* DOROTHEA DUDA: Innenarchitektur syrischer Stadthäuser des 16.–18. Jahrhunderts. Die Sammlung Henri Pharaon in Beirut, Beirut 1971, VI, 176 S., 88 Taf., 6 Farbtaf., 2 Faltpläne.

13.* WERNER DIEM: Skizzen jemenitischer Dialekte, Beirut 1973, XII, 166 S.

14.* JOSEF VAN ESS: Anfänge muslimischer Theologie. Zwei antiqadaritische Traktate aus dem ersten Jahrhundert der Hiǧra, Beirut 1977, XII, 280 S. dt., 57 S. arab. Text.

15. GREGOR SCHOELER: Arabische Naturdichtung. Die zahrīyāt, rabīʿīyāt und rauḍīyāt von ihren Anfängen bis aṣ-Ṣanaubarī, Beirut 1974, XII, 371 S.
16. HEINZ GAUBE: Ein arabischer Palast in Südsyrien. Ĭirbet el-Baiḍa, Beirut 1974, XIII, 156 S., 14 Taf., 3 Faltpläne, 12 Textabb.
17. HEINZ GAUBE: Arabische Inschriften aus Syrien, Beirut 1978, XXII, 201 S., 19 Taf.

18.* GERNOT ROTTER: Muslimische Inseln vor Ostafrika. Eine arabische Komoren-Chronik des 19. Jahrhunderts, Beirut 1976, XII, 106 S. dt., 116 S. arab. Text, 2 Taf., 2 Karten.

19.* HANS DAIBER: Das theologisch-philosophische System des Muʿammar Ibn ʿAbbād as-Sulamī (gest. 830 n. Chr.), Beirut 1975, XII, 604 S.

20.* WERNER ENDE: Arabische Nation und islamische Geschichte. Die Umayyaden im Urteil arabischer Autoren des 20. Jahrhunderts, Beirut 1977, XIII, 309 S.

21. ṢALĀḤADDĪN AL-MUNAǦǦID, STEFAN WILD, eds.: Zwei Beschreibungen des Libanon. ʿAbdalġanī an-Nābulusīs Reise durch die Biqāʿ und al-ʿUṭaifīs Reise nach Tripolis, Beirut 1979, XVII u. XXVII, 144 S. arab. Text, 1 Karte, 2 Faltkarten.

22. ULRICH HAARMANN, PETER BACHMANN, eds.: Die islamische Welt zwischen Mittelalter und Neuzeit. Festschrift für Hans Robert Roemer zum 65. Geburtstag, Beirut 1979, XVI, 702 S., 11 Taf.

23. ROTRAUD WIELANDT: Das Bild der Europäer in der modernen arabischen Erzähl- und Theaterliteratur, Beirut 1980, XVII, 652 S.

24.* REINHARD WEIPERT, ed.: Der Dīwān des Rāʿī an-Numairī, Beirut 1980, IV dt., 363 S. arab. Text.

25.* ASʿAD E. KHAIRALLAH: Love, Madness and Poetry. An Interpretation of the Maǧnūn Legend, Beirut 1980, 163 S.

26. ROTRAUD WIELANDT: Das erzählerische Frühwerk Maḥmūd Taymūrs, Beirut 1983, XII, 434 S.

27.* ANTON HEINEN: Islamic Cosmology. A study of as-Suyūṭī's al-Hayʾa as-sunnīya fī l-hayʾa as-sunnīya with critical edition, translation and commentary, Beirut 1982, VIII, 289 S. engl., 78 S. arab. Text.

28. WILFERD MADELUNG: Arabic Texts concerning the history of the Zaydī Imāms of Ṭabaristān, Daylamān and Gīlān, Beirut 1987, 23 S. engl., 377 S. arab. Text.

29. DONALD P. LITTLE: A Catalogue of the Islamic Documents from al-Ḥaram aš-Šarīf in Jerusalem. 1984, XIII, 480 S. engl., 6 S. arab. Text, 17 Taf.

30. KATALOG DER ARABISCHEN HANDSCHRIFTEN IN MAURETANIEN. Bearb. von Ulrich Rebstock, Rainer Osswald und Ahmad Wuld ʿAbdalqādir, Beirut 1988. XII, 164 S.

31. ULRICH MARZOLPH: Typologie des persischen Volksmärchens, Beirut 1984, XIII, 312 S., 5 Tab., 3 Karten.

32. STEFAN LEDER: Ibn al-Ǧauzī und seine Kompilation wider die Leidenschaft, Beirut 1984, XIV, 328 S. dt., 7 S. arab. Text, 1 Falttaf.

33. RAINER OSSWALD: Das Sokoto-Kalifat und seine ethnischen Grundlagen, Beirut 1986, VIII, 177 S.

34. ZUHAIR FATḤALLĀH, ed.: Der Diwān des ʿAbd al-Laṭīf Fatḥallāh, 2 Bde., Beirut 1984, 1196 S. arab. Text.

35. IRENE FELLMANN: Das Aqrābāʾīn al-Qalānisī. Quellenkritische und begriffsanalytische Untersuchungen zur arabisch-pharmazeutischen Literatur, Beirut 1986, VI, 304 S.

36. HÉLÈNE SADER: Les États Araméens de Syrie depuis leur Fondation jusqu'à leur Transformation en Provinces Assyriennes, Beirut 1987, XIII, 306 S. franz. Text.

37. BERND RADTKE: Adab al-Mulūk, Beirut 1991, XII, 34 S. dt., 145 S. arab. Text.

38. ULRICH HAARMANN: Das Pyramidenbuch des Abū Ǧaʿfar al-Idrīsī (gest. 649/1251), Beirut 1991, XI u. VI, 94 S. dt., 283 S. arab. Text.

39. TILMAN NAGEL, ed.: Göttinger Vorträge – Asien blickt auf Europa, Begegnungen und Irritationen, Beirut 1990, 192 S.

40. HANS R. ROEMER: Persien auf dem Weg in die Neuzeit. Iranische Geschichte von 1350–1750, Beirut 1989, unveränd. Nachdr. Beirut 2003, X, 525 S.

41. BIRGITTA RYBERG: Yūsuf Idrīs (1927–1991). Identitätskrise und gesellschaftlicher Umbruch, Beirut 1992, 226 S.

42. HARTMUT BOBZIN: Der Koran im Zeitalter der Reformation. Studien zur Frühgeschichte der Arabistik und Islamkunde in Europa, Beirut 1995, XIV, 590 S. dt. Text.

43. BEATRIX OSSENDORF-CONRAD: Das „K. al-Wāḍiḥa" des ʿAbd al-Malik b. Ḥabīb. Edition und Kommentar zu Ms. Qarawiyyīn 809/49 (Abwāb aṭ-ṭahāra), Beirut 1994, 574 S., davon 71 S. arab. Text, 45 S. Faks.

44. MATHIAS VON BREDOW: Der Heilige Krieg (ǧihād) aus der Sicht der malikitischen Rechtsschule, Beirut 1994, 547 S. arab., 197 S. dt. Text, Indices.

45. OTFRIED WEINTRITT: Formen spätmittelalterlicher islamischer Geschichtsdarstellung. Untersuchungen zu an-Nuwairī al-Iskandarānīs Kitāb al-Ilmām und verwandten zeitgenössischen Texten, Beirut 1992, X, 226 S.

46. GERHARD CONRAD: Die quḍāt Dimašq und der maḏhab al-Auzāʿī. Materialien zur syrischen Rechtsgeschichte, Beirut 1994, XVIII, 828 S.

47. MICHAEL GLÜNZ: Die panegyrische qaṣīda bei Kamāl ud-dīn Ismāʿīl aus Isfahan. Eine Studie zur persischen Lobdichtung um den Beginn des 7./13. Jahrhunderts, Beirut 1993, 290 S.

48. AYMAN FUʾĀD SAYYID: La Capitale de l'Égypte jusqu'à l'Époque Fatimide – Al-Qāhira et Al-Fusṭāṭ– Essai de Reconstitution Topographique, Beirut 1998, XL, 754 S. franz., 26 S. arab. Text, 109 Abb.

49. JEAN MAURICE FIEY: Pour un Oriens Christianus Novus, Beirut 1993, 286 S. franz. Text.

50. IRMGARD FARAH: Die deutsche Pressepolitik und Propagandatätigkeit im Osmanischen Reich von 1908–1918 unter besonderer Berücksichtigung des „Osmanischen Lloyd", Beirut 1993, 347 S.

51. BERND RADTKE: Weltgeschichte und Weltbeschreibung im mittelalterlichen Islam, Beirut 1992, XII, 544 S.

52. LUTZ RICHTER-BERNBURG: Der Syrische Blitz – Saladins Sekretär zwischen Selbstdarstellung und Geschichtsschreibung, Beirut 1998, 452 S. dt., 99 S. arab. Text.

53. FRITZ MEIER: Bausteine I-III. Ausgewählte Aufsätze zur Islamwissenschaft. Hrsg. von Erika Glassen und Gudrun Schubert, Beirut 1992, I und II 1195 S., III (Indices) 166 S.

54. FESTSCHRIFT EWALD WAGNER ZUM 65. GEBURTSTAG: Hrsg. von Wolfhart Heinrichs und Gregor Schoeler, 2 Bde., Beirut 1994, Bd. 1: Semitische Studien unter besonderer Berücksichtigung der Südsemitistik, XV, 284 S.; Bd. 2: Studien zur arabischen Dichtung, XVII, 641 S.

55. SUSANNE ENDERWITZ: Liebe als Beruf. Al-ʿAbbās Ibn al-Aḥnaf und das ġazal, Beirut 1995, IX, 246 S.

56. ESTHER PESKES: Muḥammad b. ʿAbdalwahhāb (1703–1792) im Widerstreit. Untersuchungen zur Rekonstruktion der Frühgeschichte der Wahhābīya, Beirut 1993, VII, 384 S.

57. FLORIAN SOBIEROJ: Ibn Ḫafīf aš-Šīrāzī und seine Schrift zur Novizenerziehung, Beirut 1998, IX, 442 S. dt., 48 S. arab. Text.

58.* FRITZ MEIER: Zwei Abhandlungen über die Naqšbandiyya. I. Die Herzensbindung an den Meister. II. Kraftakt und Faustrecht des Heiligen, Beirut 1994, 366 S.

59. JÜRGEN PAUL: Herrscher, Gemeinwesen, Vermittler: Ostiran und Transoxanien in vormongolischer Zeit, Beirut 1996, VIII, 310 S.

60. JOHANN CHRISTOPH BÜRGEL, STEPHAN GUTH, eds.: Gesellschaftlicher Umbruch und Historie im zeitgenössischen Drama der islamischen Welt, Beirut 1995, XII, 295 S.

61. BARBARA FINSTER, CHRISTA FRAGNER, HERTA HAFENRICHTER, eds.: Rezeption in der islamischen Kunst, Beirut 1999, 332 S. dt. Text, Abb.

62.* ROBERT B. CAMPBELL, ed.: Aʿlām al-adab al-ʿarabī al-muʿāṣir. Siyar wa-siyar ḏātiyya. (Contemporary Arab Writers. Biographies and Autobiographies), 2 Bde., Beirut 1996, 1380 S. arab. Text.

63. MONA TAKIEDDINE AMYUNI: La ville source d'inspiration. Le Caire, Khartoum, Beyrouth, Paola Scala chez quelques écrivains arabes contemporains, Beirut 1998, 230 S. franz. Text.

64. ANGELIKA NEUWIRTH, SEBASTIAN GÜNTHER, BIRGIT EMBALÓ, MAHER JARRAR, eds.: Myths, Historical Archetypes and Symbolic Figures in Arabic Literature. Proceedings of the Symposium held at the Orient-Institut Beirut, June 25th – June 30th, 1996, Beirut 1999, 640 S. engl. Text.

65. Türkische Welten 1. KLAUS KREISER, CHRISTOPH K. NEUMANN, eds.: Das Osmanische Reich in seinen Archivalien und Chroniken. Nejat Göyünç zu Ehren, Istanbul 1997, XXIII, 328 S.

66. Türkische Welten 2. CABBAR, SETTAR: Kurtulu› Yolunda: a work on Central Asian literature in a Turkish-Uzbek mixed language. Ed., transl. and linguistically revisited by A. Sumru Özsoy, Claus Schöning, Esra Karabacak, with contribution from Ingeborg Baldauf, Istanbul 2000, 335 S.

67. Türkische Welten 3. GÜNTER SEUFERT: Politischer Islam in der Türkei. Islamismus als symbolische Repräsentation einer sich modernisierenden muslimischen Gesellschaft, Istanbul 1997, 600 S.

68. EDWARD BADEEN: Zwei mystische Schriften des ʿAmmār al-Bidlīsī, Beirut 1999, VI S., 142 S. dt., 122 arab. Text.

69. THOMAS SCHEFFLER, HÉLÈNE SADER, ANGELIKA NEUWIRTH, eds.: Baalbek: Image and Monument, 1898–1998, Beirut 1998, XIV, 348 S. engl., franz. Text.

70. AMIDU SANNI: The Arabic Theory of Prosification and Versification. On ḥall and naẓm in Arabic Theoretical Discourse, Beirut 1988, XIII, 186 S.

71. ANGELIKA NEUWIRTH, BIRGIT EMBALÓ, FRIEDERIKE PANNEWICK: Kulturelle Selbstbehauptung der Palästinenser: Survey der modernen palästinensischen Dichtung, Beirut 2001, XV, 549 S.

72. STEPHAN GUTH, PRISKA FURRER, J. CHRISTOPH BÜRGEL, eds.: Conscious Voices. Concepts of Writing in the Middle East, Beirut 1999, XXI, 332 S. dt., engl., franz. Text.

73. Türkische Welten 4. SURAYA FAROQHI, CHRISTOPH K. NEUMANN, eds.: The Illuminated Table, the Prosperous House. Food and Shelter in Ottoman Material Culture, Beirut 2003, 352 S., 25 Abb.

74. BERNARD HEYBERGER, CARSTEN WALBINER, eds.: Les Européens vus par les Libanais à l'époque ottomane, Beirut 2002, VIII, 244 S.

75. Türkische Welten 5. TOBIAS HEINZELMANN: Die Balkankrise in der osmanischen Karikatur. Die Satirezeitschriften Karagöz, Kalem und Cem 1908–1914, Beirut 1999, 290 S. Text, 77 Abb., 1 Karte.

76. THOMAS SCHEFFLER, ed.: Religion between Violence and Reconciliation, Beirut 2002, XIV, 578 S. engl. u. franz. Text.

77. ANGELIKA NEUWIRTH, ANDREAS PFLITSCH, eds.: Crisis and Memory in Islamic Societies, Beirut 2001, XII, 540 S.

78. FRITZ STEPPAT: Islam als Partner: Islamkundliche Aufsätze 1944–1996, Beirut 2001, XXX, 424 S., 8 Abb.

79. PATRICK FRANKE: Begegnung mit Khidr. Quellenstudien zum Imaginären im traditionellen Islam, Beirut 2000, XV, 620 S., 23 Abb.

80. LESLIE A. TRAMONTINI: „East is East and West is West"? Talks on Dialogue in Beirut, Beirut 2006, 222 S.

81. THOMAS SCHEFFLER: Der gespaltene Orient: Orientbilder und Orientpolitik der deutschen Sozialdemokratie von 1850 bis 1950. In Vorbereitung.

82. Türkische Welten 6. GÜNTER SEUFERT, JACQUES WAARDENBURG, eds.: Türkischer Islam und Europa, Istanbul 1999, 352 S. dt., engl. Text.

83. JEAN-MAURICE FIEY: Al-Qiddīsūn as-Suryān, Beirut 2005, 358 S., 5 Karten.

84. Türkische Welten 7. ANGELIKA NEUWIRTH, JUDITH PFEIFFER, BÖRTE SAGASTER, eds.: The Ghazal as a Genre of World Literature II: The Ottoman Ghazal in its Historical Context. Würzburg 2006, XLIX, 340 S.

85. Türkische Welten 8. BARBARA PUSCH, ed.: Die neue muslimische Frau: Standpunkte Ş Analysen, Beirut 2001, 326 S.

86. Türkische Welten 9. ANKE VON KÜGELGEN: Inszenierung einer Dynastie – Geschichtsschreibung unter den frühen Mangiten Bucharas (1747–1826), Beirut 2002, XII, 518 S.

87. OLAF FARSCHID: Islamische Ökonomik und Zakat. In Vorbereitung.

88. JENS HANSSEN, THOMAS PHILIPP, STEFAN WEBER, eds.: The Empire in the City: Arab Provincial Capitals in the Late Ottoman Empire, Beirut 2002, X, 375 S., 71 Abb.

89. THOMAS BAUER, ANGELIKA NEUWIRTH, eds.: Ghazal as World Literature I: Migrations and Transformations of a Literary Genre, Beirut 2005, 447 S.

90. AXEL HAVEMANN: Geschichte und Geschichtsschreibung im Libanon des 19. und 20. Jahrhunderts: Formen und Funktionen des historischen Selbstverständnisses, Beirut 2002, XIV, 341 S.

91. HANNE SCHÖNIG: Schminken, Düfte und Räucherwerk der Jemenitinnen: Lexikon der Substanzen, Utensilien und Techniken, Beirut 2002, XI, 415 S., 130 Abb., 1 Karte.

92. BIRGIT SCHÄBLER: Aufstände im Drusenbergland. Ethnizität und Integration einer ländlichen Gesellschaft Syriens vom Osmanischen Reich bis zur staatlichen Unabhängigkeit 1850-1949, Beirut 2004, 315 S. arab. Text, 2 Karten.

93. AS-SAYYID KĀẒIM B. QĀSIM AL-ḤUSAINĪ AR-RAŠTĪ: Risālat as-sulūk fī l-aḫlāq wa-l-aʿmāl. Hrsg. von Waḥīd Bihmardī, Beirut 2004, 7 S. engl., 120 S. arab. Text.

94. JACQUES AMATEIS SDB: Yūsuf al-Ḫāl wa-Maǧallatuhu „Šiʿr". In Zusammenarbeit mit Dār al-Nahār, Beirut 2004, 313 S. arab. Text.

95. SUSANNE BRÄCKELMANN: „Wir sind die Hälfte der Welt!" Zaynab Fawwāz (1860-1914) und Malak Ḥifnī Nāṣif (1886-1918) – zwei Publizistinnen der frühen ägyptischen Frauenbewegung, Beirut 2004, 295 S. dt., 16 S. arab., 4 S. engl. Text.

96. THOMAS PHILIPP, CHRISTOPH SCHUMANN, eds.: From the Syrian Land to the State of Syria and Lebanon, Beirut 2004, 366 S. engl. Text.

97. HISTORY, SPACE AND SOCIAL CONFLICT IN BEIRUT: THE QUARTER OF ZOKAK EL-BLAT, Beirut 2005, XIV, 348 S. engl. Text, 80 S. farb. Abb., 5 Karten.

98. ABDALLAH M. KAHIL: The Sultan Ḥasan Complex in Cairo 1357-1364. In Vorbereitung.

99. OLAF FARSCHID, MANFRED KROPP, STEPHAN DÄHNE, eds.: World War One as remembered in the countries of the Eastern Mediterranean, Würzburg 2006, XIII, 452 S. engl. Text, 17 Abb.

100. Results of contemporary research on the Qurʾan: The question of a historio-critical text of the Qurʾan (Arbeitstitel). Edited by Manfred S. Kropp, Beirut; Würzburg, 2007. 198 S.

101. JOHN DONOHUE SJ, LESLIE TRAMONTINI, eds.: Crosshatching in Global Culture: A Dictionary of Modern Arab Writers. An Updated English Version of R. B. Campbell's "Contemporary Arab Writers", 2 Bde., Beirut 2004, XXIV, 1215 S. engl. Text.

102. ATTILIO PETRUCCIOLI, STEFAN WEBER et al. eds.: The Multicultural Urban Fabric. In Vorbereitung.

103. MOHAMMED MARAQTEN: Altsüdarabische Texte auf Holzstäbchen. In Vorbereitung.

104. AXEL HAVEMANN: Geschichte und Geschichtsschreibung (BTS 90). Arab. Übersetzung. In Vorbereitung.

105. SUSANNE BRÄCKELMANN: „Wir sind die Hälfte der Welt" (BTS 95). Arab. Übersetzung. In Vorbereitung.

106. MATTHIAS VOGT: Figures de califes entre histoire et fiction – al-Walīd b. Yazīd et al-Amīn dans la représentation de l'historiographie arabe de l'époque abbaside, Beirut 2006, 362 S.

107. HUBERT KAUFHOLD, ed.: Georg Graf: Christlicher Orient und schwäbische Heimat. Kleine Schriften, 2 Bde., Beirut 2005, XLVIII, 823 S.

108. LESLIE TRAMONTINI, CHIBLI MALLAT, eds.: From Baghdad to Beirut... Arab and Islamic Studies in honor of John J. Donohue sj., Beirut 2007, 496 S. engl., franz., arab. Text.

109. RICHARD BLACKBURN, ed.: Journey to the Sublime Porte. The Arabic Memoir of a Sharifian Agent's Diplomatic Mission to the Ottoman Imperial Court in the era of Suleyman the Magnificent, Beirut 2005, 366 S.

110. STEFAN REICHMUTH, FLORIAN SCHWARZ, ed.: Zwischen Alltag und Schriftkultur: Horizonte des Individuellen in der arabischen Literatur des 17. und 18. Jahrhunderts. Im Druck.

111. JUDITH PFEIFFER, MANFRED KROPP, eds.: Theoretical Approaches to the Transmission and Edition of Oriental Manuscripts, Würzburg 2006, 335 S., 43 Abb.

112. LALE BEHZADI, VAHID BEHMARDI, eds.: The Evolution of Artistic Classical Arabic Prose. In Vorbereitung.

113. SOUAD SLIM: The Greek Orthodox Waqf in Lebanon during the Ottoman Period, Beirut 2007, 257 S., maps, plates.

114. HELEN SADER, MANFRED KROPP, MOHAMMED MARAQTEN, eds.: Proceedings of the Conference on Economic and Social History of Pre-Islamic Arabia. In Vorbereitung.
115. DENIS HERMANN, SABRINA MERVIN, eds.: Courants et dynamiques chiites à l'époque moderne (1800-1925). In Vorbereitung.
116. LUTZ GREISIGER, CLAUDIA RAMMELT, JÜRGEN TUBACH, eds.: Edessa in hellenistisch-römischer Zeit: Religion, Kultur und Politik zwischen Ost und West. In Vorbereitung.
117. MARTIN TAMCKE, ed.: Christlich-muslimische Gespräche im Mittelalter. In Vorbereitung.
118. MAHMOUD HADDAD, et alii, eds.: Towards a Cultural History of Bilad al-Sham in the Mamluk Era. Prosperity or Decline, Tolerance or Persecution? In Vorbereitung.
119. TARIF KHALIDI, et alii, eds.: Al-Jahiz: A Muslim Humanist for our time. In Vorbereitung.
120. FĀRŪQ ḤUBLUṢ: Abḥāṯ fī tārīḫ wilāyat Ṭarābulus ibbān al-ḥukm al-uṯmānī. Im Druck.
121. STEFAN KNOST: Die Organisation des religiösen Raums in Aleppo. Die Rolle der islamischen Stiftungen in der Gesellschaft einer Provinzhauptstadt des Osmanischen Reiches. In Vorbereitung.
122. RALPH BODENSTEIN, STEFAN WEBER: Ottoman Sidon. The Changing Fate of a Mediterranean Port City. In Vorbereitung.
123. JOHN DONOHUE: Robert Campbells Aʿlām al-adab al-ʿarabī (Arbeitstitel). In Vorbereitung.
124. ANNE MOLLENHAUER: Mittelhallenhäuser im Bilād aš-Šām des 19. Jahrhunderts (Arbeitstitel). In Vorbereitung.
125. KIRILL DMITRIEV: Das poetische Werk des Abū Ṣaḫr al-Huḏalī. In Vorbereitung.

* Vergriffen

Die Unterreihe „Türkische Welten" geht in die unabhängige Publikationsreihe des Orient-Instituts Istanbul „Istanbuler Texte und Studien" über.

Orient-Institut Beirut
Rue Hussein Beyhum, Zokak el-Blat,
P.O.B. 11-2988, Beirut - Lebanon
Tel.: 01-372940 / 376598, Fax: 01-376599
e-mail: oib-bib@oidmg.org
homepage: www.oidmg.org

Vertrieb in Deutschland:
ERGON Verlag
Grombühlstraße 7
97080 Würzburg
Tel: 0049-931-280084, Fax: 0049-931-282872
e-mail: ergon-verlag@t-online.de
homepage: www.ergon-verlag.de

Vertrieb im Libanon:
al-Furat
Hamra Street
Rasamny Building
P.O.Box: 113-6435 Beirut
Tel: 00961-1-750054, Fax: 00961-1-750053
e-mail: info@alfurat.com

Stand: April 2007